ABOUT MENTAL ILLNESS IS AN ACTUAL ILLNESS

Documents additional progress from someone who was hospitalized due to bipolar mental illness. It is nothing short of a miracle that Mr Medl has written multiple books. What is even more amazing is that he's a mental health advocate who helps other people cope with the same disease. If you don't think mental illness is a real disease, you need to read one or more if Mr Medl's books.

Tom

John has done it again. Another fantastic book in his collection on mental illness. John gets it. John lives it. It's great to get additional insight on bipolar from John in this more recent collection, as well as a few of his interviews where he answered questions about his illness, concerns on mental illness, and police and show they interact with mental illness.

Craig A. Price Jr.

In the mental health community we often feel alone because people don't understand us. After reading through John's book I find a sense of peace. That I wasn't alone and there is hope in recovery. We can't just "get over it" there is a process to healing from the battle we experience in our own head.

Grant Williams

ABOUT THE ENTROPY OF BIPOLAR DISORDER

This is the fourth book in a series of books written by John Medl. John takes us on another journey describing his daily struggles with bipolar disorder. His story is truly amazing. 14 years after being first hospitalized for a break in reality, he is now an author and mental health advocate. He discusses how he tries to help others and how it makes him feel better about his own situation. This book is full of raw emotions and feelings; the reader can actually feel the ups and downs of a bipolar man. Mental health professionals and students would also benefit from reading John's amazing story.

Tom

John keeps it real. If someone you know is dealing with mental health struggles this book can provide some suggestions that they too can get through the journey and enter a new way of life. He is able to provide first-hand experience and I fully support promoting the message.

Grant Williams

Mr. Medl, you are an inspiration! I hope you always know that. Your honesty and openness make people feel less alone. You bring hope to others. And as you know, that is a very precious gift. Thank you for sharing your life with us all.

Shana Koehler

John's books are a must have for anyone with, or anyone who loves, someone suffering from bipolar. It is a true insight of his day to day struggle. Very open and honest.

Susan Yacapraro

This book, in journal form, lays bare the daily struggles of a man with bipolar disorder. The story and the writing are true, unforgettable, and a lesson to be learned, for the writer is true and honest about his struggles and victories. A must for those wanting to know how mental illness is a stigma but also a proving ground for the soul, the mind. I very pleased to learn from this text. It helps me with my own journey and will help others. A must read book!

Albino Carrillo

ABOUT THE LAST DAY OF JULY

How does one go from being held in a mental hospital during a psychotic episode to someone who can live on their own and then write about it? How can someone who continues to have cycles of mania and depression able to reflect back on those episodes and then write about how it felt? If you want to understand how a bipolar patient feels and their daily struggles then this is the book to read. The author made significant progress over the years but everyone should realize that there is no real "cure" for bipolar "disease". I say disease because its a chemical imbalance of the brain which we don't fully understand. Certain "triggers" can bring back some of the symptoms as the author discusses. The book also makes you wonder how bad it must be for people who don't have access to mental health professionals and if we as a country are doing enough to help these people. How many people are in jail because they didn't get help? Other more general topics/themes include giving back, helping others, living simply, and finding your purpose in life. These are things everyone should think about, not just the mentally ill. I highly recommend the book.

Tom

This is such a raw and honest book about the author's journey through mental illness. It gives a great inside to the challenges someone faces and the everyday symptoms. Even though I do not have mental illness I can relate to some battles and understand more about others. I think my favorite part is how positive his attitude continues to be through it all! Great book!!

Nyssa Darterd

This is a great account of John's life following his diagnosis in 2006 and what it's like for him to live with his bipolar one disorder every single day. He has many useful and thought-provoking insights during the course of the book, which is basically a journal he wrote on an almost daily basis. For example, on January 4, 2019, he muses: "What is my personality and what is my illness? Is it both? Was I just an active child that played sports and excelled at school or was that the beginning of mania?...When I was working 60+ hours a week and going to college full-time, was I manic or just showing a good work ethic?" These are great questions, and the reader will be surprised and pleased at some of John's answers. Highly recommend this book to anyone trying to understand their own mental illness or that of someone they care about...a nice thought collection. The only thing I think would have improved the book is if it had page numbers so it would be easier to refer back to some of John's key epiphanies.

Lori M. Balster

This is the first of Mr. Mel's books I have read. I have multiple people in my life struggling with bipolar disorder and while I see what it does on the outside, I have never had insight as to how the other person felt on the inside.

Wendi

This book is very very good. A brutally honest journal about the author's struggles with a bipolar mind and his hope for a better future. I recommend it to anyone who may be struggling with mental health issues or anyone who is willing to learn more about the effects of this disease.

Kevin C Schell

An incredibly honest and true to life story of one man's struggle to exist, A world where he is deemed insane. He struggles, he makes it through to have a promising career as a writer. Confessional, Frank, brave.

Albino Carrillo

ABOUT POEMS FROM A BIPOLAR MIND

Mr. Medl has the natural talent of being able to paint a picture with words. His poetry covers many subjects, but his imagery remains vivid and imaginative. I enjoyed the author's notes, which offered insight added context to each poem. In the end, the reader feels as if they have taken a guided journey through Medl's fascinating mind. I recommend this book on it's own or as a companion to the author's other book, "Millions Like Me". Both are great reads, and I can only hope that there will be more books to follow.

Evan Vomacka

A wonderful collection of beautifully written poems. John is clearly a poet and wonderful with prose. I've found that people with a mental illness, have absolutely wonderful minds. My mom also has bipolar, and her writing is wonderful, when she can put the discipline to sit down and do it. She's no poet, but her eulogy for grandma was absolutely heartfelt, as several other small pieces she's actually written. John's poems are clear, concise, and a promising insight into the mind of bipolar. They're beautiful, and I hope he continues to write them.

Craig A. Price Jr.

I love that John chose to add another talent to his series. Mental illness is a serious issue that often gets swept under the rug and I like that John took a different approach by embracing the disorder and providing hope and incite.

Grant Williams

Excellent poetry with excellent commentary on each poem. A look into someone's mind with mental illness with obvious creativity and talent.

Sue M

ABOUT MILLIONS LIKE ME

This man has struggled for years with his illness. He has researched it thoroughly and through personal experience he certainly understands all that he has gone through and is going through. His family must be very understanding and supportive of him. An enlightening read for me.

Ann

I. would. recommend. this. book. to. anyone. who. I. talk to. IT. was. a. very interesting. book. I enjoyed it. very much.

Robert S

A brilliant take on a man's life and struggle with mental illness. Bipolar is a condition not a lot of people understand. Even doctors are unsure about most of it. A person with bipolar is often sporadic, unrestful, and hard to concentrate. My mother has it, and so I understand it more than most. When I saw that John himself had bipolar, and wrote about his experiences, I was eager to pick up this book. I've talked to Mom over the years about it, but getting additional insight from another who had the patience to write his journey down, was inspiring. It was like hearing from a good friend. The voice for the narrative was engaging, and I consumed every word. I look forward to reading the rest of John's book for a wonderful insight into the mind of mental illness.

Craig A. Price Jr.

John has so much talent and is doing everything he can to break the stigma that mentally ill people can't function like the rest of society. Overcoming every obstacle thrown at him he has made it his mission to spread awareness of how one can recover and adapt to being productive. I enjoyed his book so much that I bought 2 copies of all five of his books. One to stock one to share.

Grant Williams

John is brave to lay bare his soul as he does in this book. It is rare that someone can look at themselves so honestly, especially someone who must admit that he is unstable and that he will always have to work to keep his mental illness under some sort of control. As he says, "Every day is a mountain." He bravely admits that he will always have mental illness but it is a part of who he is, and he is not trying to be someone he is not. Very brave...especially since talking about mental illness is still viewed as "taboo" by a significant portion of society. However, it is because of John's bravery at facing what he sees in the mirror that there is some real insight into the human condition in his prose and poetry. This book has no page numbers and many of the poems don't have names, which means while there are worthwhile insights in the book, they may be hard to refer back to once you have found them...they are more of an organic whole, a cohesive tableau of what mental illness is like. A worthwhile book. I will be reading more of John's works.

Lori M. Balster

WORKINGS OF A BIPOLAR MIND 1-7

THE INNER MIND OF SOMEONE WITH BIPOLAR DISORDER

JOHN MEDL

Formatted by Craig A. Price Jr.

CONTENTS

MILLIONS LIKE ME

POEMS FROM A BIPOLAR MIND

THE LAST DAY OF JULY

THE ENTROPY OF BIPOLAR DISORDER

MENTAL ILLNESS IS AN ACTUAL ILLNESS

MAKING BIPOLAR LEMONADE

BIPOLAR RISING

MILLIONS LIKE ME

MY STRUGGLE WITH MENTAL ILLNESS

INTRODUCTION

There are many purposes to this book. One is to educate and inform the reader of the disorders I have (and millions of others that are affected). Another is to help motivate and inspire those with mental illness. Lastly, I want the reader to try and see what mental illness looks like from someone who suffers from it. There are many people with no experience in these matters, and it is hard to convince some that mental illness is even an illness at all. Some people think you can will your way out of it either through diet and exercise, or positive thinking, prayer, or whatever "cure" they think there is. Some people believe mental illness affects the weak-minded. Mental illness affects people at all levels of intelligence. There are those that I could educate until I am blue in the face, but they will not be convinced otherwise. A friend described it as there being two types of people: the receptive and the non-receptive. As someone with mental illness, it's important to know the difference and focus on the ones who will be receptive. They could be receptive to a variety of things; my symptoms and feelings, for example. Just like any belief, really. Like politics or religion. I think this will end up being therapeutic for me also. I use humor a lot, even though this book isn't supposed to be humorous exactly. I may go on tangents as well. My mind skips around a lot. I am trying to paint a complete picture of what someone with mental illness goes through and where he/she may come from. Mental illness does not discriminate based on race, gender, social class, or any other personal factors. It affects everyone from all walks of life. There will be some of my poetry mixed in as well, and I will include as many poems as I have at the end of the book. I have been writing poetry since grade school, and I have continued into adulthood. 1 in 4 people are thought to have some form of mental illness. 1 in 3 go through anxiety, panic, or depression at some point in their lives. I think I have led an unusual and interesting life to this point, so the read should be enjoyable. I should probably mention that I have been diagnosed with bipolar disorder, panic disorder, and obsessive-compulsive disorder. I also have agoraphobia and claustrophobia.

1 SYMPTOMS OF BIPOLAR DISORDER

MANIC PHASE OF BIPOLAR DISORDER

Signs and symptoms of the manic or hypomanic phase of bipolar disorder can include:

- Euphoria
- Inflated self-esteem
- Poor judgment
- Rapid speech
- Racing thoughts
- Aggressive behavior
- Agitation or irritation
- Increased physical activity
- Risky behavior
- Spending sprees or unwise financial choices
- Increased drive to perform or achieve goals
- Increased sex drive
- Decreased need for sleep
- Easily distracted
- Careless or dangerous use of drugs or alcohol
- Frequent absences from work or school

- Delusions or a break from reality (psychosis)
- Poor performance at work or school

DEPRESSIVE PHASE OF BIPOLAR DISORDER

Signs and symptoms of the depressive phase of bipolar disorder can include:

- Sadness
- Hopelessness
- Suicidal thoughts or behavior
- Anxiety
- Guilt
- Sleep problems
- Low appetite or increased appetite
- Fatigue
- Loss of interest in activities once considered enjoyable
- Problems concentrating
- Irritability
- Chronic pain without a known cause
- Frequent absences from work or school
- Poor performance at work or school

OTHER SIGNS AND SYMPTOMS OF BIPOLAR DISORDER

Signs and symptoms of bipolar disorder can also include:

- Seasonal changes in mood. As with seasonal affective disorder (SAD), some people with bipolar disorder have moods that change with the seasons. Some people become manic or hypomanic in the spring or summer and then become depressed in the fall or winter. For other people, this cycle is reversed — they become depressed in the spring or summer and manic or hypomanic in the fall or winter.
- Rapid cycling bipolar disorder. Some people with bipolar disorder have rapid mood shifts. This is defined as having four or more

mood swings within a single year. However, in some people, mood shifts occur much more quickly, sometimes within just hours.

- Psychosis. Severe episodes of either mania or depression may result in psychosis, a detachment from reality. Symptoms of psychosis may include false but strongly held beliefs (delusions) and hearing or seeing things that aren't there (hallucinations). Courtesy of mayoclinic.com

2 WHAT ARE PANIC ATTACKS/PANIC DISORDER?

A discrete period of intense fear or discomfort, in which four (or more) of the following symptoms developed abruptly and reached a peak within 10 minutes:

1. palpitations, pounding heart, or accelerated heart rate
2. sweating
3. trembling or shaking
4. sensations of shortness of breath or smothering
5. feeling of choking
6. chest pain or discomfort
7. nausea or abdominal distress
8. feeling dizzy, unsteady, lightheaded, or faint
9. derealization (feelings of unreality) or depersonalization (being detached from oneself)
10. fear of losing control or going crazy
11. fear of dying
12. paresthesias (numbness or tingling sensations)
13. chills or hot flushes

DSM IV Criteria for Panic Disorder

A) Both (1) and (2)

(1) recurrent unexpected Panic Attacks

(2) at least one of the attacks has been followed by 1 month (or more) of one (or more) of the following:

(a) persistent concern about having additional attacks

(b) worry about the implications of the attack or its consequences (e.g., losing control, having a heart attack, "going crazy")

(c) a significant change in behavior related to the attacks

B) The Panic Attacks are not due to the direct physiological effects of a substance (e.g., a drug of abuse, a medication) or a general medical condition (e.g., hyperthyroidism).

C) The Panic Attacks are not better accounted for by another mental disorder, such as Social Phobia (e.g., occurring on exposure to feared social situations), Specific Phobia (e.g., on exposure to a specific phobic situation), Obsessive-Compulsive Disorder (e.g., on exposure to dirt in someone with an obsession about contamination),

Posttraumatic Stress Disorder (e.g., in response to stimuli associated with a severe stressor), or Separation Anxiety Disorder (e.g., in response to being away from home or close relatives).

Panic Disorder is divided into with or without agoraphobia DSM IV Criteria for Agoraphobia

A) anxiety about being in places or situations from which escape might be difficult (or embarrassing) or in which help may not be available in the event of having an unexpected or situationally predisposed Panic Attack or panic-like symptoms. Agoraphobic fears typically involve characteristic clusters of situations that include being outside the home alone; being in a crowd, or standing in a line; being on a bridge; and traveling in a bus, train, or automobile.

B) The situations are avoided (e.g., travel is restricted) or else are endured with marked distress or with anxiety about having a Panic Attack or panic-like symptoms, or require the presence of a companion.

C) The anxiety or phobic avoidance is not better accounted for by another mental disorder, such as Social Phobia (e.g., avoidance limited to social situations because of fear of embarrassment), Specific Phobia (e.g., avoidance limited to a single situation like elevators), Obsessive-Compulsive Disorder (e.g., avoidance of dirt in someone with an obsession about contamination),

Posttraumatic Stress Disorder (e.g., avoidance of stimuli associated with a severe stressor), or Separation Anxiety Disorder (e.g., avoidance of leaving home or relatives).

3 OBSESSIVE-COMPULSIVE DISORDER SYMPTOMS INCLUDE BOTH OBSESSIONS AND COMPULSIONS

Obsession symptoms

OCD obsessions are repeated, persistent and unwanted ideas, thoughts, images or impulses that you have involuntarily and that seem to make no sense. These obsessions typically intrude when you're trying to think of or do other things.

Obsessions often have themes to them, such as:

- Fear of contamination or dirt
- Having things orderly and symmetrical
- Aggressive or horrific impulses
- Sexual images or thoughts

Obsession symptoms and signs may include:

- Fear of being contaminated by shaking hands or by touching objects others have touched
- Doubts that you've locked the door or turned off the stove
- Thoughts that you've hurt someone in a traffic accident
- Intense stress when objects aren't orderly or facing the right way
- Images of hurting your child
- Impulses to shout obscenities in inappropriate situations

- Avoidance of situations that can trigger obsessions, such as shaking hands
- Replaying pornographic images in your mind
- Dermatitis because of frequent hand washing
- Skin lesions because of picking at your skin
- Hair loss or bald spots because of hair pulling

Compulsion symptoms

OCD compulsions are repetitive behaviors that you feel driven to perform. These repetitive behaviors are meant to prevent or reduce anxiety related to your obsessions. For instance, if you believe you hit someone with your car, you may return to the apparent scene over and over because you just can't shake your doubts. You may also make up rules or rituals to follow that help control the anxiety you feel when having obsessive thoughts.

As with obsessions, compulsions typically have themes, such as:

- Washing and cleaning
- Counting
- Checking
- Demanding reassurances
- Performing the same action repeatedly
- Orderliness

Compulsion symptoms and signs may include:

- Hand washing until your skin becomes raw
- Checking doors repeatedly to make sure they're locked
- Checking the stove repeatedly to make sure it's off
- Counting in certain patterns
- Arranging your canned goods to face the same way

Symptoms usually begin gradually and tend to vary in severity throughout your life. Symptoms generally worsen during times when you're experiencing more stress. OCD is considered a lifelong illness.

When to see a doctor

There's a difference between being a perfectionist and having obsessive-compulsive disorder. Perhaps you keep the floors in your house so clean that you could eat off them. Or you like your knickknacks arranged just so. That doesn't necessarily mean that you have obsessive-compulsive disorder.

Obsessive-compulsive disorder can be so severe and time-consuming that it literally becomes disabling. You may be able to do little else but spend time on your obsessions and compulsions — washing your hands for hours each day, for instance. With OCD, you may have a low quality of life because the condition rules most of your days. You may be very distressed, but you seem powerless to stop your urges. Most adults can recognize that their obsessions and compulsions don't make sense. Children, however, may not understand what's wrong.

If your obsessions and compulsions are affecting your life, see your doctor or mental health provider. People with OCD may be ashamed and embarrassed about the condition. But even if your rituals are deeply ingrained, treatment can help.

4 DSM IV PSYCHIATRIC DISORDERS

THE DSM IV IS A MANUAL USED TO CHARACTERIZE VARIOUS PSYCHIATRIC disorders. Here's how it is organized:

The DSM-IV organizes each psychiatric diagnosis into five levels (axes) relating to different aspects of disorder or disability:

- Axis I: clinical disorders, including major mental disorders, as well as developmental and learning disorders
- Axis II: underlying pervasive or personality conditions, as well as mental retardation
- Axis III: Acute medical conditions and physical disorders.
- Axis IV: psychosocial and environmental factors contributing to the disorder
- Axis V: Global Assessment of Functioning or Children's Global Assessment Scale for children and teens under the age of 18. (on a scale from 100 to 1)

Common Axis I disorders include depression, anxiety disorders, bipolar disorder, ADHD, phobias, and schizophrenia.Common Axis II disorders include personality disorders: paranoid personality disorder, schizoid personality disorder, schizotypal personality disorder, borderline personality disorder, antisocial personality disorder, narcissistic personality disorder, histrionic personality disorder, avoidant personality disorder, dependent personality disorder, obsessive-compulsive personality disorder, and mental retardation.

Common Axis III disorders include brain injuries and other medical/physical disorders which may aggravate existing diseases or present symptoms similar to other disorders.

http://uk.answers.yahoo.com/question/index?qid=20090401065653AAaGyf3

5 MY BIPOLAR DISORDER

THE TYPE OF BIPOLAR DISORDER I HAVE IS CALLED BIPOLAR I WITH PSYCHOTIC tendencies or episodes. This means that I am more manic than depressed, whereas bipolar II is vice versa. The psychotic features part, or tendencies, refers to bouts of psychosis mixed in.

A group of illnesses which disrupt the functioning of the brain which causes a condition called psychosis. Psychosis is a syndrome seen in a number of different illnesses including Schizophrenia, Schizoaffective Disorder, Delusional Disorder, Brief Psychotic Disorder, Bipolar Disorder, Major Depression or occurring as a result of the effects of illicit substances or some physical illnesses.

It consists of such symptoms as:

- Delusions - which are false beliefs that are utterly true to the one who is experiencing the psychosis, but not understandable to others from the same cultural background.
- Hallucinations - which are sensory experiences which seem entirely real to the person experiencing them, but are unable to be shared by others (e.g. hearing "voices").
- Disorganised thought, speech, or behaviour.

These symptoms may lead to social withdrawal and reduced performance in academic or occupational pursuits. The person's behaviour may change significantly. These changes may be difficult for others to understand because they occur in response to the delusions or hallucinations.

Most people are able to recover from an episode of psychosis. http://www.health.qld.gov.au/mentalhealth/abt_mental/facts_psychosis.asp

There are so many negatives that go along with this disorder, but I would not have had the energy to work and attend college and eventually graduate without these manic episodes. I try to see the positives that have come from this diagnosis. I was definitely caught up in the pursuit of financial success, and when I was diagnosed and the years after, I began to appreciate the smaller things in life. Like just living outside of the hospital. Like being able to think somewhat clearly without being delusional or psychotic. Like having food, clothing, and shelter. The one thing I miss is that I cannot read anymore. Not that I am illiterate, but my concentration and attention have deteriorated to the point of near nonexistence. That's why I am proud of this piece of work. I am passionate about helping others and sharing my story. I guess some things can hold my attention if I have enough passion about the purpose. Even TV shows are hard for me to follow. I think TV is really the lowest form of attention you can have, and it is hard for me. I watch a lot of sports, which I can kind of tune in and out of. I am pretty good with sports history though, like who is the all-time leader in whichever statistical category.

6 PANIC DISORDER

PANIC DISORDER IS MY SECONDARY DIAGNOSIS. I WAS DIAGNOSED AROUND 2009. This diagnosis is just as terrible as bipolar disorder. The physical sensations during a panic disorder are far from pleasant, and I have thought I was going to die on several occasions. I have had to go to the hospital as a result. Sometimes, even when I know it is a panic attack, it feels so real that I think I need medical attention. My last hospital visit I was there for 4 hours, and they didn't really do anything for me except give me oxygen. They listed the reason for admission as mania and panic. I have listed the symptoms previously in the book, so refer to them if you need to.

7 OBSESSIONAL OCD

There are five types of OCD, and my type is called an obsessional. Most people think that people with OCD are all neat freaks, but that's not me. I don't need things in a certain order, but I don't like change. I guess I have my own order of things that may not look organized to anyone else. I hate when my mom moves things around in her attempts to clean up or organize things the way she wants. In my unprofessional opinion, she has OCD also. I should mention I live with both of my parents, who are both in their seventies. I tend to recite prayers and song lyrics in my head obsessively, as well as facts and figures. I obsessively check the clock around my med times, which are not set in stone, but for some reason, I have made it that way. I also obsessively check my eBay sales, Facebook, and/or emails. I have nervous tics like pulling at my shirt or hat, and it's hard for me to sit still sometimes. I also smoke cigarettes, which could be obsessional, or I might like the oral fixation or, on the simplest level, addicted to nicotine. Or all of the above, which is usually the answer in psychology. A disproportionate amount of the mentally ill are smokers compared with the general population. I can't smoke in my parents' house where I live now, so I am always out on the front porch.

My parents have lived in this house where I live now since 1967, and many people in my neighborhood know me and my family. I enjoy when people wave to me when they are traveling to or from work or just out and about. I like the small-town feel, and I couldn't imagine living in a big city. I would much rather live in the middle of nowhere, although there are scary parts about that to me as well. My parents' house is the only place I have ever felt like was my home. Maybe one day it will be mine. I would be proud to carry on the legacy of the household my siblings and I grew up in.

8 CLAUSTROPHOBIA

CLAUSTROPHOBIA IS AN ANXIETY DISORDER; THE SUFFERER HAS AN IRRATIONAL fear of having no escape or being closed in. It frequently results in panic attack and can be triggered by certain stimuli or situations, such as being in a crowded elevator, a room without windows, or sitting in an airplane. Some people may even experience claustrophobia when wearing tight-necked clothing.

The word claustrophobia originates from Latin claustrum which means "a shut in place" and Greek phobos, which means "fear". Research has shown that approximately 6% of people suffer the disorder worldwide, but the majority are not receiving treatment for it.

People with claustrophobia can find the disorder hard to live with, as they will go to great lengths to avoid small spaces and situations that trigger their panic and anxiety. They will avoid certain places like the subway/underground and will prefer to take the stairs over using a lift/elevator, no matter how many floors they need to ascend/descend.

According to Medilexicon's medical dictionary, claustrophobia is: "A morbid fear of being in a confined place."

WHAT ARE THE SYMPTOMS OF CLAUSTROPHOBIA?

A symptom is something the patient feels or reports, while a sign is something that other people, including the doctor detects. A headache may be an example of a symptom, while a rash may be an example of a sign.

A claustrophobic may suffer symptoms similar to anxiety that are triggered by being in a small space. The phobia of the small space is based on the fear of running out of oxygen, along with the fear of restriction. When in an small confined space, someone with claustrophobia may start to show the following symptoms:

- Sweating
- Accelerated heart rate
- Increased blood pressure
- Hyperventilation, or 'over-breathing'
- Shaking
- Sweating
- Panic attacks
- Light-headedness
- Nausea
- Fainting
- Fear of actual harm or illness

It is not essentially the small spaces that trigger the anxiety but the fear of what can happen to the person if confined to that area, hence the fear of running out of oxygen. Examples of small spaces that could trigger a claustrophobic's anxiety are:

- elevators/lifts
- basements/cellars
- small rooms
- airplanes
- locked rooms
- cars
- trains
- crowded areas

As claustrophobia is also defined by the phobia of being restricted, being confined to one area can also trigger the anxiety (e.g. having to wait in line at a checkout/cash register). There have also been studies to support the theory that MRI machines can cause claustrophobia due to the prolonged length of time spent in a confined space with restricted movement.

As the above situations can cause a claustrophobic to suffer anxiety and panic attacks, a claustrophobic will try their best to avoid them. The following are examples of how a claustrophobic may behave:

- As soon as they enter a room, they may urgently check out where the exits are and position themselves near them. When all the doors are closed, they may feel troubled.
- In a crowded party, even if the venue is a large and spacious room, they will position themselves near the door.
- Avoid driving during peak times, when traffic is likely to be congested
- Avoid travelling as a passenger in a car during peak traffic times
- In severe cases, some individuals with claustrophobia may panic when a door is closed
- Avoid using elevators and use the stairs, even if this means getting tired, out of breath and sweating a lot

WHAT CAUSES CLAUSTROPHOBIA?

Claustrophobia is generally the result of an experience in the person's past (usually in their childhood) that has led them to associate small spaces with the feeling of panic or being in imminent danger. Examples of these kinds of past experiences are:

- falling into a deep pool and not being able to swim
- being in a crowded area and getting separated from parents/group
- crawling into a hole and getting lost/stuck

As the experience will have dealt some kind of trauma to the person, it will affect their ability to deal with a similar situation rationally. The mind links the small space/confined area to the feeling of being in danger and the body then reacts accordingly (or how it thinks it should). This type of cause is known as classic conditioning and can also be a behavior inherited from parents or peers. If for example, a claustrophobic has a child, the child may observe their parent's behavior and develop the same fears.

There are other theories behind the causes of claustrophobia, these are:

- Smaller Amygdala - the amygdala is a tiny part of the brain that is used to control how the body processes fear. During a study, Fumi Hayano discovered that people who suffered panic disorders had a smaller amygdale than average. This smaller size could interfere with how the body processes panic and anxiety.
- Prepared Phobia - there is also a theory that phobias develop on the genetic level rather than psychologically. The research behind this theory suggests that claustrophobia and some other phobias are dormant evolutionary survival mechanisms. A survival instinct buried within our genetic code that was once crucial to human survival but is no longer needed.

HOW IS CLAUSTROPHOBIA DIAGNOSED?

Claustrophobia would be diagnosed as a result of seeing a psychologist. The patient may be seeing the psychologist because they suffer the symptoms of claustrophobia, or they could be originally seeing them about another anxiety problem or phobia.

The psychologist would ask for a description of the symptoms and what triggers them. Using their knowledge and resources, the psychologist would then determine the type and severity of the patient's phobia.

There are methods put in place to help decide if the patient is suffering from claustrophobia and to what extent. These methods are:

- Claustrophobia questionnaire - Originally developed in 1993 and modified in 2001, this has been a helpful way of identifying the symptoms of claustrophobia.
- Claustrophobia Scale - Developed in 1979, this method is made up of 20 questions that when answered can help establish the levels of anxiety when diagnosing the claustrophobia.

HOW IS CLAUSTROPHOBIA TREATED?

After diagnosis has been made, the psychologist would try one or a few of the following methods to help the claustrophobic deal with their fear:

- CBT (Cognitive-Behavioral Therapy) - This is a well-recognized treatment method for many other types of anxiety disorder. The goal of CBT is to retrain the claustrophobic's brain to no longer feel threatened by the places they fear. An approach taken may be slowly exposing the patient to small spaces and helping them deal with their fear and anxiety (in vivo exposure). This is the most common way claustrophobia is treated.
- Drug Therapy - This type of therapy can help manage the anxiety symptoms, however it does not deal with the problem itself. This, along with the undesired side effects makes this method far from first choice for treating claustrophobia.
- Relaxation Exercises - Taking deep breaths, meditating and doing muscle relaxing exercises are effective at dealing with negative thoughts and anxiety.
- Alternative/Natural medicine - There are some natural products and homeopathic medicines that some patients say help them manage panic and anxiety.

Written by Mike Paddock
Original article date: 3 Feb 2006 Article updated: 22 April 2011

9 MEDICATION

I AM ON SEVERAL MEDICATIONS TO HELP WITH MY SYMPTOMS, BUT AS YOU WILL read, do not always do the job. Presently, I am on three mood stabilizers and two anti-anxiety medications. Specifically, Invega, Trileptal, Cogentin, Klonopin, and Xanax.

1. Invega (paliperidone) is an antipsychotic medication. It works by changing the effects of chemicals in the brain.
2. Invega is used to treat schizophrenia.
3. Invega may also be used for purposes not listed in this medication guide.
4. Trileptal (oxcarbazepine) is in a group of drugs called anticonvulsants, or antiepileptic drugs. It works by decreasing nerve impulses that cause seizures.
5. Trileptal is used to treat partial seizures in adults and children who are at least 2 years old. Trileptal may also be used for purposes not listed in this medication guide.
6. Cogentin/Benztropine reduces the effects of certain chemicals in the body that may become unbalanced as a result of disease (such as Parkinson's), drug therapy, or other causes.

7. Benztropine is used to treat the symptoms of Parkinson's disease, such as muscle spasms, stiffness, tremors, sweating, drooling, and poor muscle control.
8. Benztropine is also used to treat and prevent these symptoms when they are caused by drugs such as chlorpromazine (Thorazine), fluphenazine (Prolixin), perphenazine (Trilafon), and others.
9. Benztropine may also be used for purposes not listed in this medication guide.
10. Klonopin (clonazepam) is in a group of drugs called benzodiazepines (ben-zoe-dye-AZE-eh-peens). Clonazepam affects chemicals in the brain that may become unbalanced and cause anxiety.
11. Klonopin is used to treat seizure disorders or panic disorder.
12. Klonopin may also be used for purposes not listed in this medication guide.
13. Xanax (alprazolam) belongs to a group of drugs called benzodiazepines. It works by slowing down the movement of chemicals in the brain that may become unbalanced. This results in a reduction in nervous tension (anxiety).
14. Xanax is used to treat anxiety disorders, panic disorders, and anxiety caused by depression. Xanax may also be used for purposes not listed in this medication guide.

1-5 drug information found at www.drugs.com if you want to read more about side effects or other uses.

Medication regimens tend to be switched when necessary, either the drug itself or a different dosage. I have gone years without changing a thing, but just recently had to change in June 2012, but I will explain that later. The biggest side effect of my medications is lethargy. I sleep most of the day, and my days and nights are reversed. Most times, I wake up at 2AM, ready to start the day.

10 A WORK OF TRUTH

This book is not fictional whatsoever, but it may be like a story. The point of some of my stories is to show how stress may have triggered a breakdown, and also to show how out of control I was. It's a very odd feeling to look back at my past and realize how foolish I acted, when, in those moments, I didn't realize it. I also tend to be too hard on myself. I can't help that I was being manic. When you are in a manic episode, you feel terrific and just keep going and going with energy to no end. When the mania is over, sometimes the events that happened when you were in mania or psychosis are hard to remember. I just remembered I had a great time. Part of my erratic behavior could also come from my fear of being forgotten. I wanted to live my life, so that whoever meets me or is friends with me, will remember me. If you are not remembered when you are gone, it's like you never existed, in my opinion. I think I have already accomplished that. On the flip side, I believe if you are remembered, it's like you are never gone.

People with bipolar disorder can sometimes be the "life of the party", and that role seemed to fit me rather well. I like being a little wild and out of control. I like stirring things up, and making lasting memories as a result of that wildness, or whatever you want to call it. The way I see it, there are two types of people; the people who ask why, and the people who say why not. I am a why not kind of person. I have settled down quite a lot, and I don't go out much. Most of the time, I am happy staying home and sober. Every once in a while, I get a little manic and want to drink and party with my friends.

I would describe myself today as a social binge drinker. I don't drink alone, but I did in college after work to wind down for the day. I think I am really a social drinker at heart. When I am around my friends, I just want to get wild, and I usually drink to excess. I used to drink to the point of getting sick, but that was more in my younger days. I still did get sick on occasion in my late twenties. I never really feel any peer pressure, it's just that drinking to me is normalcy. It's what I'm used to. I feel restricted if I can't do things I used to do. The fact is that people change, regardless of mental state. It's just hard to accept that I may be turning the page and slowing down.

Some of the events may be out of chronological order because my memory is so bad. I will do the best I can, and I may have to refer to my medical records to be accurate, which, by the way, is as thick as a dictionary. Somehow, I keep getting denied Social Security Disability. In my most recent rejection letter, the SSA (Social Security Administration) will not even grant me the time of day to appeal the denial. Sometimes I may set things from my medical records aside with quotation marks, other times, I will be reciting from memory. Maybe a little game the reader could play is taking the aforementioned symptoms and apply them to my life and the stories I will tell. If you want to play psychologist. If not, enjoy the read.

With all that out of the way, I guess I will just start at the beginning, and let it flow. I was born in 1981 in a suburb of Cincinnati, Ohio, to my 39-year-old mother and my 40-year-old father. I was a "pleasant surprise" as they like to say. I always tease I was an accident. It doesn't matter how I got here because I am here now. I have four older siblings, three brothers and a sister, ranging in age from 48 to 41. I am now 31 years old. My siblings used to always tease me that I was adopted, and I think I believed it sometimes until about age eight. I think I finally demanded I be shown my birth certificate. My parents got married in 1963 and are still married to this day. They are coming up on 50 years of marriage. My neighborhood has basically a small-town feel. Everyone knows each other kind of thing. Middle class at best. I never went without the necessities and had few expensive things like other kids I knew. I didn't mind too much. It made me appreciate what I had; which was a solid family, and I was completely immersed in sports. Those are the great memories I have from my childhood.

I actually had a life-changing moment at the age of 5 (maybe younger), which I remember to this day. I was born with a giant nevus (basically a mole) that covered my entire leg when I was born. The nevus could have potentially become cancerous later in life, so doctors had to remove it and do a skin graft to replace the skin. I was in a cast for about six months, around the age of two. This left a lot of scar tissue, and the color of my left leg is a darker than my right. My left leg is skinnier than my right also. One day, I was playing with friends, and some kid called me "bacon leg". I was devastated. I sat on my porch and cried for at least an hour. That was the first time in my life I realized I looked different and was being made fun of for it. When I was done crying, I had an epiphany of sorts and decided that I would never treat someone like that kid did to me that day. It felt awful, and I never wanted to make anyone feel that way. It's funny that I still remember that.

I had a good childhood, in general. My father was the breadwinner and authoritarian, and my mother raised the children and kept house. Very old-fashioned and traditional. My father was not very emotional, and my mother was somewhat over emotional. I think I have only seen my dad cry once or twice, and telling me he loves me with the same frequency. That is how it was. You were just supposed to know, even if you really needed to hear it sometimes. My mother still had a traditional job when times were economically tough. In her seventies now, she still works. My mother did everything around the house. She always had dinner on the table when my father got off work, and she considered it a time for everyone in the family to catch up on what had happened that day. She still cooks dinner almost every night for my dad, except for the rare occasions they go out to dinner. My mom and my sister were basically the ones to raise me, teach me, and so forth. One of my brothers also helped. He used to tote me around and show me off to all his friends. My dad's job was to work, take care of the yard, or any other "manly" things like fixing things. He probably missed 5 days of work in 50 years, if that. He was very hardworking, and I always admired him for that. He had a bit of a temper, and would take it out on the kids sometimes physically, but I don't think he missed more than a handful of my baseball games. My parents were never drinkers, and physical violence was rare, but present. Being older now, I realize my father doesn't know how to express his emotions or communicate very well, so anger, violence, bitterness, and sarcasm was how it came out. He still doesn't know how to communicate, which doesn't surprise me. I don't think it is realistic to think he would all of a sudden change. I also played soccer, basketball, and lacrosse, to which games he rarely attended. He didn't go either because he didn't like these sports or he was just too tired from working. Either way, it would have been nice for him to be there. I tried baseball, football, and track and field in high school, but I wasn't as talented as the other kids. Maybe I wasn't as dedicated, either. I had mixed feelings towards my father, and I still do to this day.

I started reading before the age of 2, and I think people started to notice then that I was a pretty bright child. I was very social and enjoyed talking to people older than myself. I don't know if it was because I associated more with older people because my parents are older or what, or if I was socially mature for my age, maybe because of my older siblings. I was raised Catholic, and attended Mass every Sunday until about the age of 15. I refused to go one Sunday because I felt like everyone was going through the motions and forgot everything they were supposed to learn as soon as Mass let out. I didn't think that was right. I wasn't sure of my own faith either, so I didn't think it was right for me to go for that reason either. My parents were big believers in private Catholic schooling, so I can only imagine the outrageous amounts of money it cost to send all five children through private grade school and high school. I have to give them credit for being so unselfish because they could have had a lot more money freed up if we all had been sent to public school.

I found school very boring, but managed to make As or Bs all the way through college for the most part. I also worked the entire time to try to support myself the best I could in high school and college. I held a full-time job while attending college full time. My parents were always there to help me financially if I couldn't make the bills. At the worst financial times, I didn't know where my next meal was going to come from, and once, I had to sleep in my apartment with no electricity for 3 days. I regularly got in trouble for talking too much or clowning around in grade school and high school. I earned a B.A. In Psychology from the University of Dayton. I even had conflicts with some of my professors over attendance policies and what I thought was unfair subjective grading. Once again, this could have been a result of my bipolar disorder building up and having problems with authority. Or my points were valid, or both. Later, I would earn a real estate license. I had grand plans of being a millionaire, real estate mogul.

My entrance test scores for high school were nearly perfect, and I attended high school where my three brothers had gone also. I held various jobs since the age of 15, mostly of the pizza or food delivery variety. I played nearly every sport when I was a child, but could not compete with the athletes at my high school, so that is when my sports career ended. I wasn't used to being average, or even below, I guess. I don't really enjoy playing games I don't have a chance at winning. I can be a sore winner, all in fun, but I would like to think of myself as a gracious loser. I was always big and tall and towered over most children. Not the case in high school. I went to Archbishop Moeller High School, which is nationally recognized for academic and athletic excellence. I was 3rd in my class academically and after freshmen year, and would finish 22giving. I had a photographic memory in my schooling days, and I rarely studied. Maybe I just retained everything the first time. I was skipping high school and smoking a lot of marijuana. A lot of those days were spent bumming around, usually at a park just listening to new music or throwing a frisbee. Eventually, my friends and I got caught after we left fake voice messages on the school voice mail, pretending to be each other's parents. I think it was the bursting out laughing that gave us away. We were reprimanded, and we never missed a day after that. I got into photography as well. Taking pictures of nature was my interest, and I still enjoy that to this day. I went to the many parks in Cincinnati, and I took pictures of simple things like a flower arrangement or a fountain, which is amazing considering the lack of effort I was.

There was a place a lot of my friends went to hang out in high school that we called "the band room". It was my friend's upper loft in his garage where he kept his drums. He went to a public school in the area, but I had known him from sports as a child. We had lots of good times there, and his parents tolerated us as long as we didn't get too out of control. It was a place we could all go to hang out without much parental supervision. We would drink, smoke pot, and do other drugs occasionally up there. I had three girls as my best friends in high school, and two of them I went to grade school with for eight years. We used to drive around and listen to music and smoke pot, sometimes through a rich neighborhood in Cincinnati. We hung out all the time. One time we were smoking pot, and I thought I saw my deceased grandmother's face up in the clouds. It really frightened me at first, and then comforted me like she was still with me in spirit. I realize now I could have just been high, or it was a precursor hallucination from bipolar disorder.

I got along with the jocks, hippies, nerds, and everyone else. I was very outgoing and likeable. My high school was an all male high school, so ribbing and making fun of each other was a daily thing.

If you couldn't take it, you wouldn't survive. The best defense was to give it right back, and I did. I was basically a smartass, and have been my whole life. The students took a liking to that. The authority figures that didn't appreciate my humor reprimanded me for it. Some teachers actually knew how to handle me, to their credit, and would tolerate me to a certain point. I knew when to quit with these teachers because I respected them for putting up with me and teaching me so much. Not just the subject they taught, but a little about adult life along the way. The whole dynamic of my high school was to prepare you for college and manhood, and it did. I shrugged it off like it didn't, just to not give satisfaction to the higher-ups that saw me as a nuisance. There was a prayer retreat that was optional for seniors, and I was one of the two who did not attend out of a class of over 200. They acted like it was optional, but all the authority figures were not pleased I didn't go.

I earned a partial academic scholarship to the University of Dayton on account of my high ACT score, which was really a drop in the bucket considering how expensive it was. My SAT scores were in the 1100s, which really isn't that great, considering how smart I thought I was. I was lucky to score better on the ACT, with a score of 29. I guess that is good enough to get a partial scholarship. They called the University of Dayton "Moeller North" because so many people from my Cincinnati high school go there. I still have student loans to pay back from attending. I learned there is a program for the disabled to have student loan debt relieved, if deemed by the doctor and the courts. That is what I am pursuing now. I have been living my mental illness for 7 years, and the state and federal courts refuse to grant me disability. I don't think I ever will pay those student loans back, honestly. It's the only debt I have. All my credit cards got paid off with help from my father, and I am very grateful for that. He even helped with some of my student loans. I would gradually pay him back most of it.

I never met my maternal grandfather or my paternal grandmother. They both passed before I was born. I've never heard too many stories about my paternal grandmother, just that she was a farmer and a very nice lady. My grandfather would end up remarrying (too soon, according to his kids AKA my dad, aunt, and uncle). His second wife was the only grandmother I would know on my dad's side. She was very good with money, and passed away, leaving my grandfather a widower for the second time. She was a big believer in education and was always a very sweet lady to me. My grandfather passed away in 2012. He fought in WWII in the United States Navy aboard the USS Whitley. He was a mechanic for the ship. He could fix or build pretty much anything. We have an American flag in a case in our dining room commemorating his service. I never saw such a flag in real life before. I always saw them handed to families at funerals on TV or in the movies. Soon after he died, it gave me a creepy feeling, but now, it makes me proud I am his grandson. We also got a letter from President Obama thanking our family for his service. Another proud moment.

From the stories my mom tells, my maternal grandfather would have loved me. He was a drinker, smoker, gambler, and an accomplished businessman. He was also honored as a Kentucky State Colonel. He used to feed the homeless and poor right out of his own home, with my grandmother (my mom's mom). I feel like things started to go downhill when my maternal grandmother passed in 1998. I was 16 or 17 years old. The night she died, I went into my room with a fifth of whiskey and closed the door. Probably the first time I was really drunk. I remember crying too. I was no longer in sports activities. I began drinking and smoking marijuana. I experimented with mushrooms and ecstasy also. I tried acid and smoked hash oil once, and smoked opium whenever it was available, which was hardly ever. Mostly at music festivals and rock concerts. I never snorted anything in my life, nor did I ever shoot heroin or anything like that. I ate a piece of cocaine once because one of my friends always had it, but like I said, never snorted it. I quit all the drugs by age 20, except for smoking pot. The reason I quit the harder drugs is because I took too many psychedelic mushrooms and had a bad trip, as they call it. Wild, intense hallucinations, and that was the end of that. The walls and floor were moving and vibrating. I passed out in my kitchen in my apartment and woke up terrified and confused. A part of me is glad I experimented, but I don't think I could encourage any child to try what I did in good conscience. I continued to smoke marijuana every day, several times a day. It never really cost me a lot of money, because I was selling it to my friends, or at least, people who I thought were my friends.

Everyone is your friend when you have something they want. I started out small, just straight out buying it. Then, I met a few people who had more, at a discounted rate. I began to realize if I sold it; I didn't have to pay for it. That's how I got into the whole drug dealing situation. I don't like the term "drug dealer" because of the stereotype that goes with it. I didn't hurt anyone, and I wasn't on the street selling it to kids. I didn't own any guns either. I really just sold it to my friends, and I have a lot. Sometimes I would have to ride to bad parts of town to get it cheaper, which was pretty risky now that I look back on it. The guy who would take me to these neighborhoods always had a gun strapped to him under his armpit. He never had to use it when I was around, but it made me feel safer. I met him through a mutual friend, and we even hung out sometimes despite the fifteen years or so age difference. He was my first supplier. In college, I immediately found a supplier. It was all I knew how to get it for cheap and smoke for free. If I was lucky, I would even make money. Actually, I made 100% on my money, but I smoked a lot, which cut into the profits significantly. I got into it pretty heavy, transporting somewhat large amounts from Dayton to Cincinnati and back. I think I liked the easy money, the power, and the respect I got from my "customers". People tend to kiss your ass when you are supplying them. I even got respect from my dealers because I made them all so much money. Never mind that some days I could have easily gone to prison if I had been caught. I had nerves of steel. I don't know why I didn't really care. It could have been the money, or maybe I felt important. I was young too, and sometimes you feel invincible. I hope you are following my skipping around from ideas to memories. You may be asking yourself: Where were his parents at? They were both working most of the time, and I really quit listening to them when I got my first car at the age of 16. I had a job, my own money, and my own transportation. I got away with pretty much anything. I would disappear for the whole weekend while I was not in school. My mom still thinks she failed me, and she could have done more. I tell her all the time she was a good mom, and I wouldn't have listened, anyway. The most despicable behavior I displayed when I was young was stealing money and pain medication from her. It was never much, but I regret it so much. I hate thieves, and I used to be one of them.

When I was a child, my father used to say I had a "spring in my ass" because I would never sit still. That could have been a clue that I would turn out to have bipolar disorder, but a lot of kids were hyper, like I was. It may sound funny, but my obsession with numbers began with the Count from Sesame Street. I remember I used to spend days writing out numbers, starting at one and continuing into the tens of thousands. Pretty strange for someone not quite five years old.

When I was a teenager, I started going to music festivals and rock concerts. I loved it. I felt like the people understood me there and thought like me to some extent. I enjoyed traveling to them as well, from Florida to Vermont. It really changed me. I didn't realize that there were so many people that "went against the grain" of societal norms and mores. The people dressed and acted much differently than the people I encountered in parochial school. I started with a music festival called Hookahville, which was named because the headlining band was called Ekoostik Hookah. There were a lot of other bands, too. I got to see Blues Traveler, Arlo Guthrie, Ziggy Marley, and many other great bands. It was a three-day event every Memorial Day and Labor Day weekends. I probably attended around seven of those. I went to a Phish concert in Florida on a Seminole Indian reservation that had over 110,000 people. One of the best times of my life. Phish is a jam band with a cult following similar to the Grateful Dead. I was 18, and it was New Year's Eve 2000. It was a three-day event. It was an awesome and eye-opening experience. People were walking around naked, doing drugs, basically total freedom. Police were not allowed on the reservation because it is considered out of the jurisdiction of the state or federal government. Two people died that weekend. While it is a tragedy, all things considered, could have been worse. They even showed part of the concert on the Dick Clark's New Year's Eve countdown show. Phish is the name of the band I have seen most, and the atmosphere of those shows stayed with me. I still try to go whenever I can. It's hard for me to handle large crowds. It's hit or miss. Sometimes it bothers me, sometimes it doesn't, but is severe enough to label me agoraphobic. It never used to bother me, and this is more of a recent development. Another thing that is anxiety provoking for me is having to be somewhere on a certain day at a certain time. If the appointment is two weeks away, I will obsess about it almost to the point of physical illness. My anxiety ramps up the day of the appointment, too. Whether it is a psychiatric appointment or having to be at a job. Jobs are so hard for me for this reason, but also I have a phobia of being constrained or restrained. I feel like when I am at a job that requires me to be there from 9-5 for example, I feel trapped. The time goes by so slowly. The anxiety is literally choking. It feels like there is an elephant sitting on my chest while I am there. I think that this phobia comes from being hospitalized on lock-down, and basically held against my will. I spent a night in a jail cell too while I was manic, and it was a horrific experience. Somewhat related, I always hated turtlenecks as a child and clothes in general. Could be because of the restraining nature of clothes.

I was asked to write a paper in high school about what I wanted to do when I grew up, and I had no answer except to be happy. That's all I really wanted, honestly. I chose psychology as my major because I wanted to understand why people thought and acted the way they did. I was confused how some people could act so strange, heartless, mean, angry, or whatever the situation may be. I wanted to see what made people tick, while others were not motivated by these same things. My plan was to continue to get my Ph.D., but I ran out of money, interest, and energy. I graduated in 2004, and I got sick in 2006 also. I was never much of a materialistic person, although sometimes I would go on spending sprees with the money I made (people with bipolar disorder tend to do this). I still just really want to be happy, and helping others has always made me feel that way. I always had a laid back attitude, and hardly ever got mad. I don't express my emotions very well and tend to keep things inside, usually resulting in a blowup of some sorts over something miniscule. I use poetry as an outlet sometimes. I still have never been in a fight to this day. Physically, anyway. My biggest fights have been against myself and my disorders.

While attending college, I had a live-in girlfriend that I thought I might marry someday. We dated about 3 years, but broke up before I graduated college. At that time, she got pregnant. I was devastated. I was 20. I'm not going to put all the blame on her, but the one time we had unprotected sex, she told me she couldn't get pregnant for all these different reasons, and I believed her. Within weeks, she had an abortion with my persuasion. I felt tricked and betrayed. I still think about it to this day and feel pretty guilty sometimes. I think of how old my child would be in the present day. I have a 12-year-old nephew that would have been about the same age as my child, if I had chosen to have him/her/it. I don't even know the right term to use. I was raised Catholic, and this was something that was definitely against my upbringing. I rationalize it sometimes by thinking that my ex and I could have never raised a child, and that child would have maybe had mental illness, which I wouldn't want to pass on or wish on anyone. I felt like there was no other option. It is one of my dark secrets that very few people know about. This girlfriend would show up later in life, but that is a different part of the story. During college, I was always on the go. If it wasn't work, it was schoolwork, if it wasn't school work, it was partying or giving attention to my girlfriend. I was barely sleeping. I would sometimes take Adderall to help me study, but mostly so I could stay awake and drink and party more. I was never prescribed it, but someone at school had extras and would give them to me if I asked, which wasn't that frequent.

I dated another woman who was studying to be an EMT. There was nothing serious about it. We worked at a sports bar together, and all we would do was get drunk and high together. It was fun, but it wasn't going anywhere. I lost contact with her eventually, and I found out about two weeks after we stopped seeing each other, she got pregnant. It scared the hell out of me, but luckily, it was not mine.

I graduated from the University of Dayton in 2004 and struggled to find a job. I graduated with a 2.95 GPA, which is pretty good all things considered, among the partying, working, and catatonic behavior. I used to be able to cram for exams, reading a hundred pages from a textbook in one night. Now, I can barely read one page from a book. I don't have the concentration or attention span anymore. The only thing I can watch on TV really is sports because I can't keep attention on any shows with a storyline or a plot. While attending the University of Dayton, I started to notice something odd. Every time I walked under street lamps, they would go out. I thought it was some sort of celestial or heavenly sign. That could have been a foreshadowing of my illness, but I joked about it, and it never impaired my functioning. The reality is these lamps are on timers or motion sensors, and it was mere coincidence.

I still lived in Dayton for another year before I bounced around from friend's to friend's houses because I didn't want to move back home and lose the independence I had. So, I went back to school and earned a real estate license. I had grand plans of being a real estate mogul like Donald Trump, but that didn't work out, yet anyway. These are called grandiose feelings, which are a symptom of bipolar disorder. You think you are superior and are going to succeed at a high level. You feel invincible. What they don't tell you in real estate school is the outrageous amount of money it takes to start up and be successful. The advice I was given from other agents and a broker was "Just get a credit card and charge everything and pay it off when you sell a house". I was not willing to do that and get more into debt. I got a job working at a pizza place I worked at in high school in my hometown. I was basically made a manager, and began working long hours. I began acting manic with the new job stress. I signed a lease to buy a house in my mania also. I was going to buy a new car. I couldn't afford any of it, but I thought I could. I guess this is where I tell you about the day that would forever change my life and the way I thought about everything.

11 DIAGNOSED

THIS IS WHERE THINGS ARE GOING TO GET A BIT FOGGY, AND I WILL PROBABLY have to refer to my medical records at some point to be accurate. On July 31, 2006, (I will never forget the date, and always am very somber when it comes around each year) Sometimes I feel like it is a birthday though. I go through a range of feelings on this day. I am somber because the memory will never leave my mind, but grateful I am not in that place anymore. I went to the psychiatric unit of a hospital in Cincinnati. I was very paranoid, hearing voices, seeing things that weren't there, and demonstrating odd behaviors (all symptoms of bipolar disorder). I actually thought I heard the trumpets of angels calling to me. I had to lie down at my house to remain calm. I remember reading the Bible aloud in the waiting room. One of my brothers, who is as close to me as my father, noticed, and took me to the hospital. I was in such a frenzy that after I signed the papers for them to treat me; the nurses gave me a huge shot of some medicine and I went right to sleep for hours. I didn't realize I had just committed myself, and I tried to escape in my psychosis. About twelve security guards had to surround me before I would let them give me the shot. I found out later the drug was Geodon or Risperdal (I can't remember). I will tell you it was the best sleep of my life.

A doctor interviewed me and asked me questions like if I knew who the president and vice president were, and the day and date. I guess I was correct, but I don't remember. They asked me about all the drugs I have done, and I still remember the shocked looks on my parents' faces. It was all so surreal. It was like I was watching myself in a movie. I still get that feeling sometimes to this day. I think it is the brain's natural defense mechanism to withdrawal from a painful event. I spent 11 days there on a locked-down floor. I was hyper-religious, constantly reading the Bible and talking about God. I thought I could heal people and predict the future as well. I thought the end of the world was near. I almost jumped off a balcony because I thought I could fly. That's how strong the high of mania can be. Delusional thinking is also a symptom of bipolar disorder. This is what people in the psychiatric community call a "first break". Basically, when the symptoms of bipolar disorder become too intense to function, usually resulting in a hospitalization. I remember calling the governor of Ohio and leaving a message saying I was being held captive against my will. I think I also tried to order a pizza. They had a phone in the common area that the patients could use. Here is a statement from the hospital record:

"John Medl is a 24-year-old white male who endorses a history of paranoid behavior. He has no prior psychiatric diagnosis. His mother and brother brought him to University Hospital on July 31, 2006 because of his erratic behavior. Prior to admission, he broke into a car on July 29, 2006 because he believed that the CIA gave it to him. He also believed that he was receiving special messages from lottery tickets, television, and radio. He was smoking 10 to 20 joints a day" I would like to add that I wasn't smoking that much. When they interviewed me, I was psychotic, and really had no idea what was going on. And it continues," In University Hospital, the patient has been exhibiting extreme manic and psychotic symptoms, including elevated mood and labile affect. He has delusional thinking that he works for the CIA. He states that God is talking to him. He continues to be very grandiose. He has been irritable with staff on the unit. He has destroyed property and required emergency medication. He has been walking around with his backside exposed. He has decompensated since his admission.

Mr. Medl is currently suffering from Bipolar Affective Disorder, manic episode with psychotic features. His delusions and hallucinations and his irritable behavior represent a substantial risk to himself and others. It is the belief of this treatment team that the least restrictive, effective, and safe treatment option for Mr. Medl is as an inpatient in the locked down psychiatric unit. The patient will benefit from medication treatment, and the social and therapeutic milieu of the hospital."

I thought the CIA was following me and recruiting me. I thought there were microphones or "bugs" in my house to record what I was saying. I was getting messages through the TV. I could have sworn the TV changed channels by itself one time, but I probably sat on the remote control or some logical explanation. There was a gang in my neighborhood that I thought the CIA was rewarding me for exposing, which led to an arrest. In my mind, I was following clues and messages I was receiving that told me the CIA was going to give me a free car as a reward for helping to uncover this gang. I walked up to a complete stranger's car that was vacant and parked and got in. I was charged for trespassing and criminal damaging, but the charges were dropped on the account that I was not guilty by reason of insanity. Probably the best thing that could have happened to me. The police took me to jail, and I spent the night. I still remember how good the food tasted because I probably hadn't eaten in a day or so. Sauerkraut and hot dogs on white bread with water. I had to ask for the water I remember. In the morning, I saw a judge that specialized in mental illness. I was in complete psychosis, and have trouble remembering the details to this day. I know I was referred to an agency and a psychiatrist. I have received the excellent treatment I have received today in 2013 because of that arrest and hospitalization. Here is a poem that I wrote about describing that day and how I felt:

July 31, 2006

It was like lightning Struck my brain in two
A feeling I hope never happens to you.
Fueled by a combination
Of drugs and chemical failure
I never even saw it coming.
But in hindsight, they say things seem clearer
The teamwork of genetics, environment, and behavior.
A complete mental meltdown
Of someone competent and capable before
Never having a clue of what tests were in store.
I thought I would get better soon
Not months into years and more.
Confused, never in control
As the toxic cocktail took its toll

Crammed in a cell and then a bus to court
With total strangers, not knowing what I'd done Or where I was
But knowing it wasn't normal or fun
They had me sign some papers
That I couldn't focus to read
And plunged a needle deep in me
And gave me pills they said I'd need
They took me to a ward where I was greeted By shrieking vocal cords
They gave me a room, and a short tour
Life as I knew it, never more
A condition I guess they thought they could fix July thirty-first, two-thousand and six.

JOHN E MEDL

12 REVOLUTION

Around this time (not sure exactly) I felt a crazy amount of energy one night while I was on my front porch. I saw the American flag hanging off our house, and I ripped it off the house and began marching. I thought I was going to lead some kind of revolution. I marched with the flag waving from my house to a police station about 2 miles away. I felt like I could have run a marathon. Keep in mind, I was at least 400 pounds at the time, so you know the energy was at a high level. I walked into the police station and gave it to the dispatcher working at the time. I think my mindset was that I was giving the flag to the police in appreciation for their service. One of my best friends saw me in this mania around this time also. She thought I was on cocaine because I was talking so fast. I wasn't making sense, and I just kept ordering drinks. I had no control over what I was doing. My body was the vehicle, and my brain was the driver.

I forgot to mention that I starting dating a girl around 2005, and we rarely spent time apart. We would just sit around her apartment, smoke pot and/or drink beer, play games, watch TV, and eat, and that was enough for us. We went out every once in a while, but not much. She worked for a big time company, and she was consumed by it, but we still managed to hang out a lot. I never really thought it was going anywhere. The biggest clue was when I met her parents and they scolded me like a child for getting up from the dinner table without asking to be excused. A little too uptight for my taste.

She had a saying she would write on any card she gave me or present. It was "amor vincit omnia", which means "love conquers all" in Latin. She even had a watch engraved with that saying on it. I still have it, but I don't know why. I couldn't care less where it ends up. Very soon after being released from the hospital, she dumped me. Pretty hypocritical, if you ask me.

13 EXHAUSTION

From August 2006 to September 2007, I slept almost all day and all night. My couch was my favorite place to sleep, and I remember watching out of the large window above the couch watching life go by. Here is a poem that describes how I felt about that:

Quilted Sofa

Padded checkers and rings
Hold my see-saw feelings
Tragedy, triumph, good, and bad
The best rest I've ever had.
Once glued, now improved
I got back everything
I used to groggily wish for.
Now I seem to be
Trapped in my own clarity.
Truths that will haunt me for years, and fears, dried up tears
Steered by sanity now, but how?
No better time to start than now
Forcing me to stand pat
A curse worse than a black cat Labels by faces, replaces

All the old thoughts about myself.
But I know who and what I am Like it or not
Do you really think my soul forgot?

Here is a quote I really like that explains how I feel about the difference between my old self and my medicated, non-manic self:

"I compare myself with my former self, not with others. Not only that, I tend to compare my current self with the best I have been, which is when I have been mildly manic. When I am my present "normal" self, I am far removed from when I have been my liveliest, most productive, most intense, most outgoing and effervescent. In sort, for myself, I am a hard act to follow."

Kay Redfield Jamison, An Unquiet Mind: A Memoir of Moods and Madness

14 ADMITTED AGAIN

I NEVER THOUGHT I WOULD BE ABLE TO FUNCTION AGAIN. A VERY DEPRESSING feeling. The doctors explained they medicated me to "bring me down" from my mania. This was a time where I almost gave up and gained over 100lbs from eating all the time and being sedentary. I slept at least 18 hours a day. The medication warned that it may cause weight gain, so I figured if it was going to happen anyway, I would eat anything and everything I wanted. In retrospect, not such a great idea. So, I guess this brings me to 2007. I got a job at a sandwich shop and excelled delivering food and managing, too. The owner wanted to send me to Chicago to be an assistant general manager. I thought I would be there forever.

On June 13, 2008, I was admitted again to a hospital for being in a manic episode. A lot of things were happening in my life like the job stress and long hours, my mom having her hip replaced, and a friend of mine from high school and college died in a boating accident. Stress and loss of a loved one, or loss in general, almost certainly will trigger a manic episode, and it did. I was on a 24 hour watch because of my out-of-control behavior. I am referring to my medical records for the next set of dates. I pulled the fire alarm because I wanted help to escape. The pleasant things I remember were that we had a little Bible study group, and we would read the Bible and pray every day. There were about 25 people on the floor, males and females. There was a refrigerator full of apple juice and wedged cheese that there was an endless supply of for the patients. They had a lot of board games, support groups, and even arts and crafts. I was resistant to participate in any of this at first because I was very paranoid of everyone and wanted to be released immediately. I wasn't exactly thrilled to be there, either. Eventually, I calmed down and started to interact with the other patients.

I remember one night I woke up about 3AM, and I thought I had been flown to the Vatican to meet the Pope. I would wake up at these odd hours and process down the halls holding the Bible up like I was at Mass. I also remember thinking I was Jesus reincarnated at some point. I thought a major earthquake was going to hit the US, so I requested a printout of all the major fault lines in the US. There was never an earthquake in the US, but one happened in China. I thought my predictive abilities were just a little off, and I had misinterpreted the "signs". I was over analyzing everything. I was using cryptology on everything from soda cans to the microwave. I remember thinking the microwave and thermostat were just cover-ups that actually controlled all of the patients' minds.

I was released on June 16th with all new meds and I hit a parked car because I thought I was getting messages from my stereo to lose my license. Specifically, my stereo read "protect", and in my delusional world, that meant lose my license. I think I thought that I needed to be protected from the outside world, so I could accomplish some grand feat. I lost my license, but criminal charges were dropped after I told my lawyer and the judge I was the "chosen one". I don't know exactly what I meant, but it warranted another not guilty by reason of insanity. I know it doesn't make sense, but it feels like it does when you are in an episode like that. I was released on June 19. I was sending emails to the White House, criticizing President Bush. Nothing wrong with that, really, but I thought the government was going to come find me.

On June 20, I called the life squad because of an anxiety attack and was taken to the hospital and released.

On June 23, I called the life squad again for the same reason, but never hospitalized. My meds got changed again, and I was a little more stable. I had to cut my hours from about 60 to 20 and began sleeping most of the time again. This is also when panic disorder was added to my diagnoses. All the while I was battling with Social Security to be granted disability benefits, but to this day, I get denied over and over. I am still in the process 7 years later. This is where it gets blurry.

I know I quit that job because I was very paranoid and demonstrated erratic, manic behavior. It was a shame because I liked the job; I was good at it, and the owner and staff liked me. Between my symptoms and the side effects of my medication, I could not function even on the lowest of levels.

15 WEIGHT

The next date I really remember is September 11. Weight. I was 591 lbs. I used to weigh myself on a scale meant for measuring large loads of scrap metal, and the red glowing numbers that were on the meter are burned into my brain permanently. I got down to 447 lbs. by eating a very low-fat diet. I didn't even have to exercise, just eat better. In June 2012, I was about 485 lbs. In May 2013, I am about 525 pounds. A lot of the medication that people, then in 2009, when I decided I was going to lose with mental illness are prescribed cause weight gain, but not necessarily everyone. In October 2009, my sister got married, and I wore a suit with size 72 pants. I now wear a size 56. Not really that important, but I was proud of myself, and I think this confidence propelled me to be more social and outgoing, like my old self. One of the constant depressing things is that I always compared myself to my "old self" that could handle a job and stress, and had fun all the time. It takes a lot of time and therapy to get over that line of thinking, which I still struggle with. I most likely will never be as productive as I was while in high school and college, and accepting that as a reality is a tough pill to swallow, no pun intended.

I have been overweight my whole life. I was almost eleven pounds when I was born, and I never stopped growing. I was almost six feet tall in the eighth grade. My mom used to have to alter all my school or sports uniforms so that they would fit me. I had trouble fitting into the desks at school, too. I never had much confidence with the opposite sex for that reason. I always thought that all women only liked skinny boys, and that they would find me disgusting. Later in life, I learned that wasn't true, but as a child, I was very embarrassed. People loved to feed me. I would get extra portions in the school lunch line. I would eat dinner at home, and then go to a friend's house, only to have his/her parents feed me again. I didn't know any better. I ate almost everything available. In fact, my mom was overweight my whole childhood as well, until she lost over 100 pounds within the last five years or so. She is somewhat of a "health nut" now, but she didn't know any better when I was younger and she was preparing meals.

Mental illness can be very embarrassing and can break down your confidence. It was like one day; I was fully functioning, and the next day, I was in the hospital. The family and friends you had before the hospital knew you to be a certain person and then they see you psychotic in a hospital. I was lucky that some of my best friends came to visit. My parents would sneak me in my favorite Mexican food too.

It felt like the rug got pulled out from under me, and I am still traumatized and haunted by it to this day. My whole line of thought and goals and beliefs changed. When I felt better, I started to live in the moment more, and it was hard for me to make long-term goals or plans. I still carry on that way. After things like this happen, you are constantly worried it is going to happen again. I am grateful for every day that I get, so the notion of thinking about retirement or any sort of long-term goals is not possible for me. The best days are when I forget about my past, but it doesn't happen often. This is probably why I self-medicated with alcohol. To forget. Basically, the same reason others drink, I think. To forget about your worries and responsibilities for a little while. But, in addition, alcohol made my symptoms disappear. This is very reinforcing as you could imagine. Bipolar disorder can be very cyclical; you are symptomatic, so you drink because you are on Cloud 9. Your symptoms disappear for a little while. Then, the symptoms come back and the process may repeat all over again.

In 2009, I was focused on losing weight, and not much else. I know I didn't see my friends for a while because I was so ashamed at how large I was. When I started to lose weight, I started to gain confidence and be social again. I had fun just like any person in his/her twenties. Alcohol or marijuana was almost always involved, but that was familiar territory for me. No one ever forced me to do anything. It was just what we did while we were hanging out. I guess it added a little variety to whatever we were doing those nights. I tried my hand at various jobs, but would eventually quit either because of conflicts with co-workers or I would begin to get symptomatic, and the job would be too much.

16 LIVE, AND LEARN

PRESENTLY, I DO NOT HAVE A TYPICAL JOB. I RECEIVE $115 A MONTH CASH AND $200 a month in food stamps from the state of Ohio. I also have Medicaid. I do market research and eBay for money, and then I usually take that money to gamble, with some success. I have gambled since I was a child really at church festivals, which is acceptable once a year at that age. I got into it heavier in college and began to play poker. I went to Canada to gamble at a casino when I was 19 because back then, the gambling and drinking age was only 18. I went with one of my exes, and we won about 2500 dollars on the first day. That made for a great trip because our budget was around 600 bucks. The legal age is 21 now, and you need a passport. That wasn't the case when I went. When I turned 21, I started going to bars and the casino with some frequency. I enjoyed both very much. I am in a poker club too, with a bunch of great people that I enjoy playing cards with to this day. Some may think I have a problem because I gamble so frequently, but it's hard for me to admit that. I just think of it as entertainment and keeping my mind occupied. I just figure if I lose, I will cut back on some other activity. I would never steal or sell a house or anything to get a "fix". I think the people who don't have a gambling spirit are really the ones that don't understand. For instance, my parents are not gamblers, and stress out over me losing as little as thirty dollars. To me, that is not a big deal, and definitely worth the price for entertainment. What would I do with the money otherwise? I'm not materialistic. I don't like shopping. I would probably spend that money at a bar or on alcohol, so I am trading one vice for another, I guess.

I am the administrator for a Facebook page devoted to helping the mentally ill and inform others about mental illness. There are almost 300 members. I don't get paid for it, but it is rewarding nonetheless. My paternal grandfather passed away May 4, 2012. We were never that close, and I didn't realize I would miss him so much. It got me thinking about losing more people close to me and ramped up my anxiety. It made me think of my own mortality as well. He served in WWII and had a military burial. I could not attend the wake or the funeral on account of my anxiety disorders. Once again, another loss in my life. I think this set off a bout of mania that ended with my last hospitalization that was June 10 , 2012. My parents were at Mass on Sunday, like they always do, and for some reason, I couldn't sit still. My mind was going 1000 miles per hour, and I couldn't quit pacing. My arms were tingling, and I thought I was having a heart attack. I thought I was going to die. I couldn't speak either, so my mom had to talk to a doctor on-call, and he advised we go to the hospital. I was transported in an ambulance to a hospital about fifteen miles away. That was the longest car ride of my life. I had on an oxygen mask that helped regulate my breathing, which was helping me slightly. All I could think about was all the people that I never got to say goodbye to. I was convinced I was having a heart attack and was going to die. I spent about six hours at the hospital, and nothing was done for me. When I felt the panic come on originally, I took a Xanax and a Klonopin. They had no effect. The doctor described it as "my brain took over my body". That's a pretty scary thought, but not far-fetched. Your brain is the control center for everything. I guess I just had never heard it put that way before. I didn't like that there was basically nothing I could have done. I have been sober ever since. On July 13, 2012, I relapsed and had about 8 beers. I felt terrible in the morning, and I don't think it is really worth it. I equate having alcohol to drink as an option as a sense of normalcy. I feel restrained if I don't think I can drink like a lot of my friends. The reality is, I am a different person with different reactions and effects to alcohol. I may not be able to drink at all, or very rarely. I was terrified to take a drink because I did not want to end up in the hospital again. I have reduced my caffeine intake dramatically as well, but lately, that is increasing as well. I haven't smoked pot in months. I feel like there is no other option. I can do everything in my power to get better, or continue to aggravate my disorders and probably end up in the hospital again. A hospitalization is always a reality for me, whether I follow my treatment plan or not. By the way, I have always followed my treatment plan, and have never missed one dose of medicine or appointment in 7 years. My most recent appointment on July 18, 2012, I could not attend physically because of my disorders. All five of my anxiety disorders can work with each other and at the same time. My doctor was nice enough to have a phone conference with me to see how I was doing. My doctor is three miles away at the most, and even that distance is too much to handle for me. He told me that if I know I will have a panic attack doing an activity, don't do it. This is against my nature because I always want to try to overcome obstacles and challenges at all costs, but I need to realize that I simply cannot beat panic disorder, or any of the other ones. All I can do is damage control and look out for my own personal well-being. Being so compliant probably hurts my case for Social Security Disability. They want someone who is not compliant. I have been 100% compliant. At any point and time, the chemicals in my brain can literally take over my body and cause a relapse. It's not a great feeling. I am constantly assessing my thought processes to see if I am okay, to the point of an obsession. People with bipolar disorder are strongly discouraged to have caffeine, alcohol, or any recreational drugs, so I am staying away for now the best I can. The possibility of a relapse is very possible and real, but all I can do is try my best.

Some time between 2009 and 2010, I dated a girl who was studying to be a nurse. She had a young daughter, and we all got along. She has a big heart and a great personality, and we still talk to this day. We eventually broke up because I got too attached. People with bipolar disorder tend to do this, but I may have especially been attached because she was the first woman I had been with since my first hospitalization. I loved that she liked me for who I was. I was still very heavy, but she didn't mind. She liked me for what I had to offer on the inside, and I respect that. I also respected her for raising her daughter alone after a failed marriage. She was the person that sort of re-socialized me back into the world. We went to the zoo, and on a bunch of mini adventures that helped my confidence grow back.

In August 2011, I got back together with my college sweetheart I mentioned earlier in the story. Big mistake. While we were apart for 8 years or so, she was diagnosed with Multiple Sclerosis, a horrible neurological disorder. She was a recovering drug addict, and she didn't contact me until she was clean because she knew she would have had no chance with me otherwise. Again, I thought I might marry her. I basically moved in with her, and we got along okay until the end. She kicked me out of her apartment in January 2012, and I moved back in on a full-time basis with my parents. I feel like I was manic then, too. I was constantly running errands and doing chores. It was stressful to be with someone with such a horrible illness. She was always in pain, and she couldn't go out much or enjoy herself very often. Most of the time, we just sat in her apartment. We hardly ever spent time apart. Then, like I said, we broke up in January. I think I was undersexed and wanted to relive the good times we had while I was in college. Definitely a bad decision on my part. To her credit, I probably wouldn't have graduated without her financial contributions to the bills while I was in college. Life had been hard on her since then, and we were both different people. You live and you learn.

17 MEDICINAL HAZE

I have given you a pretty good background of my life to this point, but what do I go through on a daily basis? How do I feel most of the time? Well, it's no picnic, but I try to keep it in a perspective that there are others who have it much worse. I only sleep three hours at night, and wake up usually with racing thoughts about what I have to do that day. I wake up about 3AM. I usually take two naps during daylight hours near my medication times. I am anxious most of the day. I obsess about death and dying; my own, as well as others. At times, I have had suicidal idealization, but no attempts. I have trouble driving a car, or even riding in one sometimes. Appointments are the worst for me. I obsess about them to the point of physical sickness. If I have to be somewhere on a certain day at a certain time, my anxiety is almost unbearable. I pace a lot, and I have a hard time sitting still. I would love to be able to concentrate enough to read or watch a movie, but sports is really all my attention can handle. I obsessively check my email, eBay, and Facebook, probably 50 times a day. I am constantly counting or running numbers in my head about making money or the probability of this or that. I constantly check the clock, whether because it is near my med times, or just out of habit. I feel every little bodily sensation I have, usually pain. I worry that there is something physically wrong with me. I have constant headaches, and I get dizzy a lot. I make a lot of lists, from what I want to accomplish that day or in the future. It could be to organize something too. I have odd sleeping times, and my meds make me feel sedated a lot. I go through cycles of being wide awake and anxious to near comatose. Here is a poem that describes how my medicine makes me feel sometimes:

Medicinal Haze

I wake up in a medicinal haze
Left over from the night
And remember all the happy days
And all the ways I used to cope.
Those were times filled with hope
Now instead of being free,
The doctors pump me full of dope.
With the stroke of his pen
He can control my behavior
Like some holier-than-thou savior
Saving me from myself
Maybe I did need help
Maybe I'll be better off
Some people hear disorder
And think it can be cured
Like a cold or cough
But it will never go away, never will
At least the drugs keep me still
Too still sometimes, more like a zombie
I guess the challenge is
Finding a balance between the new and the old me.

18 MENTAL FOG

I AM IN A FOG A LOT. IT'S LIKE WATCHING MYSELF IN A MOVIE. I THINK THE technical term is depersonalization. I think it is my brain giving up on reality for a period of time because it is always in overdrive. It is almost comparable to sleepwalking. I can be looking someone dead in the face, trying my best to pay attention, and I don't comprehend what he/she is saying. It is so frustrating because I really do care what he/she is saying, but I may come off as if I am ignoring them. Also, when in mania or psychosis, a similar thing happens, but to a greater extent. When I get manic or have been through psychosis, I had no idea what was going on, but I could remember bits and pieces after the fact. Such an odd feeling.

After seven years of trying, I was approved for disability in October 2013. Yes, the money is nice, so I am not such a financial burden on my parents, but the validation was the best part. I almost fell over when I heard the news. After all, the hospital and doctor visits. After all, the medication changes. After all the fighting. To me, the approval is saying, "We recognize that your illness is real and debilitating. You are not lazy. Your condition is too severe to work right now." I would give all the money back if it meant I could live a normal lifestyle and work a traditional job and support myself; however, that's not the reality of the situation. At least for now. I never rule out the possibility that I will get better. I want to be able to handle being in a crowd, so maybe I could enjoy a rock concert or sporting event. I want to be able to travel further than a few miles from my house. I want many things—simple things to most. I know that giving up will get me nowhere, so working hard is my only option.

I really try to improve a little every day, but sometimes I get knocked back a few pegs. I have to realize this is going to happen, and I have to dust myself off and keep trying. This is easier said than done when I am fighting disappointment on top of my brain's faulty brain chemistry.

19 FIGHTING EVERY DAY

CURRENT UPDATE---> IT IS AUGUST 2014. NOT MUCH HAS CHANGED. MY LAST update from above (October 2013) pretty much applies. I am still fighting every day, both my illness and my weight. I have gained about forty pounds. My doctor thinks I may have Post Traumatic Stress Disorder from being in the hospital as well. Basically, I start to panic at random times when I am near a hospital or I might have flashbacks of all the times I have spent in them. Claustrophobia has been removed as part of my diagnosis, and I have gone from five prescriptions to three (Cogentin and Xanax were eliminated). If I ever need medicinal help for a panic attack, I just have to take extra Klonopin. The final part of the book will be included, which is all my poetic works, in no particular order. After reading the book, it should be pretty easy to understand where my material comes from. I have been a published poet at maverickmagazine.com for many years. Over 12,000 people have read the poems I have published. Most of the poems I am including in this book never got to publishing, due to my lack of motivation. I am available through email at johnmedl7@gmail.com, if anyone has questions or comments. You can also friend me on Facebook if you so choose. My Facebook page for the mentally ill now has 401 members. I hope you have enjoyed my story and learned something. Thank you for your time.

20 I GIVE IT ALL I'VE GOT

When I feel down,
I go back to that place.
The needles and doctors
My mind can't erase.
My concerned friends and family
Who came to visit,
And how my entire life
Is wrapped up in it.
It's everything to me.
It's what drives me to be
A good person and friend.
A success story.
I was down on the mat,
But I got up.
I don't know how or why.
I could have easily given up
And kissed my future goodbye.
I must not be done yet
Or else it would have ended.
My dreams aren't gone,
They just got suspended.

I gave it everything I had
I reached down deep
The memories still haunt me Even in sleep.
When I have a bad day,
It can always be worse
The curse of making it through.
I give it all I've got
In everything I do.

JOHN E. MEDL

21 PAIN FOR MILES

Behind the laughter and the smiles
There is pain for miles
I've cried so many times
Pleading it will stop
It always seems to
When it wants to.
Most people don't know what makes me tick
I don't even know if I do
Maybe some day I will find out
How and why I got sick.
Maybe because I used to take life for granted
I never appreciated the little things
I just went about going through the motions
Never noticing anything surrounding the path I was on.
Most people have never seen me cry
I hide my emotions well
Every day is as big as a mountain
But you will probably not be able to tell.
My life's an open book
For everyone to read
I like it that way

Nothing to hide
Everything to explain
Like why sometimes
I prefer the rain.
Or why I value the company of friends so much
Or how my thoughts got out of touch
I reach down deep every minute of every day
I try my best to get through them
As hard as they are
But at least I got a poem.

JOHN E. MEDL

22 STANDING TALL

My head is pounding
And my mind won't quit
The hospital and medications
All because of it.
The sirens scream
Getting closer and closer
Until they are clear as can be
You can imagine my terror
When I knew they were coming for me.
Laid out on a stretcher
Gasping for air
I wanted to be anywhere but there.
Every second felt like ages
And not a thousand pages
Could capture
How it has come to this.
Never a day goes by
When I don't obsess about it all
But through every single battle
At least I've stood tall.

JOHN E. MEDL

23 LEGACY

My brain is on fire and my mind won't quit
Sometimes, I get sick of all of it.
I fight and I fight, but sometimes it's not enough
I just want to be known as tough.
I have a sense of humor to keep it light
I just want to do what's right.
My purpose is to make people smile and laugh
In that, I firmly believe
You can have all the money and all that comes with it.
I just want to leave a legacy of great stories.
That's what I want to achieve.
That others will commit
To their memories and have a lasting impression in their hearts.
At one time, I was torn apart.
I keep getting up and sometimes I don't know why or how
But I'm a lot closer to knowing now.

JOHN E. MEDL

24 I CARRY IT AROUND

As I've gotten older
I carry around the hurt
As a chip on my shoulder.
I carry it around as a fire inside
When it starts burning
There's nowhere to hide.
I carry it around
As a weight on my back
Sometimes I can't shake it
Sometimes I look back.
I carry it around
Like concrete in my shoes
Hard to move forward
But refusing to lose.
Making giant steps
Stumble by stumble
Sometimes it's too much
But it keeps me humble.
A mind that doesn't stop
Cranking and cranking
It keeps me occupied

And it keeps me thanking
My lucky stars
For what could have been.
How it could be.
I focus more on that
Than how it should be.

JOHN E. MEDL

25 I'LL NEVER FORGET

And in my darkest hour You had a kind word
My brain wasn't working
But I somehow still heard.
I remember your smiles
When my memory was lost
I remember the visits
At such a cost.
I remember your concern
At every single step
I remember how sad you were
Even while I slept.
I'll never forget
When you gave me your heart
Even when our souls
Were miles apart.
Even then
I still never forgot
All the love you gave
Towards the story, and the plot I'm here today
Doing pretty well
Mostly because of you

And partly from going through hell.
There will still be those that don't believe
Everything I say
I've had some awful moments
And I still count the days.
I've learned a great deal
About life and about myself
I've taken all your acts
And placed them on a shelf
Any given moment
I can reach back in time
And remember what you gave me
Truly sublime.

JOHN E. MEDL

26 HOW MANY NIGHTS DO I HAVE LEFT?

Many times a day I wonder
How many nights I have left
I wonder if I would even want to know.
I wonder if I am living right
When the world tells me 'no'.
I wonder if Fate will smile kindly on me
And let me be around
I wonder if I have done enough work
Before they lay me in the ground.
Or let the wind take my ashes to the sea
That's really the only place I wish to be.
I try to imagine how far the stars are away
And if I will get to see one up close some day.
I only know how to live one way—
The simplest way
I possibly can.
And at the same time
Leaving the Earth a good man.

JOHN E. MEDL

27 THE GRAVEYARD

Only when you've stared death in the face
And survive
Only then are you truly alive.
Live like it is your last day
Don't make it something you just say.
I know this from experience
It's not some theoretical idea to me
I consider it a blessing to be
Reminded so soon of my mortality.
Some sail through life, no worries, and that's great
But this is not a lesson you want to learn late.
Let me be an example
And lend your ear
The struggles I have had,
I hope you are never near.
And to you, I say good luck
Painting the canvas of life
And I hope your days are filled
With not a bit of strife
But if life deals you an altering hitch
I can only wish

You find the strength to carry on
May all your troubles be short,
and your days long.
If life's so easy
And not so hard
Why do I believe
They are dancing in the graveyard?
Laughing when we drive past
With convincing looks it will all last
Stress and and blur our thoughts
At least the dead are never lost
And never feel the need for greed
No violence or destruction
Not to ever have to bleed
Or the pressure to succeed.
If you deem these thoughts bizarre
Try looking out from the graveyard.

JOHN E. MEDL

28 THE HEAVENS

I hope I soar into the heavens
Far above the sky.
I know I'll see all the angels
That too early, passed us by.
I want to meet all the saints
And ask them a lot of questions
Maybe over a nice dinner
And talk about the people I want to mention.
Maybe it will be an ocean
And I'll fall into the darkest depths
A peaceful place of silence
Filled with tears we all wept.
But maybe I'll be sent to
Hell The fire and smoky air—
A place for only a few
But I think I've already been there.

JOHN E. MEDL

29 MAKING LEMONADE

In that place
All I feel is fear
And thoughts about death
Are near.
When it is through
I just want to cry
Another step backwards
Telling myself all I can do is try.
Enough to bring a big man
To his knees
And pray for it to be over
Begging for the end, please!
A terror so potent
Minutes feel like days
Feelings so strong
My ego always pays
I never know when it will come
I just know I'm grateful when it's done
I sometimes wish I were the only one.
I just want someone to tell me it's okay
I just want the words to help convey

How awful the panic really can be
If you could only see
How crippling it really is
How painful and strong
Not matter how short, it always seems long
And I always feel wronged
What did I do?
I try to be a good person
And do what's right
I try and work hard
And I'm thankful at night
I know deep down it's not my fault
But I always retrace my actions
And my past deeds
Even though I know
I can't go back
I think if I do enough good
I can cover my tracks.
But the fact is,
Nothing I did
Has anything to do with me now
For some reason, I have been chosen
To make lemonade somehow.
I don't want your pity
That's not the point
I can't say enough
To get anyone to feel how terrible it can be
I wouldn't wish it on my worst enemy

JOHN E. MEDL

30 JUST A PARK

The sycamore and oak trees
Bow and wave to greet me
And immediately their presence
Makes me feel at peace.
One of my sanctuaries
I've been visiting for years
Not one tall building or store around
Just the trees and me
The rustling of leaves, the only sound.
Just a quiet spot to simply think
That's all I was really after
No music, conversation, or laughter.
No one to judge me by my fame or wealth
Or to criticize and scrutinize my health
Fields and woody statues
As far as I can see
At this place, in this time,
I can't think of a place I'd rather be.

JOHN E. MEDL

31 UNTOUCHED

My eyes pick out crosses everywhere
From just regular, everyday things.
I see light flashes
And I don't know if they are really there.
I dream about people far in the past
Some dreams I wish were over fast
And some I wish would last.
I've been wide awake
And I didn't know where I was.
I used to tempt the Fates
Just because.
Most of the time, I'm just sort of 'there'
Not blissful but not particularly down either.
When I'm down,
it's the worst I've ever felt
But when I feel alive,
it's the best I've ever been.
Even when crying, at least it's a feeling
What I'm implying
Is that there are very tall hills and deep, dark, holes
Sometimes I'm embarrassed when my story is told.

But as age creeps up
Talking does more good than harm
Most are inspired
But some will always be alarmed.
A boat I have elected myself the captain
Attempting to steer ashore
The turmoil rising from below
The thunder pounding from above I am surrounded—
And I am supposed to find land?
The sea sees no penalty when chaotic
But woe to the mind when disturbed
Shaken off course—
With an earthquake off the charts
My whole functioning without the parts
Vital to survive and succeed.
A persistent bleed from my heart through my skin
So the heart is where I shall begin
To repair what has failed for years.
I have survived typhoons and tidal waves countless times I have crossed uncrossable lines
And disaster has gratefully let me prepare
For the misfortunes fortunate enough to plague me.
An easy task for they have seen stronger
But they will not weaken me a minute longer
Unknown, a formidable enemy clenches his fist
Executing his plans down the list.
The resilient may at first seem meek
The strong at first weak
But victory hides in the end
A winner wins at the finish of a race
Not the beginning, soon to be erased.
Others are happy just to place
But winners all the same.
A spirit deserving of a name
But no one word could do justice
Call it a spark or flame
They wonder whom to blame

For these countless, relentless tries—
The sun dies, the wind cries, and the sea subsides.
You will not hold me back, turbulent sea
For my soul will set fire
As the kindling lay before me.
Fuel for my motor
A motivation unseen by woe or worry
A whirlwind of fury—
Let it strike down
Those who dare subjugate me
Under an umbrella of expectations
That even God would fall short.
But I will not, I refuse
To let abuse—abuse me
I remain untouched and will forever be.

JOHN MEDL

32 POSER FRIENDS

Self-reflection has revealed
An ejection of delusions and false hope.
A more quiet way to cope
Than screaming what I really think of you.
You are the weaker link of a chain now broken
Not even a sentimental token am I left with
A revelation freed from a dark hole
Like a mole, poking its head out for air
Far away in some hand-me-down chair
If you only knew what you lost
But that's just my perception
No better than the rest, no exception
You are no better friend than I am to you
Never have been
I'd like to cram, all your lies back in your mouth
One by one, 'til you choke
Our "friendship" was just a horrible, cruel joke.
Thanks, once again, poser friend
Your memory will never make me laugh again
I must have run out of what you wanted
Or you would still be around.

All I can say, and I hope you take with you
As penance for all your faults
Locked down tight in mental vaults
I could delicately unravel
But I would rather see you crack and explode
Blow the doors off, and the landing won't be soft, no loft Smack against a wall
I could watch you fall over and over again
I saw the end from afar
And now I'm glad to see who you really are.
You piece of nothing, trash on the street
Rancid and sour
And in your final hours, you can explore
The dark abysses you created
And I'm elated to see you doing so poorly
I used to be concerned, surely
When you were someone else...

JOHN MEDL

33 QUILTED SOFA

Padded checkers and rings
Hold my see-saw feelings
Tragedy, triumph, good, and bad
The best rest I've ever had.
Once glued, now improved
I got back everything
I used to groggily wish for.
Now I seem to be
Trapped in my own clarity.
Truths that will haunt me for years, and fears, dried up tears
Steered by sanity now, but how?
No better time to start than now
Forcing me to stand pat
A curse worse than a black cat
Labels by faces, replaces
All the old thoughts about myself.
But I know who and what I am
Like it or not
Do you really think my soul forgot?

JOHN E. MEDL

34 MY MIND IS ON REPLAY

My mind is on replay
Day after day
I saw a man strapped to his bed
Nurses approaching with needles Inhuman cries and moans
He was trapped inside his head
Every day I think about being dead
Going on seven years
It gets old really fast
The same old fears
My mind is on replay
Day after day
I take medication for some relief
I wish there were some other way
My mind is on replay
Day after day
My thoughts race in circles
The acts in some strange play
My mind is on replay
Day after day
I talk myself out of giving up
But sometimes I stray

My mind is on replay
Day after day
I have to check the clocks
To make sure time is okay
I don't check the locks
Those don't bother me much
I do check my own thoughts
To make sure I'm in touch
My mind is on replay
Day after day
Sometimes I get frustrated
Recovery seems so far away
My mind is on replay
Day after day
I have to write it all down
And put it on display
It helps to express some things In a creative way
My mind is on replay
Day after day

JOHN E. MEDL

35 I DON'T NEED YOUR SYMPATHY

I don't need your sympathy.
I'll make some coffee
And have a cup with me.
Our roads crossed for some reason
Time don't matter or the season
But I don't need your sympathy.
We can talk until our tongues go dry
And if we need to
We can wipe each other's eyes.
I just love your company
But I don't need your sympathy.
I'll light a smoke while you're talking
And I'll listen the best I can
I want to hear your point of view
And all the things that make up you
But I don't need your sympathy.
I don't have close to all the answers
But maybe we have some common ground.
I just want to make you feel better
I know pain and I know healing
But I don't need your sympathy.

Our talk is over now and it's time to go
Maybe we can do this again
If I say I am your friend,
I will be one to the end,
But I don't need your sympathy.

JOHN E. MEDL

36 THERE IS HOPE

I lose my mind from time to time
But I always seem to find it
I sometimes get excited about the future
But my past looms right behind it
Pain that pity and recovery can't resolve
An assortment of memories involved
And plans that never blossomed.
But if anyone thinks for one second
I will give up my hopes and dreams
Just to spite the daily screams
There's just some things I can't repress
I try to give my all and nothing less.

JOHN E. MEDL

37 WHEN THE SUNSHINE WENT AWAY

As I watched clouds explode
And stars collide
The sky swallowed itself in submission
An event for no one's eyes
But that night
With my mind's permission
I witnessed the grim possibility of the future.
The catastrophic, violent images
Disturbed me enough to retreat
And run from the Creator and Destroyer
No hope for success, the inevitable demise
But that's not what our state implies
And when greed, power, and money combine
They will leave nothing behind.
As soon as I woke
I pleaded to the silence
To never let me see the day
When the sunshine goes away

JOHN E. MEDL

38 NEVER BREAK

Usually when my mind is racing
I write my best
But today my mind is taking a rest.
Not thinking much at all
Unusual for me.
A sense of peace and calm
Bathed in mirth and security.
My thoughts are not frantic
Unusual for me.
Feeling pretty fantastic
But never to the highest degree.
Not too sluggish
Or nerves standing on end.
No negative thinking
And realizing I just bend
Never break.
If I could only find which road to take.

JOHN E. MEDL

39 WHO YOU WERE MEANT TO BE

Most of all I wish you joy
Happiness beyond measure
Infinite pleasure
And satisfaction with your life.
Only you are you
And it is who you were meant to be
Don't wish to be someone else
You were made perfectly.
If you should fall,
pick yourself up
And I wish for you,
an overflowing cup.
Try to be kind and increasingly wise
There isn't much else
As much as I can surmise.
I want for you the very best
And I mean that more than you know
I hope you find a blissful place
A respite, in your mind, you can go.
Don't spend too much time
On sadness and despair

Seconds are precious
And there are no flowers there.
Pick up the pieces, one by one
Until you feel whole
Nothing will ever be perfect
Not everything you can control.
Try to be your best
Every single day
Show the world your greatness
In every single way.

JOHN E. MEDL

POEMS FROM A BIPOLAR MIND

A COLLECTION OF JOURNAL ENTRIES RELATED TO MENTAL ILLNESS AND BIPOLAR DISORDER

I want to dedicate this book to my parents, family, and friends who have never left my side through my battles with mental illness. I also want to dedicate this book to the millions of people who suffer from mental illness around the world. I hope I have done well in being the voice of the suffering.

INTRODUCTION

This is the second book I have written. My first book is titled, "Millions Like Me: My Struggle with Mental Illness". That's my whole life story up until 2013. This book is a book of poetry, with commentary mixed in. For clarity purposes, I wanted to give you a brief introduction. I have been writing poems since grade school. I am now 35 years old. These are all the poems I could find. There is no real order to any of the poems. I hope that my commentary will help clarify what I was thinking and feeling at the time. In 2006, I was diagnosed with bipolar disorder with psychotic features. Since 2006, the doctors have added Post Traumatic Stress Disorder, Generalized Anxiety Disorder/Panic Disorder, Obsessive Compulsive Disorder, agoraphobia, and claustrophobia. For the full story, reference my first book. I wanted a book completely devoted to the poetic arts. Just as with my first book, I hope this book leaves a positive, lasting impression on the readers.

1 NAVIGATING TROUBLED WATERS

A boat I have elected myself the captain
Attempting to steer ashore
The turmoil rising from below
The thunder pounding from above
I am surrounded—
And I am supposed to find land?
The sea sees no penalty when chaotic
But woe to the mind when disturbed
Shaken off course—
With an earthquake off the charts
My whole functioning without the parts
Vital to survive and succeed.
A persistent bleed from my heart through my skin
So the heart is where I shall begin
To repair what has failed for years.
I have survived typhoons and tidal waves countless times
I have crossed uncrossable lines
And disaster has gratefully let me prepare
For the misfortunes fortunate enough to plague me.
An easy task for they have seen stronger

But they will not weaken me a minute longer
Unknown, a formidable enemy clenches his fist
Executing his plans down the list.
The resilient may at first seem meek
The strong at first, weak
But victory hides in the end
A winner wins at the finish of a race
Not the beginning, soon to be erased.
Others are happy just to place
But winners all the same.
A spirit deserving of a name
But no one word could do justice
Call it a spark or flame
They wonder whom to blame.
For these countless, relentless tries—
The sun dies, the wind cries, and the sea subsides.
You will not hold me back, turbulent sea
For my soul will set fire
As the kindling lay before me.
Fuel for my motor
A motivation unseen by woe or worry
A whirlwind of fury—
Let it strike down
Those who dare subjugate me
Under an umbrella of expectations
That even God would fall short.
But I will not, I refuse
To let abuse abuse me
I remain untouched and will forever be.

This was the first poem I ever had published in 2004, two years before I was diagnosed with bipolar disorder. I remember that this was an assignment for one of my poetry classes at the University of Dayton. This is one of my most polished poems, for it was edited several times before publication. I remember that when I wrote this poem, I felt like there was so much chaos in my life—attending college full-time, and working full-time. I also had a live-in girlfriend, and I was constantly drinking alcohol and smoking marijuana. I was barely sleeping. I did this for almost three years straight. I believe that this chaos was a catalyst in making me ill, but no one really knows.

2 FIRST BREAK

It was like lightning
Struck my brain in two
A feeling I hope never happens to you.
Fueled by a combination
Of drugs and chemical failure
I never even saw it coming.
But in hindsight, they say things seem clearer
The teamwork of genetics, environment, and behavior.
A complete mental meltdown
Of someone competent and capable before
Never having a clue of what tests were in store.
I thought I would get better soon
Not months, into years and more.
Confused, never in control
As the toxic cocktail took its toll
Crammed in a cell and then a bus to court
With total strangers, not knowing what I'd done
Or where I was
But knowing it wasn't normal or fun.
They had me sign some papers
That I couldn't focus to read

And plunged a needle deep in me
And gave me pills they said I'd need.
They took me to a ward where I was greeted
By shrieking vocal cords
They gave me a room, and a short tour
Life as I knew it, never more.
A condition I guess they thought they could fix
July thirty-first, two-thousand and six.

July 31, 2006

This is the day that I was rushed to the hospital, and then diagnosed with bipolar disorder with psychotic features. I had to stay in the psychiatric unit for eleven days. I would have to be hospitalized a few times after this too. I haven't been hospitalized since 2012. On that occasion, it was for mania and anxiety/panic. The doctors called it my "first break", which basically means the symptoms of bipolar disorder had become so severe that I was a danger to myself and others and needed to be hospitalized.

3 QUILTED SOFA

Padded checkers and rings
Hold my see-saw feelings
Tragedy, triumph, good, and bad
The best rest I've ever had.
Once glued, now improved
I got back everything
I used to groggily wish for.
Now I seem to be
Trapped in my own clarity.
Truths that will haunt me for years, and fears, dried up tears
Steered by sanity now, but how?
No better time to start than now
Forcing me to stand pat
A curse worse than a black cat
Labels by faces, replaces
All the old thoughts about myself.
But I know who and what I am
Like it or not
Do you really think my soul forgot?

After I was released from the hospital in 2006, I was heavily sedated. I slept on the sofa mentioned in this poem most of the day. All I could manage was to eat and go to the bathroom for the most part.

4 MEDICINAL HAZE

I wake up in a medicinal haze
Left over from the night
And remember all the happy days
And all the ways I used to cope.
Those were times filled with hope.
Now instead of being free,
The doctors pump me full of dope.
With the stroke of his pen
He can control my behavior
Like some holier-than-thou savior.
Saving me from myself
Maybe I did need help
Maybe I'll be better off.
Some people hear disorder
And think it can be cured Like a cold or cough.
But it will never go away, never will
At least the drugs keep me still.
Too still sometimes, more like a zombie
I guess the challenge is
Finding a balance between the new and the old me.

I REMEMBER WRITING THIS POEM ON A REGULAR OLD MORNING. I WAS STILL pretty heavily sedated. I was learning to adjust to my "new self", i.e. how the drugs had changed me.

5 JUST A PARK

The sycamore and oak trees
Bow and wave to greet me
And immediately their presence
Makes me feel at peace.
One of my sanctuaries
I've been visiting for years
Not one tall building or store around
Just the trees and me
The rustling of leaves,
the only sound.
Just a quiet spot to simply think
That's all I was really after
No music, conversation, or laughter.
No one to judge me by my fame or wealth
Or to criticize and scrutinize my health
Fields and woody statues
As far as I can see
At this place, in this time,
I can't think of a place I'd rather be.

When I started to become a little more alert, I used to drive to this park about ten minutes from my house. I would just read a book or write poetry or just sit peacefully and be one with nature. I remember feeling very at peace there. It was near a place called Camp Dennison, near a town called Indian Hill. I haven't been back in years. I need to find time to visit again.

6 POSER FRIENDS

Self-reflection has revealed
An ejection of delusions and false hope.
A more quiet way to cope
Than screaming what I really think of you.
You are the weaker link of a chain now broken
Not even a sentimental token am I left with
A revelation freed from a dark hole
Like a mole, poking its head out for air
Far away in some hand-me-down chair.
If you only knew what you lost
But that's just my perception
No better than the rest, no exception
You are no better friend than I am to you
Never have been
I'd like to cram, all your lies back in your mouth
One by one, 'til you choke
Our "friendship" was just a horrible, cruel joke.
Thanks, once again, poser friend
Your memory will never make me laugh again
I must have run out of what you wanted
Or you would still be around.

All I can say, and I hope you take with you
As penance for all your faults
Locked down tight in mental vaults
I could delicately unravel
But I would rather see you crack and explode.
Blow the doors off, and the landing won't be soft, no loft
Smack against a wall
I could watch you fall over and over again
I saw the end from afar
And now I'm glad to see who you really are.
You piece of nothing, trash on the street
Rancid and sour
And in your final hours, you can explore
The dark abysses you created
And I'm elated to see you doing so poorly.
I used to be concerned surely
When you were someone else...

I was angry at some of my "poser friends" that had left my side when I really needed them. The type of people who claimed to be my friends, but then left my side when I was sick.

7 THERE IS HOPE

I lose my mind from time to time
But I always seem to find it
I sometimes get excited about the future
But my past looms right behind it.
Pain that pity and recovery can't resolve
An assortment of memories involved
And plans that never blossomed.
But if anyone thinks for one second
I will give up my hopes and dreams
Just to spite the daily screams.
There's just some things I can't repress
I try to give my all and nothing less.

When I started to come out of "the fog" of the sedatives, I was feeling hopeful because my life was starting to come back together again. I want everyone to know that there is life beyond mental illness, and that "there is hope".

8 STANDING TALL

My head is pounding
And my mind won't quit
The hospital and medications
All because of it.
The sirens scream
Getting closer and closer
Until they are clear as can be.
You can imagine my terror
When I knew they were coming for me.
Laid out on a stretcher
Gasping for air
I wanted to be anywhere but there.
Every second felt like ages
And not a thousand pages
Could capture
How it has come to this.
Never a day goes by
When I don't obsess about it all
But through every single battle
At least I've stood tall.

I'VE HAD THOUSANDS OF PANIC ATTACKS. THIS IS HOW I FELT DURING AND AFTER. I remember hearing the sirens of the ambulance. I remember not being able to think clearly. At the end of this poem, I'm trying to make myself feel better by thinking and feeling, "At least I've stood tall", and that I have put up a fight.

9 CAME FROM A LONG WAY

When I feel down,
I go back to that place.
The needles and doctors
My mind can't erase.
My concerned friends and family
Who came to visit,
And how my entire life
Is wrapped up in it.
It's everything to me.
It's what drives me to be
A good person and friend.
A success story.
I was down on the mat,
But I got up.
I don't know how or why.
I could have easily given up
And kissed my future goodbye.
I must not be done yet
Or else it would have ended.
My dreams aren't gone,
They just got suspended.

I gave it everything I had
I reached down deep
The memories still haunt me
Even in sleep.
When I have a bad day,
It can always be worse
The curse of making it through.
I give it all I've got
In everything I do.

THIS IS DESCRIBING MY POST TRAUMATIC STRESS DISORDER THAT I HAVE FROM being in the hospital several times, with a touch of hope at the end. My PTSD results in flashbacks and nightmares. I have severe anxiety when I am confronted with anything medically related, or anything that resembles the experiences I've had in hospitals.

10 MONSTER OF PAIN

Behind the laughter and the smiles
There is pain for miles
I've cried so many times
Pleading it will stop.
It always seems to
When it wants to.
Most people don't know what makes me tick.
I don't even know if I do.
Maybe some day I will find out
How and why I got sick.
Maybe because I used to take life for granted
I never appreciated the little things
I just went about going through the motions
Never noticing anything surrounding the path I was on.
Most people have never seen me cry
I hide my emotions well
Every day is as big as a mountain
But you will probably not be able to tell.
My life's an open book
For everyone to read
I like it that way

Nothing to hide
Everything to explain
Like why sometimes
I prefer the rain.
Or why I value the company of friends so much
Or how my thoughts got out of touch.

Around 2011-2012, I started advocating for mental illness and telling my story. This poem touches on that a bit. When I finally started to "snap out of it", I decided I wanted to be an advocate. I still am to this day, in 2017. I talk about basically putting on a tough front so others don't seem to notice that I am struggling. I wonder what makes me tick, and I wonder if my mental illness is somehow a punishment because I took life for granted when I was younger.

11 BRAIN ON FIRE

My brain is on fire and my mind won't quit
Sometimes, I get sick of all of it.
I fight and I fight, but sometimes it's not enough
I just want to be known as tough.
I have a sense of humor to keep it light
I just want to do what's right.
My purpose is to make people smile and laugh
In that, I firmly believe
You can have all the money and all that comes with it.
I just want to leave a legacy of great stories.
That's what I want to achieve.
That others will commit
To their memories and have a lasting impression in their hearts.
At one time, I was torn apart.
I keep getting up and sometimes I don't know why or how
But I'm a lot closer to knowing now.

THIS POEM IS ABOUT HOW I WANT TO BE REMEMBERED. ONE OF MY LIFE GOALS IS never to be forgotten, or at least not for a very long time. I want to be known as tough and as someone that didn't give up. I want to be that person that makes the best of a bad situation. I talk about finding myself in this battle at the end of the poem. I allude to this battle as being something that has happened for a reason.

12 SMALL TOWN MAN

Right near where the local roads meet the highway,
A man sits and thinks.
He is well-known around his home,
But the small town could not keep him forever.
One day, his name will be heard for miles
And all he can do is smile
Because he knew it would happen all along.
He had dreams about being famous
As long as he could remember
And everything was falling into place.
Not much grace, but there was something special about him.
Intangible, but real.
He could steal hearts in a matter of moments
And he would keep them forever
Because he was loving and loyal.
Far from royal, but he had a distinct strut
Like he had just won at a game.
Many people seem the same,
so he sought out the different to be his friends.
He couldn't care less about trends.
Or money, houses, or cars.

He liked to look up at the stars.
He survived on a little, but it felt like a lot to him.
He knew what it was like to have nothing,
And that feeling always stayed with him.
It helped him be humble and grateful.
Loving, not hateful. Positive, not skeptical.
He never wanted to be a spotlight spectacle.
Just always in others' thoughts
And hopefully those thoughts are fond.
And every time it was needed,
He would answer the bell and respond.

I have a nice front porch on my house that I like to sit and think and smoke cigarettes. This poem describes my desire to be somewhat famous, but not valuing material things. I want to be well known, but remain humble. You will definitely keep seeing the theme of me not wanting to be forgotten anytime soon, and to be remembered in a positive light, which really relates to my obsession with death and dying.

13 BEACH

The sun shoots its rays
Across the expansive sky
Reflected off the water like glass
And I start to wonder why.
Anyone would wake to anything else
The clouds hanging over like cream
This is the morning most are forced to dream.
For some, an actuality
But they probably stopped looking
Thinking about bills, or errands for the day
While the sorrowful are longing
For such a sight to behold.
A scene, to some, has turned old.
But if I ever have a chance
To hear the waves crash and see the foam dance
The amazing sun and clouds overhead
I will rush to meet the sea.
But then what would I think about
To keep me restful in my bed?

I live in Cincinnati, Ohio, so I am far from the ocean. This poem is basically just me describing a daydream about the beach and ocean. I describe the daydream, but then wonder if it would be ruined if I actually got to experience my daydream (i.e. "but then what would I think about to keep me restful in my bed?").

14 LET ME GO

If you are done with me, let me go.
I've died several times.
I obsess over death. I dream about it.
I pray for it.
Until that time comes, let me live.
I don't want to be here halfway.
I have a job to do, and we both know it.
I need all the strength and courage I can hold.
I will leave nothing left untold.
My soul was meant to be shared.
It was really never mine.
It wasn't supposed to be like this, but here we are.
I've already come so far.
Don't let me go just yet. I have work to do.
I just need a little relief.
Forgive me for my beliefs, and all I have done wrong.
I want my list of good deeds to be long.
So when we meet, I can stand proud.
So when I sing, I can sing out loud.
The only thing I have ever been sure of is that I wanted to be a good person

And help those in need.
Why must I bleed?

THIS POEM IS ABOUT MY FRUSTRATION WITH STRUGGLING TO DO SMALL TASKS. I am frustrated, but at the same time, I have "work to do" (advocate for the mentally ill). I am almost pleading to God, or gods, or the Fates, to "let me go, if you are finished with me". This also fits the theme of death that you have seen in other poems.

15 BROKEN DOWN

I feel broken
Usually unspoken.
It's a trembling,
Sometimes it seems unending.
My chest hurts,
In short bursts,
But I've learned it's not alarming.
It's disarming, I'm charming,
When I feel like myself.
And it all figures somehow
But don't ask me how.
I'm dizzy, light-headed
Scary memories, embedded.
I can't shake it, or take it
I just try to survive and make it.
I feel shattered,
I matter,
At least that's what they tell me.
I don't trust my instincts,
Or gut feels
My mind runs like hamster wheels.

It's be nice not to think at all for a while
And when I hit a wall,
I go around it or through it.
It's like I always knew it.

THIS IS BASICALLY JUST HOW I FEEL ON A REGULAR BASIS. THIS ALLUDES TO racing thoughts ("my mind races like hamster wheels"), and also mania, where it's hard to trust my own judgment (instincts).

16 LUCKY STARS

As I've gotten older
I carry around the hurt
As a chip on my shoulder.
I carry it around as a fire inside
When it starts burning
There's nowhere to hide.
I carry it around
As a weight on my back
Sometimes I can't shake it
Sometimes I look back.
I carry it around
Like concrete in my shoes
Hard to move forward
But refusing to lose.
Making giant steps
Stumble by stumble
Sometimes it's too much
But it keeps me humble.
A mind that doesn't stop
Cranking and cranking
It keeps me occupied

And it keeps me thanking
My lucky stars
For what could have been.
How it could be.
I focus more on that
Than how it should be.

THIS POEM IS ABOUT HAVING A POSITIVE ATTITUDE, AND NEVER GIVING UP. I allude to focusing on how it is and how it should be. I don't think it's therapeutic to think of the way things should or could be. I don't think it's productive to think life's not fair. I think it's in my best interest to deal with life as it has been given to me.

17 CHILD GIANT

They all knew
He didn't belong
In a chair, anywhere
The desk wouldn't even hold him.
He sat in discomfort
Most of the time
And the teachers would often scold him.
He towered over the children
And more wit than the teachers
He disobeyed most rules
And challenged the preachers.
He was told things he had already been taught
Five years earlier, and never forgot.
A class clown
And a teacher's pet
All the lessons he would never forget.
A kind and gentle giant of a child
Calm and collected, with a touch of wild
Slow to anger
Quick to peace
A hunger for knowledge

Never ceased

This is my perception of how I was when I was a child. Or maybe other people's perception. In a way, it is arrogant to think I didn't belong "in a chair, anywhere" (i.e. a desk as in school). People with bipolar disorder often think highly of themselves. Also called grandiose feelings.

18 MY DARKEST HOUR

And in my darkest hour
You had a kind word
My brain wasn't working
But I somehow still heard.
I remember your smiles
When my memory was lost
I remember the visits
At such a cost.
I remember your concern
At every single step
I remember how sad you were
Even while I slept.
I'll never forget
When you gave me your heart
Even when our souls
Were miles apart.
Even then
I still never forgot
All the love you gave
Towards the story, and the plot
I'm here today

Doing pretty well
Mostly because of you
And partly from going through hell.
There will still be those that don't believe
Everything I say
I've had some awful moments
And I still count the days.
I've learned a great deal
About life and about myself
I've taken all your acts
And placed them on a shelf
Any given moment I can reach back in time
And remember what you gave me
Truly sublime.

This poem is about all the support I have received since 2006 from family and friends. It's worth mentioning that some people with mental illness have little to no support.

19 WONDERING ABOUT EVERYTHING

Many times a day I wonder
How many nights I have left
I wonder if I would even want to know.
I wonder if I am living right
When the world tells me 'no'.
I wonder if Fate will smile kindly on me
And let me be around.
I wonder if I have done enough work
Before they lay me in the ground.
Or let the wind take my ashes to the sea
That's really the only place I wish to be.
I try to imagine how far the stars are away
And if I will get to see one up-close some day.
I only know how to live one way—
The simplest way I possibly can.
And at the same time
Leaving the Earth a good man.

HERE IS THE THEME OF NOT BEING FORGOTTEN EASILY AGAIN. I OFTEN THINK about death. It's listed as one of the symptoms of bipolar disorder. Death or dying is a theme that you will see.

20 DEATH STARE

Only when you've stared death in the face
And survive
Only then are you truly alive.
Live like it is your last day
Don't make it something you just say.
I know this from experience
It's not some theoretical idea to me
I consider it a blessing to be
Reminded so soon of my mortality.
Some sail through life, no worries, and that's great
But this is not a lesson you want to learn late.
Let me be an example
And lend your ear
The struggles I have had, I hope you are never near.
And to you, I say good luck
Painting the canvas of life
And I hope your days are filled
With not a bit of strife.
But if life deals you an altering hitch
I can only wish

You find the strength to carry on
May all your troubles be short, and your days be long.

THIS IS ME TRYING TO BE POSITIVE AFTER A PANIC ATTACK. I TRULY WISH THE BEST for everyone. That is another theme you might see. I have a lot of love in my heart, despite everything.

21 WHILE IN SLEEP

Words that are jumbled
Explosions of neon greens...
And brilliant bursts of blue.
A nervous, unsettling, spasm of moves.
Sleep comes in spurts
But it's never enough.
Dreams hardly come
And nightmares are plenty.
Wide awake and sweating.
The damage has been done.
If only memories had filters
And we could pick and choose
The ones to forget, and the ones we don't want to lose.
Work with what you're given,
As hard as that may be
You may find it will suffice.
Always know your worth
But never tag yourself a price.

I WROTE THIS POEM AFTER A BAD NIGHT'S SLEEP. I TRY TO BE ENCOURAGING AS well. There is another theme. Sometimes when I close my eyes, I see colors that I can only describe as pink and blue cotton candy, and they burst and dance like some kind of visual effects show.

22 THE GRAVEYARD DANCERS

If life's so easy
And not so hard
Why do I believe
They are dancing in the graveyard?
Laughing when we drive past
With convincing looks it will all last
Stress and and blur our thoughts
At least the dead are never lost
And never feel the need for greed
No violence or destruction
Not to ever have to bleed
Or the pressure to succeed.
If you deem these thoughts bizarre
Try looking out from the graveyard.

Here is the theme of death and dying again. I wrote about wondering if the dead have any pain or problems. I also wonder if I would be better off dead because at least I wouldn't be suffering.

23 THE WINDS OF LOVE

His heart settled for a draw,
But it felt more like a loss.
He tried to adjust his sails,
But the winds of love
Would just blow across.
He could only do things halfway
Because he never felt complete.
He found solace in solitude,
And the material world could not compete.
He surrounded himself in knowledge,
And learned and taught many things.
But he could never find, in any book,
The joy that love brings.

THIS IS ABOUT THE HEARTBREAK OF NOT BEING ABLE TO FIND LOVE IN A MATE. I also don't value material things too much anymore. I love learning, and I'm still unsure whether solitude is what I want.

24 MAN ON A MISSION

I hope Heaven and Hell can wait.
I hope I arrive surrounded by love and late.
It's not my decision,
I'm just a man on a mission.
My life is in the hands of Fate.
I hope Heaven and Hell can wait.

THIS IS ANOTHER POEM ABOUT MY MORTALITY. I FEEL LIKE MY "MISSION" IS TO BE a mental health advocate and spread the word about mental illness.

25 SOAR INTO THE HEAVENS

I hope I soar into the heavens
Far above the sky.
I know I'll see all the angels
That too early, passed us by.
I want to meet all the saints
And ask them a lot of questions
Maybe over a nice dinner
And talk about the people I want to mention.
Maybe it will be an ocean
And I'll fall into the darkest depths
A peaceful place of silence
Filled with tears we all wept.
But maybe I'll be sent to Hell
The fire and smoky air—
A place for only a few
But I think I've already been there.

HERE IS THE THEME OF DEATH AGAIN AND ME WONDERING ABOUT THE AFTERLIFE. Also describing the "Hell" that I have been through.

26 A STURDY HOUSE

I built a house made of paper,
But it all came crashing down.
It all came crashing down.
I drove a car as far as I could drive,
But I wrecked along the way.
I wrecked along the way.
I took a bus to the end of the line,
But it went spinning of the road.
Spinning off the road.
I took a plane to the edge of the world,
But it fell before I got there.
It fell before I got there.
I built a boat that could stand a mighty wind,
But it sank to the bottom.
It sank to the bottom.
I built a life made of promises and hope,
But it all came crashing down.
It all came crashing down.
And then I stopped building,
And I just started creating things.

And nothing could bring them down.
Nothing could bring them down.

This is a celebration of the creative arts, and the denouncement of material things.

27 IF IT'S THE LAST THING I DO

If it's the last thing I do,
Let it be kind,
So I can have a clear mind.
If it's the last thing I do,
Let it be courageous
Because no one respects a coward.
If it's the last thing I do,
Let it be out of love
Because I want to leave it all for you,
And I have so much to give.
If it's the last thing I do,
Let it be noble
Because I want to leave proud.
If it's the last thing I do,
Let it show my strength
Because I have the heart of a lion.
If it's the last thing I do,
Let it be thoughtful
Because my intentions are good.
If it's the last thing I do,
Let it be creative

Because I have so much to share.
If it's the last I do,
Let it show character.
And if it's the last thing I do,
Let it be memorable.

Common themes of death and being remembered are repeated again here. Also my unwillingness to quit.

28 THE TERROR OF PANIC

In that place
All I feel is fear
And thoughts about death Are near.
When it is through,
I just want to cry.
Another step backwards
Telling myself all I can do is try.
Enough to bring a big man
To his knees
And pray for it to be over
Begging for the end, please!
A terror so potent
Minutes feel like days
Feelings so strong
My ego always pays.
I never know when it will come
I just know I'm grateful when it's done
I sometimes wish I were the only one.
I just want someone to tell me it's okay
I just want the words to help convey
How awful the panic really can be

If you could only see
How crippling it really is
How painful and strong.
Not matter how short, it always seems long.
And I always feel wronged.
What did I do?
I try to be a good person
And do what's right
I try and work hard
And I'm thankful at night.
I know deep down it's not my fault
But I always retrace my actions
And my past deeds
Even though I know I can't go back
I think if I do enough good
I can cover my tracks.
But the fact is,
Nothing I did
Has anything to do with me now
For some reason, I have been chosen
To make lemonade somehow.
I don't want your pity
That's not the point
I can't say enough
To get anyone to feel how terrible it can be
I wouldn't wish it on my worst enemy.

My description and feelings about a panic attack.

29 LIFE CREEPS UP

We all want perfect little lives,
With everything in a row,
But that's rarely how it goes.
Life creeps up, and life creeps in,
And it forces us to change plans.
Some things are best unplanned,
While others seem too much to bear.
We are left gasping for air,
But soon it all passes.
And we start to pick up the pieces,
Pretending nothing ever happened.
But then, life creeps up, and life creeps in,
Forcing us to change the plans again.

This poem is about how life can be very unorganized, as much as we want everything planned out.

30 NOT A TIME FOR SYMPATHY

I don't need your sympathy.
I'll make some coffee
And have a cup with me.
Our roads crossed for some reason
Time don't matter or the season
But I don't need your sympathy.
We can talk until our tongues go dry
And if we need to
We can wipe each other's eyes.
I just love your company
But I don't need your sympathy.
I'll light a smoke while you're talking
And I'll listen the best I can
I want to hear your point of view
And all the things that make up you
But I don't need your sympathy.
I don't have close to all the answers
But maybe we have some common ground.
I just want to make you feel better
I know pain and I know healing
But I don't need your sympathy.

Our talk is over now and it's time to go
Maybe we can do this again
If I say I am your friend,
I will be one to the end,
But I don't need your sympathy.

THIS POEM IS ABOUT HOW I DON'T WANT PEOPLE TO FEEL SORRY FOR ME, AND HOW I am almost always available to listen to a friend's problems. Also, that I enjoy just sitting and talking about life and whatever else. On a lighter note, I really enjoy coffee and smoking cigarettes on my front porch.

31 PSYCH WARD

Nightmares from the psych ward....
Nightmares from the psych ward....
Flashed back to the day
When I was locked away
They all tell me
That it was the only way.
Meet your new master, the Queen of Disaster,
She's going to let you know how it goes.
I had to behave, so that I could have a shave
I was lucky to even remember my name.
Every single day, trying to find a way to get out
And I wondered what this was all about.
Every so often, I would hear a shout
Either staff or the committed.
They said I belonged there,
But I refused to admit it.
I still don't know what they dosed me with,
But I took a long, deep sleep.
I woke up so foggy that they knew they could keep me.
Nice and calm now, here's a bunch of questions.
We'll let you know when we think you're alright.

This poem describes nightmares and flashbacks to when I was hospitalized in the psychiatric unit in 2006.

32 FINALLY ON TOP

He was broken down,
Stepped on,
And will be buried in the ground.
But the demons will not go with him.
His soul shined bright as a star
Reflected through a diamond prism.
While alive, he kept marching,
And after every single fall, he got up.
He would not quit and refused to lose.
A battle he didn't get to choose.
A peaceful man, with a warrior's fight
Even though he didn't sleep at night.
The shadows danced wherever he looked,
But he just learned to ignore them.
The voices never stopped either,
But again, he lived through it.
Even he didn't understand why he kept getting up.
Maybe he wanted to be a legend.
Maybe when he's finally at rest,
He wants to be remembered as a man that never gave up.
Maybe he wants to be an inspiration and example

To everyone that is facing hard times.
Although he didn't always understand,
He understood never to stop.
And when it's all said and done,
With any luck,
He will finally end up on top.

THIS FITS THE THEME ABOUT DEATH AND BEING REMEMBERED AGAIN. I WAS thinking that when my life is over, I can finally rest and "end up on top". I hope I have left a positive imprint on the world. To me, that's what it means to "end up on top".

33 STANDING MY GROUND

I will not lay down my sword in defeat.
I will die with it in my hand.
I will not retreat.
You can kill me where I stand.
I've already faced the worst,
So nothing really scares me.
I have nothing to lose,
So all your threats, you can spare me.
I don't back down. I don't quit.
Yes, sometimes I get sick of all of it. I will admit.
But fear and me got to be friends through the years.
So you can speak your negative talk into someone else's ears.

This poem is about staying positive in the face of adversity and not giving up.

34 YOU CAN'T TAKE EVERYTHING

The tears sting sweetly
As they roll down my face.
And things were taken from me
That can't be replaced.
But I'm not bitter or angry or sad.
I can't go on that feeling that way.
But it's still hard to believe
All the words that you say.
Like you love me and you are proud.
Down deep, I know them to be true.
But when I hear them out loud,
There's only so much healing they can do.

I wrote this poem after I had been crying. It speaks to how I feel that I am damaged and broken, no matter how much everyone encourages me.

35 THE END

As I watched clouds explode
And stars collide
The sky swallowed itself in submission.
An event for no one's eyes—
But that night
With my mind's permission
I witnessed the grim possibility of the future.
The catastrophic, violent images
Disturbed me enough to retreat
And run from the Creator and Destroyer
No hope for success, the inevitable demise
But that's not what our state implies
And when greed, power, and money combine
They will leave nothing behind.
As soon as I woke
I pleaded to the silence
To never let me see the day
When the sunshine goes away.

This is about a dream I had about the end of the world.

36 MY RESTING MIND

Usually when my mind is racing
I write my best
But today my mind is taking a rest.
Not thinking much at all
Unusual for me.
A sense of peace and calm
Bathed in mirth and security.
My thoughts are not frantic
Unusual for me.
Feeling pretty fantastic
But never to the highest degree.
Not too sluggish
Or nerves standing on end.
No negative thinking
And realizing I just bend
Never break.
If I could only find which road to take.

THIS IS DESCRIBING MY USUAL SYMPTOMS AND HOW THEY ARE ABSENT WHILE I was writing this. It also alludes to not really having a set direction and general uncertainty with my life.

37 PAINT YOU A PICTURE

I tried to paint you a picture.
I'm not much of an artist, but I can get by.
I don't have many secrets left,
Or too many lies.
I told you my feelings that I kept inside.
It seems like so long now.
I wonder who noticed. I wonder who read.
I wonder who chose to ignore it all instead.
I do what I can with what I have.
And I'm giving it all I can.
The words had to come out,
From my head straight out my hands.
I don't ask for much, because I really don't need it
I can do without a lot.
I prefer it that way actually,
Life can make you ill, the more that is sought.
I do better with less. Less mess. Less hassle.
Less stress. Less worry.
But it's still all a little blurry.
I'm feeling my way through

To fight another day.
I wonder if it will all ever go away.

This poem is about how I tried to "paint a picture" of what mental illness looks like in my first book. One last theme that you have seen throughout this book is that I keep fighting and don't give up.

38 MY LASTING WISH

Most of all I wish you joy
Happiness beyond measure
Infinite pleasure
And satisfaction with your life.
Only you are you
And it is who you were meant to be
Don't wish to be someone else
You were made perfectly.
If you should fall, pick yourself up
And I wish for you, an overflowing cup.
Try to be kind and increasingly wise
There isn't much else
As much as I can surmise.
I want for you the very best
And I mean that more than you know
I hope you find a blissful place
A respite, in your mind, you can go.
Don't spend too much time
On sadness and despair
Seconds are precious
And there are no flowers there.

Pick up the pieces, one by one
Until you feel whole
Nothing will ever be perfect
Not everything you can control.
Try to be your best
Every single day
Show the world your greatness
In every single way.

I WANTED TO END THE BOOK WITH THIS POEM. I TRULY, FROM THE BOTTOM OF MY heart, wish everyone the best. Friend or foe. I have no hostility towards anyone. I want every person to be the best that they can be and to try their best. Love and best wishes, always....

THE LAST DAY OF JULY

13 YEARS OF MADNESS

INTRODUCTION

This book is a collection of journal entries about my life and symptoms along with letters to various people and organizations. Many of the journal entries are out of order, but I will do my best to explain each entry. My entire purpose of being an author and mental health advocate is to help people not feel so alone, and also to inspire others with my life story. Mental illness is a constant struggle, and often times, just getting through the day is a victory. I've tried to set the standards for my life at a higher level, but I am also struggling along with a lot of my readers too. My writings are not just for the ill, but their friends and family as well to help understand what someone who has a mental disorder may go through in a day, week, or years.

1 SENIOR REFLECTION PAPER

John Medl
Senior Reflection Paper
English 4 CP1

THE KEYSTONE READS 1959. I APPROACH THE LUMINOUS STRUCTURE, MY collared shirt and khaki shorts drenched in sweat on a hot late-August day. I am a freshman attending Archbishop Moeller High School for the first day in my high school career. The walls loom over my head as if to mock me, complemented by brass figurines perched on top of championship pedestals. All around are strange faces, except the dozen or so children that I had known since I was in first grade. I planned to sneak into Moeller without talking to too many people, get good grades, a diploma, go to college, and have Moeller not bat an eye at my existence. Familiarity and popularity were very familiar to me as a smaller child. I excelled in knothole sports (biggest kid on the team and probably the best). I've lived in the same house all my life in a small town, and I was somewhat of a troublemaker. All those combined with myself being a nice kid, funny for my age, and I could not walk two blocks in Deer Park without recognition. I wanted to stay away from that, not because I didn't like it, but simply because I knew the feeling. I wanted to be different at Moeller, just for the adventure and unpredictability of different. I would talk to my old friends who knew me already, stay in my corner of the school, and just get out. I realize how immature this train of thought was, but I believe I was very immature when I entered Moeller. I thought smart people got good grades, and bad people were the ones in jail. I thought that was how the world worked when I entered high school.

As I proceeded through my education at Moeller, I maintained decent grades, but learned more important lessons in the process. I learned that everyone is so different, and no one can be generalized. I learned that when I treat others how I want to be treated, it might work or not, but I did my part. Those who responded positively I began to pursue relationships with, and those who responded negatively, I did not. I knew they wanted to be nice, but there was something about them I probably didn't understand. I also realized that people are not always the person I see every day, but may be hiding behind something. I've struggled to realize if that is my job, to try and help those people, or simply let them figure it out like I did. I began to develop pretty close friends that I had not known three years earlier. I was amazed at the concept of a new friendship. It had been so long for me to remember what a NEW friendship was like. I started to see the majority of the class as individuals instead of the people I didn't go to grade school with. I really started to enjoy my participation at Moeller. The epitome of when I felt the most unified in my class at Moeller was the state basketball game in Columbus versus Shaker Heights, a team heavily favored to win. The emotions, the unity, the excitement of winning our first state basketball title made me feel like I was almost the one who received the alley-oop pass to slam the game-clincher home. I felt I was out there along with the entire student body. I will never forget that.

Looking back, I will always remember that I am not always right and I should listen to everyone's opinion in search for the best result. Maturity is the acceptance of your faults, I believe, and then dealing with these faults. I will always remember how it feels to be made fun of, excluded, so that I may be able to help those who feel excluded. I have used those instances only to make me stronger. I know that not necessarily all overachievers have it together, and have problems just like underachievers. I like that the main thing I have learned about life while at Moeller can be summed up in three sentences: All people are unique and have distinct personalities, but all deserving of equal respect. Do not judge other lest you be judged. Treat your neighbor as yourself. I never thought Bible quotes would ever be applicable to my own life, but I realize that I was being close-minded to familiarity again. It's funny most people want to be known or popular, but I wanted to be common. I eventually broke out of that idea and became a pretty well-known figure on campus. I will take all that I have learned at Moeller and use it to help me succeed, and the hallowed hallways of Moeller have produced another man, John Medl.

2 1N5.ORG

This is a letter I wrote to the Cincinnati-based non-profit organization, 1N5.org. Their mission is to stop the stigma surrounding mental illness through advocacy. They have fundraisers and share stories of people who are fighting the battle of mental illness. They have a website and can also be found all across social media.

To Whom It May Concern,

I hope that sharing my story helps others within your organization. I was first diagnosed with bipolar disorder with psychotic features in 2006. Since then, I have been diagnosed with panic disorder/generalized anxiety disorder, posttraumatic stress disorder, obsessive-compulsive disorder, agoraphobia, and claustrophobia. I have dedicated my life to helping others, spreading awareness, and ending stigma. I have a social media page, for which I am the administrator named "Mental Health Awareness and Online Support". I am also a published poet at maverickmagazine.com. Both are free resources for anyone interested. I have written 3 books, with my newest book just published titled, "The Last Day of July: 13 Years of Madness". All 3 books are available online. Thanks for your time in reading my story.

Sincerely,
John E. Medl

3 38TH BIRTHDAY

This next entry was when I was reflecting on my life on my 38th birthday in October of 2019.

38 THINGS I'VE LEARNED IN THE LAST 38 YEARS:

1. Love is the most powerful force on Earth
2. Most things we worry about don't matter
3. Kindness is never the wrong thing to do
4. You don't have to be rich to be charitable and generous
5. Broad social change starts with an individual. (Thanks, Prof. Connelly)
6. Every day has the potential to be a good day
7. A loving family and good friends are priceless
8. The world is full of good people. If you can't find one, be one.
9. People who put you down don't like something about themselves
10. The world is changed by your example, not your opinion
11. Apologize whenever necessary
12. Everyone runs this race we call life at all different paces
13. Money can be a great thing, but don't let it run your life
14. Being positive and having a grateful heart really helps in tough situations

15. The world is full of suffering, but it is also full of people overcoming it
16. Recovery from tragedy is not linear
17. Perfection is not an option
18. There are many varieties of intelligence
19. If you tell the truth, you don't have to remember anything
20. Even the smartest person on the planet only knows a small amount of all there is to know
21. Dream big
22. Don't let mistakes define you
23. You don't get an award for being right. Sometimes, it's worth it to walk away from arguments.
24. Forgiveness is an attribute of the strong.
25. Sometimes a kick in the teeth is what you need at the time
26. Never give up; there is dignity in fighting
27. Integrity is doing the right thing even when no one is looking
28. Fix the cause. Not just the symptoms.
29. Practice your craft. You will statistically get better.
30. A career is a job. A vocation is a calling.
31. The thing people will remember most about you is how you treated them.
32. It is not any of our jobs to judge others
33. Everyone you meet is fighting a battle you know nothing about
34. You meet everyone for a reason
35. Not everyone you lose is a loss
36. Eat, drink, and be merry
37. Prayer never hurts
38. You only get so many birthdays

4 HOME BOUND SENIOR CITIZENS

This next entry is a letter I wrote to home bound senior citizens for Christmas.

Hello, I hope this card brightens your day and your holidays! My name is John, and I attended St. Saviour school for all 8 years, and then Moeller High School and The University of Dayton. I wanted to send you a Christmas card to let you know that there are so many people that care about you and are praying for you this Christmas season. I'm hoping for a white Christmas, but I don't have to travel. I hope you have plenty of loved ones to share the season with, and if you don't, this card is a reminder that people care about you, even people you have never met before. MERRY CHRISTMAS!

5 COMMISSIONER OF MAJOR LEAGUE BASEBALL

I was given a signed baseball by the Commissioner of Major League Baseball after I wrote him this letter.

Dear Commissioner Manfred,

I would like to request an autographed baseball from you. I'm not exactly sure if that is how it works. It seems very generous of you. I collect Cincinnati sports memorabilia, so that's why I am interested in an autographed baseball. I will include my address at the end of this letter. If you can't oblige, that's okay. I will just tell you a few of my thoughts about baseball. I was lucky to play on a little league team for ten years when I was a child. I am thirty-three years old now. Those were the best times of my life. My dad and I watch every Cincinnati Reds game that is available on TV/Cable. It's one of the only things we have always had in common.

I really like what you have done for the speed of the game. The games go much quicker, but not too fast. I know people get touchy when you start talking about changing in general, but the rules of baseball more so. I think you are doing a fantastic job with suspensions and penalties as well. Criminals, PEDs, and any form of cheating belittles the integrity of the game and should not be tolerated.

I would not be a good Reds fan (for my whole life) unless I give a mention to Pete Rose being allowed to be on the ballot for the Hall of Fame. I know you know that many players, former and current, have done much worse. I think the man has done his time for his crimes against baseball. Regardless, he is the greatest hitter of all time. No one can take that away from him. It would be nice if he took his rightful spot in the Hall with all the other greats.

There is a topic that is near and dear to my heart that I need to mention too. That's mental illness. I was diagnosed with bipolar disorder in 2006, and since then, Obsessive Compulsive Disorder, Panic Disorder, Generalized Anxiety Disorder, and agoraphobia have been added to my complete diagnosis. I have not seen a night in baseball in any stadium devoted to mental illness, and to the people who are suffering and the ones we have lost to suicide. I know it is not a happy topic, but it would be great if MLB could do something for one night in every stadium. A lime green ribbon is our symbol. The statistics are staggering for how common mental illness is. I believe that as many as one in three people have some type of mental illness. I volunteer my time every day to a social media page that I created for mental illness awareness. I am also a published author of my life story titled, "Millions Like Me: My Struggle with Mental Illness". I am a published poet at maverick-magazine.com as well. Thank you so much for your time and devotion to the betterment of the game.

Sincerely,
John E. Medl

6 MUNCHIES

MANY YEARS AGO, I HIT A PARKED CAR GOING ABOUT 10MPH. NOTHING BAD happened, but they took me by ambulance to the hospital to get checked out. I had about two beers and I took a hit or two off a joint. They did a blood test to check for drugs, and nothing significant showed up.

I was sitting there with two African-American police officers, and I kinda had the munchies, and I said, "Do you have anything to eat around here?"

One of the cops said, "We might have some juice or crackers."

So I said, "What did you call me?" We all had a good laugh.

7 THE DOCTOR

I HAVE TO SEE THE DOCTOR TODAY, WHICH IS USUALLY UNPLEASANT, BUT I FEEL pretty good today. I've been upset about this appointment for weeks. Luckily, I was able to still enjoy the holidays the best I could, although I'm not much of a festive person. I'm lucky that I have a doctor I like, and we are on a first name basis. He reminds me of a "bro"....maybe someone I would be friends with outside of the clinical setting. He is very proud of me, and he's very easygoing and easy to talk to.

I have some good news to tell him today, but I also have a lot of questions about my progress. I am getting to the point where my anxiety when leaving the house is too much to bear, and I have extreme irritability on a fairly regular basis. I don't know how much I can expect from my brain and body, which really is the whole mystery about mental illness. It's a lot of trial and error, whether it be medication or cognitive therapy.

There's no road map, and there's no magic pill. Some of the work has to be done by the patient (me). Right now, I have high anxiety when leaving the house and low energy, almost always. I want to see if that can be improved, either with a medicine change or other cognitive therapy. One thing is for sure: I have fought the whole time. It's one of my redeeming qualities. I hope when my life is over that being a fighter is one of the main things people remember about me, followed by how much I loved and gave to others.

8 DOCTOR BEN

I HAVEN'T DONE MUCH JOURNALING SINCE I FINISHED MY LAST BOOK IN JULY 2019, which has been a nice break, but I wanted to share a few things today about my progress and mental illness in general. I have to see my doctor today, who simply wants me to call him Ben. Really awesome, younger guy. Very smart, kind, and approachable. I really like him as my doctor. It's going to be a great feeling when I hand him a copy of my new book. He was very impressed that I had written so much the last time I saw him. It seemed like he was just generally impressed by the work I do, and my insight into my illness.

I'm glad the day of my appointment is finally here, so I know that it will all be over by this afternoon. I'm in better shape, anxiety-wise than usual, and overall, it is getting easier to see the doctor now that I am on a 3 month schedule rather than every month. Within the last few years, I used to have major anxiety and panic attacks at the doctor. My chest hurt and my head felt foggy every time I saw the doctor. I used to have to steady myself against the wall sometimes just to keep my balance.

One thing I want to say about mental illness is that there's no real clear cut objectives. No finish line or deadlines for improvement. Yes, things like taking a shower, driving, and socializing have gotten easier for me, and I guess that's because I kept trying. When I drove myself downtown the other day, that was a major accomplishment, but there's no guarantee that I can do it today or tomorrow. It's all so subjective and case-by-case. I know people with bipolar disorder that have full-time careers. That is not possible for me right now. If I was in proper shape, mentally and physically, I would try to apply for a career other than writing. It's just frustrating that there's no end game. Am I a success now? I would say yes. Is it possible that I could return to work eventually? Probably, but again, there's no guarantees. Just wanted to share my thoughts for a minute.

9 PROGRESS

When I saw the doctor yesterday, I was totally ready to change my medications, as scary as that idea sounded. I talked to my doctor, and he was actually happy with my progress. He told me he took the time to read through my medical records (over 13 years' worth) and my books, and I really have come a long way. Like almost miraculous.

I feel pretty good most of the time. It's at least tolerable. I don't expect to feel perfect all the time. I told him a lot of feelings and thoughts I have, and he basically pointed out that I overthink a lot of things, which I kinda already knew.

He told me I have to find ways to turn my brain off, per se. Music, crossword puzzles, whatever works. Writing about all of this really helps me, and I know it helps others as well. Another part of shutting down my brain is taking time for myself to recharge my batteries before I do too much advocating. Everything I do doesn't have to be for a cause or to help others.

The doctor was more concerned with my mood being stable and that I was getting enough sleep. He wasn't even concerned that I gained 12 pounds, but I am. I have to work on that. I'm still down 38 pounds overall, however, so I'm not starting from scratch. My BP was 138/88, which I have no idea what that means, but I know it's always high at the doctor's office. My pulse is always elevated too.

I had a brief panic attack when I got in my mom's van to go to the appointment, but I got out, and took some deep breaths, and I was able to keep the appointment. I'm really glad it's over until almost April. I found that riding in the back seat helps, for whatever reason. Maybe because I'm not right up on the dash or something.

He recommended therapy (CBT) for my cognition, but I'm still thinking if I want to make that commitment. It was nice to be reminded that I have made so much progress, but I'm also looking forward to the challenge of improving little things in my life that might make a big difference.

10 ELLEN DEGENERES

THIS IS A LETTER I WROTE TO ELLEN DEGENERES, AND I INCLUDED A COPY OF MY first book. I think this was sometime around 2014.

Hi Ellen! (Ms. DeGeneres is probably more appropriate, but it doesn't feel right. I think of you as such a kind, humble person)

Here is a copy of my book. It's my life story, detailing my struggle with mental illness. I have been diagnosed with bipolar disorder with psychotic features, generalized anxiety disorder/panic disorder, posttraumatic stress disorder, claustrophobia, and agoraphobia. I would be honored if you just gave it a read. I remember watching your sitcom as a younger adult, and it was hilarious. As I started watching your talk show, I saw again how funny you are, but I also saw such a humble, happy, and kind soul. Thanks for any time you give me.

Love and Best Wishes,
John Edward Medl
johnmedl7@gmail.com

11 QUEEN BEE

I HOPE YOU FIND THIS AS FUNNY AS I DO....THE DYNAMIC OF MY HOUSEHOLD GOES like this—Mom pretty much controls the household and knows everything that's going on. My dad has veto power, but in a limited capacity. I am the low man on the totem pole, and I try to just mind my own business and keep to myself whenever possible. All of us get along fairly well, all things considered, UNTIL the balance of power is messed with. All of this leads me to the day when my dad said something so funny to my mom. My mom was trying to tell my dad what clothes to wear or that he needed a jacket or something, and my dad was just like, "I think I can do what I want". Wrong thing to say to Queen Bee! LOL

12 HOOKAHVILLE

I have been to many Hookahvilles, starting around 1998. Hookahville is a weekend-long music festival where the band Ekoostik Hookah is the main act. My last Hookahville was Spring 2006, or whichever one that was when Blues Traveler was there.

I used to go to all kinds of concerts, but I was diagnosed with bipolar disorder and anxiety, so I don't leave my house much, and large crowds intimidate me. Well, I decided to step outside my comfort zone and go see my friends' band, The Summit, (with Ekoostik Hookah) around November of last year. My buddy, Mike Hennel, (drummer for The Summit), introduced me to Eric, the drummer for Hookah. I told Eric a little about my story and he asked if I had any requests. I honestly couldn't believe Eric was even asking me. When I was growing up, Hookah were some of my heroes. You never really think of ever meeting them or connecting with them on a personal level. The only songs I could think of were Ohio Grown and Loner. Sure enough, right as I was about to leave (early) for the night, Hookah played Loner! I like to believe it was for me :) Much love to you all! (Hookah later confirmed that the song Loner was, in fact, for me). What a great night.

13 PANIC ATTACK

SOMETIMES, IT'S OUR OWN BULLSHIT THAT IS HOLDING US BACK. NO ONE TRIES TO trigger me or upset me. It just happens. It's hard to know how much I can actually control how I react. I have to train my mind to not worry and overthink so much, which is quite a battle. I have to work at it.

The worst panic attack I've had in the last couple months was in the beginning of November 2019, and I was tempting the Fates. I drank coffee and didn't allow my medicine to work properly before getting in the car. I knew better. I don't know why I thought I could sneak something like that past my illness that day. Being successful takes extreme care, caution, maintenance, and constant attempts to improve.

14 GETTING CAUGHT UP

I'VE BEEN FOOLISH LATELY, OR PERHAPS, JUST HUMAN. I HAVE BEEN GETTING caught up in the struggle and stress of daily life, and I have been forgetting how blessed I am. I can't believe my life has turned out the way it has. Thank you all to everyone who has supported me in any way. I don't really know anyone with a mental illness who has as much support as I do, not that it's a competition, obviously. I have everything and everyone that I need, but the more good people, the merrier.

15 FEAR

Fear is a part of anxiety, but I wouldn't say I'm always scared when I have anxiety. I bring this up because I need to drive and run some errands today. Not an emergency or anything. My mom will run them for me if I can't do it. I'm lucky in that regard. But driving is so difficult for me because there is definitely a fear present, but I also have physical symptoms like numbness in my arms, dizziness, and chest pains. It's really hard for me to understand because I used to drive for a living. I guess I'm scared to drive because I don't want to cause an accident. I don't know if that's a reasonable concern or if I'm just guilty of over-thinking again. For me to successfully run errands, I have to shut down my mind enough to drive without a ton of worry, and I have to make sure my body is ready for the trip so that I don't get symptomatic while I'm driving. It would be easy if I could predict when all this is going to happen. It's just kind of a confident feeling and I guess a leap of faith that my medicine will work enough to drive. When I get excited about driving somewhere successfully, it really is an accomplishment for me. Sometimes, I just don't think people understand how bad it can be, and also I don't want others to feel ashamed if they struggle with driving too.

16 WORKING AND THINKING

I LEFT MY LAST DOCTOR'S APPOINTMENT A FEW WEEKS AGO WITH A LOT OF THINGS to work on and think about. My two main challenges right now are driving/leaving the house and over-thinking. I've started to put together a Lego set, filling in crosswords, and trying to read, both for pleasure and education of my illnesses. I'm trying to improve my mood and patience with others. I always wonder how much I can actually control my reaction to things. I have an open relationship with my parents where I can say things like, "Give me a minute. It's time for my medication." and things of that nature. My weight has been a battle my whole life, so I'm always trying to improve my physical health, mainly through weight loss. I am doing a better job of that since the holidays have passed. I only weigh myself a few times a year, but I can tell by how my clothes fit. I would like to start walking in my neighborhood. Hopefully, I can get up the energy and motivation when it's warmer outside, but if it's cold and if it's time, I will walk in the cold. I am even smoking less and drinking less coffee. I have extreme OCD when it comes to my medication times, and I still refuse to take my medicine early, but I have relaxed and allowed to take them later than scheduled. It's a trick of mine to have more energy, but I would never skip a dose entirely, on purpose anyway. Journaling like this has always helped me cope, and I probably have enough material for another book, but I'm not planning on doing that. I might look for a writing job somewhere. "The medicine works" my doctor tells me, so I tell myself that when I don't feel great. It really is amazing how far I've come. I have a lot to work on, but I'm in a great position to do whatever I want to do with my life from here on out. I'm grateful and blessed in many ways.

17 SIGNATURE

I GOT A SMALL SHIPMENT OF MY OLDER TWO BOOKS TODAY. I WILL BE GETTING another shipment of my newest book on February 4, 2020. I always enjoy autographing them all. It's a personal touch, and I feel like a part of me goes with every copy. My super secret wish is that my signature would be worth money some day, and my friends could sell my books for a lot of money. I used to practice my signature in grade school because I dreamed of being a professional baseball player. I dreamed of signing baseballs and roaring fans in a packed stadium. I guess a writer is close enough haha. I just don't think I was meant to be rich because I don't love money enough. When I have money, the greatest joy I get is to share it. It's part of my desire to help others and make other people happy. There are downsides to having that kind of personality, but overall, it has worked out for me. I was able to drive my car again to give it some work with no real issues, and I had a nice dinner with my parents. I finished my Lego set I was working on, and I'm almost finished with my article for The Antioch Review that's due at the end of February. Just writing about some pleasant thoughts that I had this evening.

18 GENETIC PREDISPOSITION

I BELIEVE THAT MENTAL ILLNESS IS MOSTLY A GENETIC PREDISPOSITION THAT COMES to the surface after a variety of environmental factors take place. It would be hard to pinpoint exactly what led to my diagnosis(es), but most of it had nothing to do with anything I did wrong morally or otherwise. I guess what I am getting at is that it doesn't help myself or anyone else to beat myself up for past behavior or feel sorry for myself. I try not to fall into that trap. I have work to do, and I can't accomplish treatment goals or help others if I am constantly looking back and wondering what I could have done differently. The past is over. There's very literally nothing I can do about it now, so I have to ask myself 'Now what?'. My medication helps calm my symptoms, but I have to do a lot of the work myself to gain progress. I am testing my anxiety every day, more and more, and I have had some great results. What did I have to lose? A panic attack? I've survived hundreds of those. Whenever I try to leave the house, most of the time every signal in my body is telling me "No, you can't do that". My brain is sending fear signals. I guess at some point I made a leap of faith that my medication will work and the fear would go away. If you are stuck in your progress, ask yourself what you have to lose. My memory isn't very good, but in the past year, I have made a lot of progress, and I have gained so much. If you have severe anxiety or other mental illness, please keep trying. It can get better. I can't promise you anything, but it has gotten better for me. I don't know how to give away that resiliency that comes with not giving up. All I can do is try to be a good example and tell you what has worked for me and that my life has gotten better. I never quit on anyone.

19 SOCIAL MEDIA ON MENTAL ILLNESS

ONLY A FEW PEOPLE IN MY CIRCLE ON SOCIAL MEDIA TALK ABOUT MENTAL illness, and I only know them in a professional capacity. It helps me to talk about my illness because it helps others, which in turn, helps me. It makes me feel like my struggles are all worth it. So, I just want to mention that people "let themselves go" for a variety of reasons, but it tends to happen a lot with people with mental illness. Hygiene can be a big challenge, which includes things like taking a shower, weight control, and other personal cleanliness. I have lost over 50 pounds now, and of course I'm proud of myself, but I have a long way to go before I really feel like I'm at a healthy weight. I think it's important to celebrate small successes along the way, but I try not to get too comfortable. I'm not really ready to declare victory over my illness, and I probably never will. I am always on high alert for triggers and red flags, which may sidetrack my progress. I fail sometimes, but I always try to put forth the best effort I can. I took a shower this morning and did some personal grooming. I also went out to lunch with my mom. All of these things are victories over my illness in that I both couldn't do them before, and that these tasks are still hard for me. I guess what I am getting at is that I'm starting to feel better mentally/psychologically, so I hope it will be easier for me to lose weight and take better care of myself physically. Just trying to hang tough, live right, and do the right thing.

20 DOWNTOWN

I DROVE MYSELF DOWNTOWN AGAIN. I'M SO PROUD OF MYSELF AND JUST SO grateful and happy (not always). If some of you knew what I have bounced back from, you would be amazed. My recovery and recent success is really something special. The best gift that mental illness gave me was appreciating every little success along the way. This is a lifelong illness. There is no cure. I am going to have to manage it the rest of my life, but when I can enjoy life at the same time, the struggles don't seem so bad. I have made so much progress!

21 I AM AN AUTHOR

WHEN I THINK OF AUTHORS, I THINK ABOUT PEOPLE LIKE STEPHEN KING AND James Patterson, but not myself, for some reason. When I was a kid, authors of books that I read were just otherworldly or something. I never thought I would become one, especially three times over. I am lucky to know some amazing authors and writers, and they have taught me a lot. I always think that I couldn't be a writer for a living, but here I am, writing again. I've thought about getting my MA in Counseling or doing some public speaking too. This whole journey has been very surreal in a lot of ways.

When strangers meet me, a lot of the time, they say it seems like they have known me for years. I think I'm pretty transparent. What you see is what you get. Maybe it's good vibes or something. A lot of people confide in me, which is a compliment that people trust me so much with their life stories. I very rarely get overwhelmed with all of it. I just feel like this is what I am supposed to be doing right now. I haven't changed too much, and if I have, I would like to think I'm just a better version of my old self. I'm always trying to improve myself, and every day, I am getting better at coping with mental illness. I am surrounded by so many people that love me. It really helps me deal with life. It's also a pretty amazing feeling to think that I am helping others by simply telling my story, perhaps even saving lives. I've come so far.

22 POSITIVE IMPACT

I HOPE I HAVE MADE A POSITIVE IMPACT ON YOUR LIFE IN SOME CAPACITY. YOU probably don't have to read my books to know a lot of my story. If you aren't feeling well mentally, please reach out. There's the crisis line, or even calling the police or an ambulance. You can reach out to me, but I can only help so much if you need medical attention. I've lost a few friends to suicide and drug overdoses, and I want it to stop. 10-20% of bipolar sufferers die by suicide, and 50% have attempted suicide. One in five people has a mental illness. These are staggering numbers when considered to scale of the general population. I know I can't save everyone, but no one is going to stop me from trying. I guess I am a little greedy in that I want to have an impact on more than one person because a lot of people say, "If I could just help one person..." I want to help a lot of people, and I hope my story is read and told for many years after I expire.

23 MENTAL ILLNESS IS NOT FAIR

I'VE HAD 2 PANIC ATTACKS IN THE LAST TWO DAYS, AND SOME GENERAL ANXIETY. The panic attacks are less than a minute usually, but I was hyperventilating, which I haven't experienced in some time. General anxiety can last much longer. For me, it lasts until I eat a meal and take a nap. Mental illness is not fair, nor is life. I miss out on a lot of things to remain stable. If you think mental illness is "all in our heads", you are simply wrong and don't understand mental illness. I hope you never have to understand. It's physical, emotional, and psychological. It's a daily struggle to remain stable. I am physically sore and exhausted from the panic and anxiety. I had planned to go see my friends' band play today, but I simply don't feel up to it. I had been planning on it for months.

A panic attack that lasts a minute can bruise my ego and confidence. One minute is all it takes for me to be less confident about my progress. I am kind of a veteran of panic and anxiety, so I know I just have to build my confidence up again. I also know that a meal and a nap will take care of the problem. Just a little disappointed today, but I'm sure it will be better after I rest.

24 BOOKS

I DON'T KNOW IF THIS IS A SURPRISE TO ANYONE, BUT I'M NOT THAT CONFIDENT OF a writer. Sometimes I think people are just being nice when they buy my books. Maybe they believe in supporting local artists. All of that is great, and I appreciate the support, but when you delve into my books, you will find more than a little valuable information about mental illness. My second book was a poetry book, which was more my creative side, but my first book is very clinical, and my third book is journal style, detailing life with mental illness. I say that my books have value because it's just an amazing story. Not a lot of people talk about mental illness, and a lot don't even survive for a variety of reasons. Then, for someone like me to have a clear enough mind to write about all of it. It's just a rare thing.

25 RAGE

I feel rage sometimes. It's not rational anger. It's not me, but I can get fixated on something I don't like about life, or I can feel rage for seemingly no reason at all. Usually, it is when my medicine hasn't started working yet. I feel awful when I am mean to my parents, but they know it's not me acting out. They know it's not in my character. I always apologize if I think I was being irrational too. I have some things in place that I do that help ease my anger/rage until it passes. I want to share because maybe these techniques will help you:

I go into a quiet room. If I feel like listening to music, I put on relaxing music, emphasis on relaxing. Sometimes, I close my eyes and just breathe in and out in silence. I roll my own cigarettes, so that monotonous action helps calm me and helps spend unnecessary anger energy. I sit on my porch and have a cigarette, and watch the traffic go by. I try to think of myself as separate from the race everyone is running. I might text a friend and ask that person how their day went. I might crack jokes on social media to help cheer me up. I might go out of my way to be kind to someone else.

I am basically trying to distract myself and my rage long enough for the medicine to work. Rage is rare for me, but it's a strong emotion that I have. I absolutely hate it because it's not in my character or personality. I have a hard time being mean to people that deserve it, much less for no reason. Also, journaling like this helps too.

26 PLAYING WITH FIRE

For the longest time, I thought I was jealous of people who can drink alcohol all the time, have a good time, and still function. That's not it. Alcohol and drugs have and always will be there for me if I choose. Stability, productivity, sanity, and peace of mind were gone from my life for a long time, and I have been fighting very hard to get it all back. These are the qualities that I lost and that I value so much. I don't value being fucked up anymore. I don't need to self-medicate because my medicine works most of time. I have slip ups. I had 5 beers about a week ago, and I had a good time actually, but I'm playing with fire. Shit man, I'm playing with fire when I have something as harmless as coffee. Maybe I have more to lose now than I did before, because stability, sanity, and all those great qualities are priceless to me. I'm not willing to risk a night of drunkenness for everything I have fought for. Overall, I'm doing a pretty good job, all things considered.

27 PEP TALK

My really good buddy called me out of the blue around midnight a few nights ago. He just felt the urge to give me a pep talk of sorts, which I didn't think I needed at the time, but I did. He told me that I have to let the things go that I've done that I'm not exactly proud of. He's right. I think my biggest regret is not what I've done or not done, it's how much energy and guilt I gave to my regrets, and how much I cared what other people thought of me. All that really matters is who I am today, and I'm proud of that person. There's no need to beat myself for things that happened a long time ago. It's not fair to myself, and it's not productive if I want to help and love others. I think when we are young; we are taught to feel guilt and remorse for things we've done wrong, which is a good way to learn right from wrong, but at some point in our adult lives, we have to let it all go. I'm the only person I'm going to have to live with my whole life. I have to love and forgive myself, and I'm still learning.

28 GIFT OF MENTAL ILLNESS

I TELL PEOPLE ALL THE TIME THAT THE BEST GIFT MENTAL ILLNESS HAS GIVEN TO me is an appreciation for the little things (which maybe are big things) and a general sense of gratitude. I was never a bad person. I just didn't fully appreciate how blessed I was, and I took life for granted. I use the word blessed instead of lucky or fortunate because I feel like blessed is a superlative word, and that's the degree to which I feel the gratitude, if that makes sense. When I use the word blessed, I am basically just describing the overwhelming sense of gratitude that I feel quite often now.

29 JUST BE YOU

My good buddy told me at my birthday party, "Just be you". Such a simple statement. This good friend thought that me being myself was good enough for him. I think we complicate things sometimes by always striving to be better and obtain more "stuff". There's nothing wrong with trying to better yourself and move up the money ladder, of course, but sometimes we define ourselves by status symbols and whatever else society says makes us good enough. Being myself is good enough for my friends, and that's actually an amazing thing, and takes a lot of pressure off me. I know how to be me. I can do that. I just want my friends to be themselves too. I wouldn't keep them around if I didn't think they were good, solid people. If you are a good person with good intentions, just be you. The world doesn't need more successful people (again, nothing wrong with that). The world needs more good, kind, and loving people.

I'm really proud of myself. I fought hard today. Today wasn't terrible, but it certainly wasn't easy. I had some anxiety and racing thoughts throughout the day, but I managed to do some housework, which helps calm me and also helps my mom. I shaved my face, which may seem very minor to most, but when I was first hospitalized in 2006, I had to earn the trust of the nurses to use a razor. Razors and sharp objects were only allowed by patients at the nurses' discretion for (hopefully) obvious reasons. I always think about the tiny drab community bathrooms and showers when I shave my face.

Shaving my face is a reminder of the freedom I have earned in recovery, and it gives me a sense of pride every time I shave. I have traumatic memories from the hospital too, but shaving my face elicits mostly good feelings. I don't even take shaving my face for granted anymore. I am also budgeting money better this month and improving my general mood.

I use social media for a lot of the same reasons everyone else does—sharing memes and photos, random status updates, etc. I definitely like to make people laugh, but I also like to use social media for a purpose. I run my own page devoted to mental health awareness, and it's a great tool for a small time author like me to promote my books. Social media has also allowed me to stay in contact with so many people when I was super sick. I also like all the live music venue feeds because I can't always be there in person.

30 PILE OF BOOKS

I'M SITTING HERE LOOKING AT A PILE OF MY BOOKS THAT I ORDERED, AND IT'S JUST such a wild feeling that I turned out to be an author/writer. When I got a degree in psychology, I thought I was going to be a psychologist. Being a writer was something so far from my plans. You may as well told me I was going to be an astronaut. Weird how stuff works out sometimes when you think it isn't. I'm helping at least as many people as I would have had I become a psychologist. It's just such a weird feeling to look at a book and know that I wrote it. I'm not trying to toot my own horn or anything. Just being honest.

31 FIGHTING THIS ILLNESS

My anxiety got the best of me just now. I tried 3 times to get into my mom's car to go get my truck from having repairs, and I couldn't sit still, and I had chest pains from anxiety. The reason I had an anxiety attack or whatever it was, was because I had just taken my medicine and it hadn't kicked in yet (usually takes about an hour or so). Luckily, my awesome parents picked up my car for me, so now I don't have to worry about it. I can't stress enough how important it is to have support with mental illness. I am truly blessed with great friends and family who I know are always going to be there for me. Others are not as fortunate, which is one of the big reasons I try to be a good example by fighting this illness and trying to be there for others. Usually, the best cure for a panic attack like that is a good meal and a nap, so that's what I'm going to do.

32 NOT OKAY

It really freaked me out when I couldn't sit still from panic and ride in my mom's car yesterday. I had a doctor's appointment scheduled for tomorrow, and I had to reschedule. I contacted my case manager, and I told him I wasn't feeling well or confident enough to endure a doctor's appointment tomorrow. Props to my case manager for responding to my texts when he was out of the office. I told my parents I wasn't feeling well too. That's all I can do I think. I'm a little upset because I feel like some of my progress was taken away, but hopefully, I will be okay shortly. It's been a lot worse before.

33 STRUGGLES AND TRIUMPHS

THE REASON I WRITE ABOUT MY STRUGGLES AND TRIUMPHS IS TO INSPIRE OTHERS and make others feel like they are not alone. I'm not suffering. I struggle sometimes, and there's a big difference. I don't want anyone to feel sorry for me, but of course, I appreciate the support and prayers. I would rather you pray for people who are really suffering, but I guess there's enough to go around.

34 DR. PHIL

I'M NOT A BIG FAN OF DR. PHIL, BUT SOMETIMES MY DAD WATCHES HIS SHOW because it's on TV right before the local news. He was talking to a 28-year-old female drug addict today, and he said something very powerful. He said, "You are 28 years old. You might have another 60 years on this planet. If you get help now, this could all just be a bad memory." What a wonderful thought for anyone who wants to change or put their past behind them. Maybe parts of my life can just be bad memories too, and I can move on (if I haven't already).

35 INSPIRED

I'M GOING TO SELL HOWEVER MANY BOOKS, BUT I REALLY JUST WANT PEOPLE TO BE inspired by my story. Maybe I can open some eyes as to what it's like to live with mental illness and how severe it can be, and how it's such a wide spectrum. Bills are bills, and money is money, but it doesn't matter to me if we have a chat about mental illness or you read about it in one of my books. It's just the same to me.

36 LIBRARY POEMS

My driving anxiety has come back in the last week or so, but today, I drove to the library to submit my second book, "Poems from a Bipolar Mind" for their catalog. This book should be on the shelves in the next month or so. No anxiety issues at all really. I was a little nervous when I left the house, but I'm really glad I was able to drive and get a little exercise. Anxiety and panic is only a little bit logical, so there's only so much that therapy can do. Usually, it's just a baby steps process to get back where I was, which I totally hate, but it is what it is. Just thankful I was able to overcome my fears today.

37 WHITE CASTLE

I just went to White Castle, and they were short 2 workers. They called off. Happens all the time in food service. Knowing this, instead of choosing to be angry and frustrated, I chose to just be happy that I was getting food that I was cheating on my diet. I was making conversation with other people in line, and smiling. I also gave the cashier a $5 bill and thanked her for showing up. We make lots of choices every day. Choose to be the bigger person and the exception to the rule. Maybe on another day, I would have been upset. I don't know. I just think today was the day to show compassion and humility to these human beings who were serving me food.

38 SHAKESPEARE

"The robbed that smiles steals something from the thief" is a Shakespearean quote that I've always liked. I thought about going so far as to get it tattooed on me. I feel like when I have a positive attitude and sense of humor in the face of mental illness (The thief, if you will), I feel like I am getting something back that mental illness stole from me. Mental illness took everything I had at the time, and then it tried to take my life. I have survived over 13 years since those days many years ago. Looking back on my journey, a lot of people would call it a success story. I don't know about all that, but I'm definitely proud of how I have handled everything and how my life has turned out.

39 SINGING

I'm always looking for natural ways to alleviate my bipolar and anxiety symptoms, and I read that singing out loud can help anxiety. This might explain why I don't have many problems singing karaoke, but why I still have problems driving to the bar to get there. Sometimes, I sing around the house without even thinking about it. Just a fun and weird thing about anxiety. I should say MY anxiety because what works for one person, might not work for another. That's why mental illness is so hard to treat, whether with cognitive therapy and/or medication. Everyone experiences mental illness differently.

40 DON'T WASTE YOUR LIFE

Sometimes, life can be overwhelming, and I let it get to me, and other times, I laugh at the magnitude of it all and my very small part in all of it. I laugh at all the dumb jokes I know or ironically, the daily tasks when they seem never-ending. Of all the atoms that could have formed anything, a tiny fraction made me and you. Yes, I know the science. The fertilized egg, yada yada yada. But there still had to be a pretty incredible happening to form your being. Don't waste it. Have something to offer to others. As far as I know and believe, we only get one shot at this thing, so make it memorable. I always keep love and kindness in my heart, which I think helps me deal with a lot of things. Oh yeah, and as much comedy as I can fit into a day without annoying others.

41 HEARTBREAK

I THINK BY THE TIME YOU GET TO BE MY AGE, YOU HAVE EXPERIENCED SOME kind(s) of heartbreak and trauma that has left you a different person, if you are wise. I wish for myself that I have become a more grateful person, and a better all around person since I was first diagnosed. I lost everything—my house, my car, my mind, my reputation—literally everything. I have spent so much time trying to get my life back on track, with a lot of success. I never thought I would be an author and writer. I have touched many lives and helped many people, and that makes me happy and gives me purpose and the will to continue the journey. My mission in life has almost nothing to do with longevity, but rather making an impact. I'm not planning ongoing anywhere any time soon, but then again, no one really ever does. I want my life to be a celebration like the stupid birthday parties I have been throwing for about 10 years. I'm never going to be confident enough to say that I beat my illness, but it certainly didn't beat me.

42 EPISODIC

I WILL SEE THE DOCTOR IN A FEW WEEKS. I'M STARTING TO THINK ABOUT WHAT I want to talk to him about, and it's frustrating. I feel like I should want to do things, but I'm not interested in a lot of things. My energy level is low, and I'm sore from being overweight and inactive for a few months. It looks like depression symptoms, but I'm not really sad. I had enough energy to write my third book, but I don't think it would take this long to recover. For a few months, I was going out and driving and really enjoying myself. When the time and weather changed, and I had a massive panic attack. It was like the rug got pulled out from under me again. It's so frustrating. I finally have enough money to do things and maybe take a trip somewhere, but I can barely drive up the street. Bipolar disorder is episodic, which is a hope I am holding onto right now, and that this is just another phase. I'm very grateful that I got out and drove places when I could. I always try to seize those moments when I feel well because lately I haven't been able to do much.

43 DEAR LAUREN

There was a courageous woman from my area who was diagnosed with a fatal brain injury. In her last days, all she wanted was letters of hope. Here is the letter I wrote her. She played basketball for a college called Mount St. Joseph's, and scored a basket in one of her final days.

Dear Lauren,

There is so much I want to say to you. I wish I could just talk to you over coffee or something. I also hope you get this message. You are such a hero to so many people, including myself. I hope you realize how big of an impact your story has had on everyone, near and far. You have shown everyone how to face adversity with dignity and courage. You have turned a negative into a positive. Even that is such an understatement. Your story will be told for such a long time. That is something so special. Your impact is on the same level as famous authors, scientists, and dignitaries. My friends and family are praying for you, and we all wish you a Merry Christmas! Keep fighting!

Love,

John Edward Medl, Age 33 Cincinnati

44 KINDHEARTED STRANGER

WEIRD HAPPENINGS ON THE PORCH THIS MORNING...A MAN STOPPED HIS CAR IN front of my house and started walking towards the porch. I thought it was my overdue package, but it was a guy my age who lived in the neighborhood. He said he drives by every day, and he saw me sleeping one day, and he wanted to make sure I was okay. He said it had been bothering him for a week because he didn't know if I was okay. I explained to him that I fall asleep sometimes on the porch because I'm groggy from medication. I told him I had bipolar disorder, and I take medication for it. He said he had bipolar disorder, too. He also has anxiety, panic attacks, and PTSD from the military. Same as me, although I was never in the military. He was 38 years old. I will be 38 in 9 days. He was first diagnosed in 2006. Same as me. This was just some random, kindhearted stranger from the neighborhood checking on me. So cool of him to do. Just a very nice, weird thing that happened this morning.

Having a positive attitude doesn't mean I'm happy all the time. I get in bad moods. Some (parts) of my days are bad sometimes. Mental illness and depression are very real and powerful, but if you start out deciding you are going to have a positive attitude, it's hard to say that you are a failure. I get enjoyment out of making people laugh and smile. I am also very candid about my struggles and illness. At the end of the day, when I'm laying in bed at night, I look back on the day. If I can look back on the day and see that someone was happier or inspired because of my life, I won that day. It's a daily measuring stick that I use to decide if I was successful for the day. I may not have had a great day, but if someone else did because of me, everything I go through is worth it. I am winning at life, despite everything. This is just simply my philosophy of life. It's not something that can be measured. It's not logical like mathematics. I'm just telling you what helps me get through hard days. I know it works because I feel it and live it.

I think most people know that bipolar disorder is a disease of extremes, especially moods. I am somewhat stable most of the time. I don't like it. I like being manic, but it's not good for me. I think I'm so addicted to coffee because it makes me manic sometimes, even at my anxiety's expense. Conversely, I can be in a good mood one minute, and the next minute, it feels like someone punched me in the gut with depression. It's strange and fascinating. I try my best to describe it.

45 DETACHED OBSERVER

Here's another poem and commentary I found from 20 years ago, when I was a senior at Moeller High School. Some of these old writings of mine are really weird because you can almost see and feel my mental problems coming on. This was written in the year 2000. I wasn't officially diagnosed until 2006. I guess it just feels weird to me because I wrote it and I remember vaguely how I felt. Like I said before, I'm still the same guy, and maybe my life turned out exactly how it was supposed to. I just took a few detours.

DETACHED OBSERVER

Don't want to ruin the mood,
I'd never think to intrude,
Upon such important matters dear to you.
I care about everyone else because of all I have felt,
I will emerge in the end,
To see the vision of mirth again.
Dissipate the groups I've come familiar with,
Take away the sanity, which fades to a myth.
Move me along the world with no trace of a journey,
For no trace for anyone to find myself.

Commentary

This poem I wrote when I started to feel that my life was becoming too hectic and rapid for my own mind. I felt that I would be lost in the shuffle of adulthood, and everything was going to change now that I'm entering the real world. I guess I'm scared, but more anxious. I wasn't a very happy person when I wrote this because I feel the pain of other people, and I'm oversensitive to negative occurrences in life. I think the world is coming down on me sometimes, and I wonder why I'm here. I think that I may have a mission on this Earth to just simply be funny and nice to others, and I think that's an important vocation. It seems rather simple, but I think I can help others a great deal in the field of psychology to help those who have struggled like myself.

46 GROWING APART

Do you think that others naturally grow apart as everyone gets older? I always wonder if it's because of my illness that I have lost so many friends and acquaintances. I don't want to believe that my former friends forgot about me on purpose or for any other reason than everyone is busy and has families now and such. When I go out, which is hardly ever, I'm trying really hard to keep the conversation about my books and my illness to a minimum. I care less about being liked, and more about being too much for people or having the conversation get too heavy when people just want to have fun. I also need a break. I have to deal with my illness almost every second, and then I'm advocating on top of that. I don't want my illness and work to define me. I have a lot of substance to my personality.

47 EMERGENCY WAITING

I REMEMBER SITTING IN THE EMERGENCY WAITING ROOM. I WAS READING BIBLE verses to an older black woman. She didn't seem to mind. She was friendly. I remember that much. I went to use the bathroom, and my urine was bright orange, like orange soda. I'm pretty sure I was hallucinating. The doctors took me back into the treatment part of the building. I couldn't calm down. A doctor asked me a bunch of questions—if I knew who the president was and if I was on drugs. She asked me all the drugs I have done, and I had to answer with embarrassment in front of my parents. The nurses gave me a big shot of medicine in my right arm. Shortly after, I laid down in a bed in a room off to the side and slept peacefully for many hours.

48 POLITICS AND WAR

And everything was about politics and war
And now it's always more
Until everything had been bought from every store.
No one wants to leave home
Safety in their gadgets
All the information in the world,
And no one uses it.
Where do we go now?
What's it all for?
Nothing is much use if you don't
Venture from your doors.
To explore everything that has always been there
Just waiting to be enjoyed
But people would rather argue and play with their toys.

John E. Medl

I KNOW I'M A STRONG PERSON, BUT I GUESS I DOUBT HOW STRONG I AM GOING about this whole driving anxiety problem. There's a lot of moments in my life when I say to myself, "Wow. That took a lot of strength". You are a strong person. I guess I just wonder if I'm being too cautious about driving. When I have physical symptoms of anxiety and panic—chest pains, dizziness, numbness in limbs—I feel like I am a danger on the road. Not to mention these symptoms make it extremely difficult to drive.

49 I AM

I AM MANY THINGS. I'M A SON, BROTHER, AND UNCLE. I'M A ST. SAVIOUR Golden Bear, a Moeller Crusader, and a Dayton Flyer. I'm a good person and a good friend. Some days I feel like I have the magic in me, and some days I feel like I'm just fighting to survive. One thing I am not is a quitter, and no one can take that away from me.

50 GRANDMOTHER

My maternal grandmother passed away around 1998-1999. Within days of her passing, I started to self medicate with drugs and alcohol. I never thought I'd be a party person like that. I think I was looking for emotional pain relief. I was hurt badly to a point that I had rarely experienced, if ever. In 2006, I was first hospitalized and diagnosed with bipolar disorder. She was a wonderful person. I've never met anyone so devoted to God. If there's anything after this life, I like to think she's looking down on us all, and that I've made her proud. We have a lamp that flickers from old wiring, and my mom says it's my grandma saying hello. It just happened, so I thought I'd write something about her. She never drove a car and loved getting her hair done. She liked a little wine, and she was a smoker, except for the last few years of her life. I guess it hurt so badly because I thought she'd always be there because she had always been there. I know this sounds like a sad post, but I'm actually reminiscing about her fondly before sleep.

A big problem I have is with confidence. In almost every sense of the word. With my mom breaking her wrist, I've had to do housework that she can't do. I don't know if I thought I couldn't take care of myself or what, but I'm learning that I can should I ever move out on my own. My mom has devoted most of her life to taking care of my dad and my siblings. With me doing some of the housework, it's a good reminder of how much my mom has done for all of us. I cooked dinner tonight for the most part. Laundry. Garbage. I don't take it for granted how much my mom does.

51 DISABILITY AND PUBLIC ASSISTANCE

I SEE STUFF ALL THE TIME ON SOCIAL MEDIA AND WHEREVER ELSE THAT TALK about people on disability or public assistance. It's almost always negative and judgemental. Yes, some people abuse the system and fake disability, but I don't believe that's usually the case. But guess what? It's not anyone's business. Yes, tax dollars pay for public assistance, but what about the people who become disabled who paid into Social Security for years? God forbid anything happens to you or your family where you need public assistance. Mr. or Mrs. Jones is allowed to have nice things even if they are food stamps. Maybe they bought their nice items before they became disabled. Maybe they have a rich uncle or something. You just never know. That's why being judgmental makes people look ignorant. Personally, it took me 7 years to get approved for disability. The whole process was ridiculous and nearly impossible. I had a lawyer, but I dumped every one finally, and I was losing hope. The way I got approved was my mother took all my records with a picture of me to the Social Security/Disability office, and shortly after, I was approved. It was a miracle for my family. I don't know where all these people are who are rich off the government, but it's not me. I would kill to be able to work a normal job. I would make a hell of a lot more money. My parents taught me the values of hard work, so I try to do what I can to feel like I am earning those disability payments and $38 a month in food assistance. I know not everyone is like that, but that's me. I don't worry about everyone else.

52 PANDEMIC

DURING THIS PANDEMIC, I SEE PEOPLE BEING KINDER TO EACH OTHER, IN general, of course. I see people respecting the elderly again. I see musicians finding new ways to perform. I see people making art and enjoying the outdoors. I see parents cherishing lost time with their kids. Maybe we needed a break and the world to stop for a minute... (obviously I know all of this has come at a great cost to a lot of people)

53 DEPRESSED

I'VE BEEN DEPRESSED FOR A FEW WEEKS OFF AND ON. IT'S ALWAYS OFF AND ON because of the duality of bipolar disorder. I've thought about what I might say if I knew it was the last of my time on Earth. I've thought about what my eulogy might sound like. Thoughts about death and dying are common with anxiety, depression, and bipolar disorder. There's as high as a 20% suicide rate for bipolar disorder as well. If I ever get to that point, I have faith that I would tell someone. Or write about it as I'm doing now. I've thought about my parents aging, and the real possibility that they might not be around some day. As always, the reason I'm writing this is for the greater good. You are not alone. If my symptoms aren't too bad, you can talk to me. Please get help if you need it or find an outlet that gives you relief.

54 NOTE FROM A READER

From a reader: Dear Mr. Medl,

I am a freshman student at the University of Vermont, enrolled in a class to discuss mental health disorders.

I have just read your book Millions Like Me, so I know reading is difficult for you.

Perhaps you have someone to help you read, but if not, I will try to keep this email short and space it so hopefully, it's easier.

I just wanted to say thank you for your book.

I do not currently think I have any mental disorders (I just turned 18) but this book was incredibly helpful and insightful for me, regardless.

I of course, cannot begin to imagine the work you put into writing it, but it's so valuable to learn from.

Your poems, while tinted with sadness and isolation, are truly powerful and beautiful to read.

Again, thank you.

55 ANOTHER REALITY

Going through psychosis and being delusional is a strange thing, especially when I snapped out of it and back to another reality. I remember a lot of the insane things I thought and acted upon, and it just hurts. I think because it's so embarrassing. Not to mention how painful it was to go through that trauma. People I've known for a very long time witnessed my insanity, and like I said, it's so embarrassing. I'm sure when some people think of me, they think of the insane things I did, and not the actual person who I really am. I am not my illness. I've had a lot of great times in my life, and it seems like good times are rare for me anymore. I get in moods where I get so agitated that not even my mother's voice is comforting. I think about how nice eternal silence is going to be. I don't really believe in complaining, but I still experience a lot of pain—physical, mental, and emotional. Some days, I think I'm ready to call it quits, or if my life ended, I would be fine with it. I've paid back society and done my time. This is what bipolar depression looks and sounds like. I'm lost as to what helps or what can help me bring me out of a funk like this. I can't even think straight except for negative and depressing thoughts. I hold on to the hopes that it will pass as it always does. It helps when I joke around and make people laugh, or when I feel like I really reached someone who is also struggling. I felt like I didn't really know what to do right now, so I wrote it down, and I feel a little better. I'm going to try to practice some self-care tonight and just take it easy. Find something relaxing to do. I haven't read a single page of any book in a while, and I have a lot of interesting books I want to read. Self care might mean taking a shower or watching something mindless on TV. I wish I could figure it out like a math problem, but depression is rarely logical.

56 MENTAL ILLNESS IS UNFORGIVING

I was supposed to have a phone call meeting/assessment with my psychiatrist today, but he was out of the office. I was looking forward to it because I wanted to talk about some emotional issues I've been having lately. I got rescheduled for 10 days from now, so it's all good. As much as I've written, I don't think I've ever just flat out said that mental illness is really hard to deal with. Maybe a few times, but not often. I don't like talking about it, and I hate complaining and excuses. Mental illness and not having a properly functioning brain has BY FAR been the hardest thing I've ever had to deal with. The worst day of my life was when I was first hospitalized in 2006, although I wasn't completely coherent, but I remember more than I should. I've tried to make the most of my situation and stay positive by writing and cracking jokes, etc., but it's really hard on me sometimes. I know a lot of you out there have to deal with all sorts of things that maybe you don't talk about. No matter what the ailment, you are not alone. I struggle a lot too. Like I said, I do a pretty good job of playing it off, but my mental illness can be unforgiving.

57 MENTAL COMFORT

I had a meeting over the phone with my psychiatrist today. He's very positive. He reminded me of how far I have come and told me I am doing a good job. If I could only internalize what others see in me. I am an overthinker and my own biggest critic and enemy. Even after all this time, I am still a work in progress. I don't know if I will ever be satisfied. My doctor even said that he wishes he could put me on payroll to talk to some of his other clients. I have been completely compliant, especially with medication, which is not my nature at all. I put my trust in the experts' hands, and they delivered. Before my diagnosis, I never even took Advil or Tylenol, much less psychotropic medications. Somewhere deep down, I know I am a success story. I know I inspire people. I know I am blessed, and I am grateful for everything I have and everything I've worked for. I have a sick brain that tells me lies and sometimes I can't convince myself that I'm actually doing pretty well compared to my mental health history. I guess it was nice to hear from my doctor. I've been humbled to the point of rock bottom, but I still believe there is something special about me. I've emptied the tank, so to speak, for so long and so many days trying to fight this illness. It's exhausting and frustrating, but I've never quit, which is something to hang my hat on. When I try to sleep at night, I remind myself that I am doing the best I can to provide some sort of mental comfort.

58 LINGERING FEARS

I CONQUERED ONE OF MY BIGGEST AND LONGEST LINGERING FEARS TODAY. I SAW A primary care doctor and had blood drawn. It had been about 10 years since both events. Everyone who gave me medical attention was great. My blood pressure was a little high, but not concerning. The blood work is the standard tests—kidney and liver functions, sugars, and metabolism. I guess you can't just be fat anymore haha. I have faith and hope in humanity, even if it is only temporary. What matters to me more is having faith and confidence in myself. It's a lot easier for me to help humanity when I feel good about myself. I can't help anyone if I don't believe in my abilities. I don't need faith in humanity. I've seen what it is—good and evil, ups and downs, lies and truth. It's always going to be that way. I just try to do my part, and I can't do that to my fullest ability without confidence, faith, and trust in myself.

59 MANIA

There's noise coming from the magic box
As I roll up another cigarette
The actors have rehearsed their lines
Handed down to them by people
Who have never had to fight for anything
The brave warriors slave away
For a hundred dollars a day
If they're lucky
So the privileged can live in decadence
It's been this way for such a long time
When will this change like society has?
Fear and masks
All we know how to do is pray
I wonder if anyone is listening

Mania is a hallmark feature of bipolar disorder. When manic, a person can impulsively spend money or have trouble budgeting money. I have experienced this many times, and it's something I struggle with. Today, I was able to open my own checking account. For years, I have been sharing an account with my mom, and it has caused a lot of stress in my family. Glad to check another thing off the list, working towards more independence and responsibility.

60 HARDEST LESSONS

One of the hardest lessons I'm still trying to learn is that not everyone is going to like me. There's a saying that goes, "You could be the ripest, juiciest peach in the world, and there's still going to be people who don't like peaches". Honestly, it's their loss. I'm loyal to a fault, and I have a lot to offer. I would never screw anyone over intentionally, and I don't wish harm on anyone, not even the people who have done me wrong.

61 WHY NOT ME?

SOMETIMES, I THINK TO MYSELF, "WHY DOES ANYONE CARE WHAT I WRITE about?", but then I think, "Why does anyone care what anyone writes about? Why not me?" I'm not some expert who is just writing about something I've read in books. I've lived the Hell that I write about. I think that's one of many reasons why people gravitate towards me and are interested in reading my books. If you read my books, you will find that I am brutally honest about my symptoms and my experiences. Just something to think about for any aspiring writers. I also hope that my honestly does not come off as complaining because sometimes I think there's nothing worse. It's a toxic trait that creates a negative environment. I try to be grateful and humble. It's a challenge. It's much harder to be grateful and courageous in the face of adversity than the alternative.

62 TREATMENT PLAN

Yesterday, I had a meeting with my clinical diagnostician, and today with my case manager. Relatively painless stuff. We basically laid out a treatment plan for the year. I wish I didn't have to do stuff like this, but it's probably for my own good. I really just want to be free and left alone most of the time, but all my meetings are good reminders of my goals and progress, I suppose.

63 RANTINGS

My parents are sleeping, so y'all are going to have to deal with my rantings. Before I wrote this, the office chair broke, which is supposed to have an 800 pound capacity or something. This is like the third one that has broken on me. I'm not slim, but I'm not 800 pounds.

We had to have a new sump pump installed in the basement today, which is basically not my territory of business, but it's just something that happened today.

The Department of Education forgave the remaining balance of my student loans years ago, but they still send mail to check up on me to make sure I haven't become wealthy or gainfully employed. Not a huge deal, but stressful and annoying in some small way.

Here's the really annoying thing. I started a checking account with $40 a few weeks ago, and it was overdrawn this morning. Every time I made a transaction, I checked the banking app first to make sure the money was there. When I set up the account, I told the people to make sure that no purchases would be approved if the money wasn't there. When I went to bed last night, I had about a dollar in my account, which is fine because when I set up the account, I made sure there was no minimum balance requirement. I MADE SURE all of these things to safeguard against an over withdrawal. When I woke up this morning, I had to deal with the stress of my account being way overdrawn, and not just by a little. No one at the bank wanted to take responsibility, and everyone around me just assumed it was my fault because I've had a few bouts of financial irresponsibility. I guess it's at least partially my fault because I was the one at the controls, but I was so careful. I was even keeping track with pen and paper because I felt like something wasn't right. Long story short, fuck today. Let's hope for a better tomorrow.

64 PANIC ATTACKS ARE NOT FOR THE WEAK

Panic attacks are shocking in a lot of ways. I'm not sure if that's the right word. I'm just always shocked at how painful they are and that I've survived so many. I just had a brief panic attack, and they are not for the weak. My entire body gets stiff, and my mind races in nonsensical words and phrases. I get dizzy and I get stomach cramps. I just took an Advil to try and kill some of the physical pain. Loud noises are almost unbearable to tolerate, but soft and familiar music sometimes helps me. I roll cigarettes to try and distract myself. I try to move around to make the body stiffness better. When my stomach settles, I'm going to eat dinner and rest. That's how I deal with them. It's over after that. Then the battle begins again. This doesn't happen to me often, and I've actually been making some good progress.

65 VICTORIES

Some victories that I've had lately:

1. I opened my own checking account so that I could be financially independent.
2. Some of my family members visited for dinner, so I got to see them. I had anxiety almost the whole time, but I got through it.
3. I successfully completed 3 meetings this week--- one with my clinical diagnostician, one with my case manager, and one with my psychiatrist. We laid out a treatment plan for the next year, and my medications are staying the same, but that may change. My doctor didn't want to change anything because he hasn't seen me in person for months. I've been on the same medication for about 8 years now.
4. I filled out some official paperwork regarding the forgiveness of my student loans
5. I drove myself to the store and to the bank. I have major driving anxiety, and sometimes I can't drive at all.

All of these things are hard for me. They are challenges and considered victories when I complete them. I think I had too many things going on in one week, so that's probably why I have had increased anxiety and panic attacks.

66 ARE YOU HEARING VOICES?

Whenever I have a visit with my psychiatrist, he always asks the same beginning questions...."Do you think you can fly or do you think you have superpowers?" and "Are you hearing voices?". These may seem like strange questions to the average person, but I have answered "yes" to these questions before. Quick example. When I was first hospitalized in 2006, I was convinced that I could jump off the balcony at the hospital and "fly" or land safely below. I have no idea what stopped me. I have a "loud brain", which basically means I have an active inner dialogue. Not everyone has that, so I've found out. It serves me well with writing, but it's extremely annoying and exhausting when I'm trying to rest. As long as the "voices" aren't directive (telling me to do a specific thing), then I'm considered stable enough, I guess. I've had problems with directive voices/psychosis before also. I can only explain psychosis as watching myself in a movie and someone or something else is at the controls. I've always had a loud brain, but I haven't had problems with psychosis or extreme grandeur in a long time.

Am I angry at life because of my mental illness? Not usually. I don't see how that's productive, and the world doesn't owe me anything. It could always be worse. Even when I don't have any money, I'm richer than a lot of people across the world. I wish I were a stronger person so that I acted as blessed as I feel, but I'm just human with limitations. I've tried not to use my illness as a crutch, but it is a good explanation for a lot of my behavior. For me, mental illness is frustrating, painful, and exhausting. I've prayed for death and thought about taking my own life. My best days are when I get some relief. It doesn't happen often, as my illness is mostly relentless. I've chosen to educate others through my books and volunteer my time to help others find some relief. So many positive things have come from my illness, and it helps me to focus on all the good things rather than feel sorry for myself.

67 RACIAL PROTESTS

June 9, 2020: In the middle of a global pandemic and racial protests

I don't feel guilty for being white. I didn't get to choose my skin color as much as anyone. But I do understand what white privilege means. As a white person, I'm more likely to have access to all kinds of resources and less likely to be harassed by the police. It doesn't mean that my life is easy. I know good cops. I've known them almost my whole life. But once you are mistreated by the police, how do you forget that? My former professor is Latino and he was brutalized and beaten by police in Minnesota. He won a lawsuit against them. I'm seeing a lot of positive changes in the form of diversity programs and funding for minority causes. It's very strange as a white person. I think I was so used to everyday racism that I was comfortable. Change is usually uncomfortable, and I want to be part of the solution, and I want to be on the right side of history. If racial equality is going to happen, white people need to help because we're still running the show.

I had a pretty good day today:

1. I took a shower. Embarrassingly, it had been a while.
2. I balanced my checking account, and the balance is positive.
3. I drove myself to the doctor for a sore jaw. He prescribed me antibiotics for the infection. I'll probably have to see a dentist, barring some miracle, but still a victory for me.

I’ve got to learn to not be so hard on myself

68 BLESSED

I'M A LUCKY, BLESSED MAN. EVERYONE IS SO KIND TO ME, ESPECIALLY MY MOM, the rest of my family, and close friends. I know this sounds stupid, but I feel like if I remind myself of my blessings even in hard times, that I will somehow heal faster. In a way, it does help me heal faster. Reminding myself of my good fortune at the very least occupies my mind with positive thoughts. I'm a simple man. I don't need much to be happy.

69 MANIA HIGH

Mania is often referred to as a "high", like a drug. It's like the highest you've ever been off drugs that are in your brain. No street drugs compare. That's how intense it is. I've heard, "Medication took my superpowers away." That high. Delusional and psychotic high.

70 NOTCH IN MY BELT

I'VE HAD PROBABLY THOUSANDS OF PANIC ATTACKS, BUT I REMEMBER THIS ONE IN particular. I remember smoking 9 cigarettes in a row. I just couldn't calm down. It goes that way sometimes. I remember because I counted. It's an OCD thing. I also roll my cigarettes in even numbers because I smoke 2 in a row while I'm out on the porch. I will always contend that mental illness is the hardest thing I've ever had to endure. Every day I survive is a notch in my belt. I'm extremely proud of myself for never giving up.

71 DELUSION

I SHOULD HAVE KNOWN SOMETHING WAS WRONG IN COLLEGE, BUT THEN AGAIN, I showed symptoms in high school and childhood. We all just had no idea. In college, I engaged in risky behavior, but I had this delusion that lights turned off when I was around. Like street lamps. It seemed like it had happened a lot. Then, I told my friends, and they noticed too, which reinforced my delusion. The logical explanation is that these lights were on timers, and it was coincidental that the lights would turn off. I thought it was some kind of supernatural thing, but I didn't take it very seriously and kind of brushed it off.

72 LIFE ISN'T A WALK IN THE PARK

One of my best friends visited the other day. He's known me since high school. He visited me in the hospital and has bought all my books. I try not to talk about my illness in regular conversation, but it always seems to come up. It occurred to me that I never really asked about this friend's mental health. So I simply asked, "Do you have depression or anxiety or anything?" And he simply said, "No". It kind of blew my mind because I thought about how nice it would be to not have anxiety or depression, but I do remember a long time ago when I didn't have to worry about my mental health. It's an incredible blessing to not have to deal with. However, my buddy has physical health problems that I don't have to deal with, so his life is far from being a walk in the park.

73 14 YEAR SURVIVOR

On July 31, 2020, I will celebrate being a 14 year survivor of mental illness from the first time I was hospitalized. Mental illness tried to take my life many times, but my spirit was not having any of it. I really hope I get a chance to talk to the students of Moeller HS about mental health. When I attended Moeller, there wasn't much talk about mental health. All the advocacy work I do makes me feel like I'm fulfilling my purpose. That somehow, some way, makes me feel I am exactly where I am supposed to be, and I'm doing exactly what I am supposed to be doing. It's a great feeling to feel like you are fulfilling your purpose in life. The fear of dying with unfinished business goes away. The age old question of "Have I done enough with my life?" goes away. Whatever I have sacrificed for stability (most of the time), I have gained in perspective and purpose. I am extremely grateful for my life and how it turned out. I wasn't always so optimistic. I had to work at it. I've lost plenty of battles, but I feel like I am winning the war. That's as close to beating mental illness as you can get, in my opinion.

I just want to talk about intelligence for a minute because it's on my mind. I am going to describe my family because there are 7 of us (my parents and 5 siblings) because I think it is a good example of the varieties of intelligence. You don't need a college degree to be smart, but I think it helps. I also know people who didn't graduate high school who are master musicians and carpenters.

I guess I will start with my dad. My dad has a two-year degree from The University of Cincinnati. He is an electrical engineer by trade. He must be good with money too because we don't have a whole lot of it, but we rarely go without necessities. My mom didn't finish college. It wasn't really a popular thing for women to do in the 1960s. However, she has raised 5 kids with good values and morals with not too many injuries haha. She is an extremely hard worker, which I think is a type of intelligence in a way. She is also very organized, which I think is another kind of intelligence. My oldest brother is a radar specialist for a government contractor out in Arizona. He has a Master's Degree. My next brother never finished college, but he is a master carpenter and very good with investing and money. My sister never finished college, but she is an office manager who oversees collecting invoices for a billboard company. My closest brother has a Master's Degree in Mathematics and is extremely book smart and computer smart. He's the brother we call when our computer screws up. Then there's me, the youngest of all of us. I consider myself intelligent, but like everyone else, I have my moments of dim bulbness. I just wanted to write about my family because I love them all, of course, but I think we are all intelligent in our own way. Some of us have degrees, and some don't. It doesn't have to be an either/or thing where you are smart if you have a degree, and dumb if you do not. All of this probably just relates to the fact that you shouldn't judge people, and it seems like it comes down to that a lot.

74 OUT OF CONTROL

My spending was out of control this month, so I gave control of my finances to my brother. My checking account is closed, credit cards are frozen, and I don't have any way to move money with apps like Venmo and PayPal. I'm a little disappointed in myself, but I know it's for the best. I was borrowing money from a lot of people, mainly to gamble, and it had to stop to get this household's finances in order, and also to plan for the future. Gambling gave me hope that I could win a lot of money in a short time because I can't work in a standard job. The writing job I was hoping for isn't going to work out either. On the bright side, I drove myself to the store, and I'm getting closer to finishing my fourth book each day. I'm just having a difficult time.

75 HEAVENLY

So here's a story that I've never told before. Damn, I remember it like it was yesterday. It was at least 10 years ago at Good Samaritan Hospital. I was being treated for psychosis and panic. One of the nurses gave me a pill and asked me how I felt.

"Heavenly," I said.

I was looking out into the sun-setting sky, and that's really how I felt. Several times. I've felt a supernatural force acting upon me, usually good, but sometimes evil feeling. I found out later that the pill was just for heartburn, but I think I answered in that way because that's what I thought the nurses wanted me to say. I'm not really sure. I do vaguely remember actually feeling that supernatural, heavenly way. I don't think anyone can truly understand psychosis and mania unless you have been through it. I don't care how many degrees you have. You have to feel it and experience it. Some people describe mania as a high, but that doesn't fully encompass the feeling. It's not like a let's smoke a blunt in high school high. It's like the best drug you have ever taken, combined with the worst hallucinogenic drug you have ever taken times a million. And psychosis is like watching yourself in a movie, with someone else at the controls.

76 NOT TAUGHT TO QUIT

WHEN I WAS 618 POUNDS, I SHOULD HAVE JUST HUNG IT UP AND LET NATURE take its course. I didn't. I don't use a scale, but I'm almost certain that I've lost over 100 pounds. Every time I was hospitalized, people would have understood if I quit. When I had to take medication, that made me feel absolutely awful. I should have given up. When I was lying on the couch in a medicinal haze, I should have just stayed down. I kept getting up and forcing myself to take showers when it felt impossible. When I had panic attacks while driving, people would have understood if I quit trying to drive. I wasn't raised that way. We (my siblings) weren't taught to quit. We were taught to fight. Our parents led by example in many ways, but the most impressive was that my mom and dad each beat cancer twice. My dad only has one kidney. In all honesty, I don't know how I survived a lot of things I have. I don't know why I didn't quit when I didn't know what I was doing. My mind was gone, and I still didn't quit. Now, I'm about to be an author for the fourth time. I'm going to be mentioned in the Fall Newsletter for my alma mater, Moeller High School. I'm also trying to get a mention from my college alma mater, The University of Dayton, but they have been unresponsive to my messages. I've worked with the Cincinnati-based non-profit 1N5.org on several projects. I'm the founder and administrator of a social media page devoted to mental illness and inspiration for 8 years now. We have almost

800 members. At times, I don't know how I've come this far, but I'm glad I did. Yes, I'm bragging about myself. I've earned it.

77 SURVIVED ANOTHER YEAR

Well, today's the day. I survived another year. Fourteen years ago today (July 31, 2006), my life fell apart. I lost my house, car, job, girlfriend, and any reputation I had as a sane person. I was rushed to the hospital with what they call a psychotic first break of bipolar disorder. I stayed in a locked down psychiatric unit for 11 days. It was a nightmare, and I still have flashbacks sometimes, even after all these years. I am extremely proud of how I have handled all my diagnoses and what I have accomplished. I have made my family and friends proud. I have a grateful and loving heart. I appreciate life now more than I ever did before. I tell everyone that I am blessed. I have everything I need, which is more than a lot of people have. At some point in my recovery, I decided I wanted to do more than just survive and exist. I've made lemonade, as they say, and I've played the cards I have been dealt to the best of my abilities. I can't express enough my gratitude for all the support, in every capacity. The love that has been shown to me, by all sorts of people, has been tremendous. I am just a humble servant trying to carry out a mission of kindness and awareness of mental health issues. Thank you all support for being there for me. It absolutely makes a difference.

78 BACK IN TIME

I DON'T WANT TO BE YOUNG AGAIN, BUT IF I COULD GO BACK IN TIME FOR A weekend in high school, I think I would agree to that. Party all weekend without a care or responsibility. Barely sleep, except on Sunday to recover for the upcoming week of classes. No smart phones or every app imaginable. Not many people had cell phones, either. I can't remember if I did or not. I remember people having pagers, which I never had. No Netflix and the like or social media. We took pictures with disposable cameras and actually had to wait to get the pictures developed. Weekend long binges at music festivals with a bunch of mostly kindhearted strangers just camping and listening to music. I think of those days fondly, but I still would only want to go back for a weekend. I enjoy my life now as a writer and mental health advocate. I appreciate peace of mind and silence. I don't like party atmospheres anymore. I don't think I'm boring. I just lived the party lifestyle already, and I'm done with it all. I want to keep those fond memories just as memories, and thank my lucky stars that I survived. Now, at age 38, I feel like I don't know about so many things, and I was so confident, borderline cocky in high school, which is amazing, because I was incredibly stupid compared to now. But I would still go back for a weekend if I had the chance. Maybe I am just feeling nostalgic today.

79 NOTHING IS BLACK AND WHITE

I used to believe in the good in everyone. The world has shown me that's not true. I used to think that bad people were just good people who did bad and evil things. I think people either chose to be evil or they are born that way, or some combination. That's usually how it goes in psychology. Nothing is really ever black and white. On a psychology exam, the answer is rarely straightforward. The answer is usually all of the above, none of the above, or both A and C. Things like that. I studied out of a philosophy book that was titled, "Taking Sides", and if I remember correctly, it was all about how people don't have to always take a side on every topic. You can agree or disagree with some parts of one side or the other. I think people get trapped into thinking in black and white terms, so when they are confronted with conflicting evidence of their beliefs, they won't give an inch because they have chosen a side. It's very hard for people to change their minds once they are made up. I believe this is the spirit of cognitive dissonance.

I remember writing a whole term paper on rationalization. It was either a psychology or philosophy course. In many ways, those two subjects overlap and are related. Anyway, the thesis of my paper is that rationalization is extremely dangerous because you can rationalize almost anything. Right now, I am fighting a gambling addiction. I have been gambling half of my life. It turned from recreational to a maniacal addiction. I don't like to use bipolar disorder as an excuse, but it definitely is an explanation and played a role. I was so stressed out about my parents' finances and their health. Every time I gambled, I thought I was going to win. It's really hard to give up because I have won a lot of money gambling. It was getting to the point where I was borrowing money and losing control. It had to stop. Maybe one day, I can recreationally gamble again, but for now, I am sickened by the idea, and I am trying to find myself again and finish this book. Getting back to my point, I rationalized my gambling habit because I don't drink alcohol or do drugs. I thought my gambling was acceptable because I didn't have those other coping mechanisms that most people have. You can rationalize anything if you lie to yourself enough.

80 COPING

I DON'T EVEN KNOW WHERE TO START. LAST NIGHT, I WAS EXTREMELY DEPRESSED. I was watching a poker tournament on my phone, and I was just thinking about how nice it would be to have the money to play. I've been in a poker club for about 10 years now, and the tournament entrants were my friends. We usually play in person, but because of the pandemic virus, everyone plays on an online computer application. I haven't been able to play in person for several years now, with the exception of one night, because it's hard for me to concentrate that long and sit still. The key to live poker is to be as unreadable (a la poker faced) as possible, and my anxiety gives me away every time. It's not even fun anymore.

My checking account is closed. All my credit cards are cut up and my credit is frozen. I have no access to any gambling sites on the computer. I have no access to money applications on my phone to move money around. All of this is for the betterment of myself and my situation, as well as lightening the worry and burden on my parents and siblings. I know that. I'm trying to accept that. I don't know if I need a night out with my friends or if I need someone to visit me, or what. Sometimes I just feel like running away and starting a new life. I think about living in a tiny place with few possessions by a body of water and just living there until I die without talking to anyone again. I feel stuck. I don't know if I should live here with my parents or go start a new life somewhere. I don't even know if I could handle living on my own or afford it, for that matter. I don't want to abandon everyone, but I really do get that urge a lot. Maybe I'm just tired or anxious or otherwise symptomatic right now. I could barely sit still enough to write this entry.

Journaling is a coping mechanism for me, but it's also a force where I feel compelled to write like my brain needs to throw up, per se. Writing helps release the pressure in my mind of all my thoughts. I wonder if other writers or artists or musicians feel that creative force too.

I don't know if it's possible for the living to understand suicide, but I feel like I do. A long time ago, I was suicidal, but I never attempted it. I've had suicidal thoughts too. Mental illness and anguish is incredible pain, and my best guess is that it gets to be too great for some people. I don't think people who commit or attempt suicide are cowards. I think they're just humans who have had too much pain to bear. My writing and mental health advocacy have given me purpose, which helps me when my thoughts get dark. I don't really have suicidal thoughts anymore. I've had to call my case manager several times because I was in mental anguish, and I'm always confident that I will ask for help if I need it. I know the world is a better place with me in it. I know my family and friends would be sad, and I want to go down swinging with dignity. Even with all these great reasons to live, the dark thoughts still creep in sometimes. Mental illness is incredible pain, as I mentioned. Most of the time, I feel okay. I feel good about my life and my contribution to society. But the small amount of time when I am symptomatic is incredibly painful.

It is currently August of the year 2020. I live in Cincinnati, Ohio. There's a global pandemic ravaging through the world with staggering infection rates and fatalities. I don't know if life will ever be the same again. I'm hoping and praying that the pandemic eventually subsides, and a sense of normalcy returns.

81 NAMI

I WILL HAVE 7 MORE COPIES OF MY NEWEST BOOK AROUND SEPTEMBER 24, 2019. Around that time, I will be shipping a variety of my books to NAMI (National Alliance for Mental Illness) in New Mexico, totaling around 10 copies. Thanks to my readers, friends, family, and even strangers who love and support me. It truly makes a difference. If I hear that I'm doing the right thing from others, it seems like life has been treating me well, which I take as a sign from the universe that I am doing the right thing. I am wise and humble enough to not declare victory just yet over my illness. It's going to be a lifelong battle. I hope I am up to the challenge. So far, so good I guess. Whatever mental illness has taken from me, I have gotten back exponentially, and I am grateful and blessed.

82 SUPPORT TEAM

Every so often, I like to thank my whole support team, which includes my readers, family, and friends. It makes a world of difference in my fight to stay positive and stable with my illness. Kindness matters. A few months ago, a woman at the grocery deli called me fat to someone she was talking to on her phone. I still think about it. It hurt a little bit emotionally, but I know I am doing the best I can to control my weight, and I also know I have been big my whole life. My point is that this woman probably had no idea the physical, emotional, and mental strength it took me to drive myself to the grocery. This was a time when driving for me was near impossible, and social interactions made me extremely anxious. She also didn't know that I had $5 to my name, and all I wanted was my favorite pasta salad to treat myself. Would she have cared had she known all of that? Maybe, but probably not. The world has gotten more unkind over the years, in my opinion. A lot of people have a psychological need to put others down to make themselves feel better about their own lives, which they are probably unsatisfied with, hence this psychological need to put others down. "In a world where you can be anything, be kind". Simple words from Dr. Seuss, but it can make a huge difference. I am lucky and blessed to have so many who support me and my writing. I care more about others being comforted by my story than any amount of money I make off my books. I donate them whenever I can. If you think my story is disturbing or outstanding or tragic or whatever, you should see some of the cases of people who have no support. So, a simple thank you to all of you. I would like to take credit individually for my successes, but I am not much of a success without all of your support. I think of myself as a humble servant or vessel just carrying out a mission.

83 ATTITUDE

My attitude has been pretty shitty off and on lately, and that's on me. It's a little more challenging to control my emotional reaction to things because of my illness, but I'm not the guy who likes excuses. I drove to the tobacco store today, which is only a few miles away, but I didn't have much anxiety. I was worried that I was relapsing or something, which would have been devastating to my confidence. I can't tell you how annoying it is for me to have to wait almost an hour to be calm enough to drive, BUT I'm thankful I have a car and that I can drive at all because I used to pretty much be confined to the house. With me, it's all about perspective and gratitude, and I lose sight of everything I'm blessed with sometimes. I'm a good person, and I know it, but I'm not perfect, and I know that too. No one is.

84 CHANGED

LESSON,MY ILLNESS HAS CHANGED ME IN MANY WAYS, SOME FOR THE BETTER, AND some for the worse. I would like to think more for the better. I have trouble relating to a lot of people because they just don't have an illness to contend with on a daily basis, so their priorities and outlook are different than mine. I really just want to make a difference through my books and otherwise, and be happy most of the time. Anything above that is great too. I've had more money than I could spend, and I was definitely happy. I bought a bunch of stuff I didn't need and went to bars and bought everyone drinks. I had a great time, but I didn't save a dime. I learned my lesson I guess. I still have trouble budgeting money, but it's not like I have some kind of million dollar trust fund to work with. I know that the white picket fence idea is not for me, at least not for the time being. I guess I understand the draw to that kind of life, but I'm selfish with my time and energy, and I'm not willing to share it with anyone right now in a relationship kind of way. I have plenty of people who love me in a familial and friendly way to keep me busy with my love. I guess it's hard to explain, and I certainly don't owe anyone an explanation, but everything changed when I got sick.

85 MENTAL ILLNESS ISN'T POPULAR

My books and my writings about mental illness will never be popular or well circulated. There are many reasons for that. Most people simply don't care about mental illness at all. The ones who do care either have an illness or someone close to them has it. Even some people with loved ones who have mental illness don't care. Some people don't even believe in modern medicine to treat mental illness. But, oh don't people love to blame mental illness, especially mass shootings, since they somehow have become trendy and popular. Everyone is in denial that the US has a gun problem. People actually think that people like me want to take their guns. Most people, even in their right mind, aren't responsible enough to own guns. They are dangerous killing weapons. Some guns' sole purpose is to kill as many people in as short a time as possible. Oh, but it's the mentally ill that's the problem. It couldn't be the access to guns. Then you have people who suffer from mental illness who are ashamed to even talk about it. Gee, I wonder why. The mentally ill are demonized by most of society and pill shamed if they need to take medicine.

86 PAPERWORK

I HAVE A MEETING WITH MY CASE MANAGER TODAY. HE HELPS ME A LITTLE BIT with cognitive therapy, but mainly, he helps me fill out all the long, confusing paperwork associated with my illness. He was a Green Beret, which I think is cool, so I will have to wish him a belated Happy Veterans' Day. He was shot in the back in combat, and he's had back problems ever since. I think he fought around the time of the Vietnam War. I don't have to see the doctor until January 6th, so another "fun" thing I have to do is get my medication refills approved so that I have enough medication until I see the doctor. You have no idea how many times I've wanted to say to my doctor, "Okay, I'm ready for the good shit" haha.

87 MURKY INDIFFERENCE

My medicine is designed to keep my mood and behavior somewhere in the middle of the mood and behavioral spectrum, and it does for the most part, but it results in this murky indifference and numbness. If I ever feel emotions like sadness or happiness, they are usually to the extreme, and usually accompanied by anxiety. I absolutely hate being in a bad mood, and I try to do things that make me happy to get out of that mindset. I enjoy lots of things—reading, music, watching sports, talking with friends, acts of kindness, etc. etc. etc. Most of the time, these things help my bad mood, but I have a feeling I don't experience emotions like most people. There's no concrete way to know, but I know a lot of people, and they don't seem to have the same emotional spectrum as I do. Just something interesting I've observed about my illness.

88 FED UP

EVEN THE BEST OF US GET FED UP—I'M SICK OF ALL THE PAPERWORK THAT GOES along with being on government assistance. I'm sick of doctor's appointments and medications. I'm sick of being sober because I'm so worried about everyone else's health, and if something happened when I was drinking, I would feel completely awful. I would lose so much progress, but again, I'm worried how my actions affect others. I think that a night out with my friends would solve these frustrations, or maybe even just a nice meal and nap, but don't think that I don't get upset and angry about all of this. I've been compliant ever since I entered treatment, but it's not my nature at all. I just hope I can settle down enough to continue to be on every else's time and schedules. I try my best to not complain and be a good boy and comply, but trust me, I want to break free of everything sometimes.

89 SURVIVAL MODE

Many years ago, when I was in an emergency situation, my instincts and survival mode kicked in. And some sort of amazing pain tolerance that I have no idea where that came from. I don't really see surviving the emergencies I've had as courageous. What took courage was facing the aftermath each time, and dealing with mental illness day after day, week after week, year after year. I may have given up if I didn't have some solid support from family, friends, and readers of my books. I mention this because a few people have stopped by lately just to see me, and one of my friends brought me some homemade food. I just want people to know that kindness and support like this matter to people with mental illness, and I would think anyone, really. So many people don't have this kind of support, and that makes a negative difference, too. I don't really know what my point is here. I guess I just want to say that the support I have has helped me greatly, and if you are able, be that support for others. It matters.

90 STRIPPER

Here's my funny story for the day to make you laugh. My mom will probably kill me, but oh well, I'll just unfriend her on social media again haha. So....I've only been to the strip club as a patron a few times. Not really my thing. But when I was working as a pizza delivery driver in Dayton, Ohio, we delivered to 3 strip clubs in our area. One night, I got such a delivery to a place called Pizazz (lol). Not classy at all. As soon as I walked through the door, I was in the middle of everything. I bring a pizza over to these 3 businessmen type people, and they tell me to sit down and have a drink with them. First of all, I wasn't old enough to drink, and second, I was driving all night. When I turned down the drinks, they gave me a $10 tip and told me to sit down and called over a stripper. They explained to me that I was going to get a lap dance too, whether I liked it or not. They didn't have to twist my arm or anything, but I felt so awkward because I'm pretty shy about this kind of thing. To make it even more awkward, when the stripper is doing her thing, she says, "MMM, you smell like pizza" WTF? I have no idea what I'm supposed to say. 'Oh yeah baby, it's a meat lovers'. I can get you pizza all night long. LOL. Anyway, hope that made you laugh. True story, of course.

91 ETERNAL DIRT NAP

There's nothing for me on the other side
And I'm fine with that
Even if it is just an eternal dirt nap
What if there's more?
I'm tired and sore
I'm tired of thinking
My thoughts have always been my enemy
I just want to live silently
Head down.
Put in my days.
I just want to feel the sun's rays.
But the rain has its place.
You might even see a smile on my face
I want to feel content enough to be kind
My mind has failed me
But I trust my heart
Even when I fell apart

92 EULOGY

I'VE BEEN DEPRESSED FOR A FEW WEEKS OFF AND ON. IT'S ALWAYS OFF AND ON because of the duality of bipolar disorder. I've thought about what I might say if I knew it was the last of my time on Earth. I've thought about what my eulogy might sound like. Thoughts about death and dying are common with anxiety, depression, and bipolar disorder. There's as high as a 20% suicide rate for bipolar disorder as well. If I ever get to that point, I have faith that I would tell someone. Or write about it as I'm doing now. I've thought about my parents aging, and the real possibility that they might not be around some day. As always, the reason I'm writing this is for the greater good. You are not alone. If my symptoms aren't too bad, you can talk to me. Please get help if you need it or find an outlet that gives you relief.

AFTERWORD

This book is random in a lot of ways, but I wanted it to be that way. Mental illness can be very fluid and different every day. I think the goal of any treatment and medication regimen is stability, but it doesn't always work that way. I can have a span of a month where every day is a different battle, but I can also have a span of a month or several that are stable and much easier to contend with. I can't tell you exactly when I wrote all of the entries in this book, but I think it represents the volatility of my illness and mental illness in general. When I decided to become a writer and mental health advocate, my main goal was to bring awareness to mental health issues and to make others feel like they are not alone. I hope I have done that in this book and all my books. Much love to you all.

THE ENTROPY OF BIPOLAR DISORDER

A COLLECTION OF JOURNAL ENTRIES RELATED TO MENTAL ILLNESS AND BIPOLAR DISORDER

INTRODUCTION

This book is a collection of journal entries about my life and symptoms, along with letters to various people and organizations. Many of the journal entries are out of order, but I will do my best to explain each entry. My entire purpose of being an author and mental health advocate is to help people not feel so alone, and also to inspire others with my life story. Mental illness is a constant struggle, and often times, just getting through the day is a victory. I've tried to set the standards for my life at a higher level, but I am also struggling along with a lot of my readers, too. My writings are not just for the ill, but for their friends and family as well to help understand what someone who has a mental disorder may go through in a day, week, or years.

1 ENTRY 1

John Medl
Senior Reflection Paper
English 4 CP1

THE KEYSTONE READS 1959. I APPROACH THE LUMINOUS STRUCTURE, MY collared shirt and khaki shorts drenched in sweat on a hot late-August day. I am a freshman attending Archbishop Moeller High School for the first day in my high school career. The walls loom over my head as if to mock me, complemented by brass figurines perched on top of championship pedestals. All around are strange faces, except the dozen or so children that I had known since I was in first grade. I planned to sneak into Moeller without talking to too many people, get good grades, a diploma, go to college, and have Moeller not bat an eye at my existence. Familiarity and popularity were very familiar to me as a smaller child. I excelled in knothole sports (biggest kid on the team and probably the best). I've lived in the same house all my life in a small town, and I was somewhat of a troublemaker. All those combined with myself being a nice kid, funny for my age, and I could not walk two blocks in Deer Park without recognition. I wanted to stay away from that, not because I didn't like it, but simply because I knew the feeling. I wanted to be different at Moeller, just for the adventure and unpredictability of different. I would talk to my old friends who knew me already, stay in my corner of the school, and just get out. I realize how immature this train of thought was, but I believe I was very immature when I entered Moeller. I thought smart people got good grades, and bad people were the ones in jail. I thought that is how the world worked when I entered high school.

As I proceeded through my education at Moeller, I maintained decent grades, but learned more important lessons in the process. I learned that everyone is so different, and no one can be generalized. I learned that when I treat others how I want to be treated, it might work or not, but I did my part. Those who responded positively I began to pursue relationships with, and those who responded negatively, I did not. I knew they wanted to be nice, but there was something about them I probably didn't understand. I also realized that people are not always the person I see every day, but may be hiding behind something. I've struggled to realize if that is my job, to try and help those people, or simply let them figure it out like I did. I began to develop pretty close friends that I had not known three years earlier. I was amazed at the concept of a new friendship. It had been so long for me to remember what a NEW friendship was like. I started to see the majority of the class as individuals instead of the people I didn't go to grade school with. I really started to enjoy my participation at Moeller. The epitome of when I felt the most unified in my class at Moeller was the state basketball game in Columbus versus Shaker Heights, a team heavily favored to win. The emotions, the unity, the excitement of winning our first state basketball title made me feel like I was almost the one who received the alley-oop pass to slam the game-clincher home. I felt I was out there along with the entire student body. I will never forget that.

Looking back, I will always remember that I am not always right and I should listen to everyone's opinion in search for the best result. Maturity is the acceptance of your faults, I believe, and then dealing with these faults. I will always remember how it feels to be made fun of, excluded, so that I may be able to help those who feel excluded. I have used those instances only to make me stronger. I know that not necessarily all overachievers have it together, and have problems just like underachievers. I like that the main thing I have learned about life while at Moeller can be summed up in three sentences: All people are unique and have distinct personalities, but all deserving of equal respect. Do not judge other lest you be judged. Treat your neighbor as yourself. I never thought Bible quotes would ever be applicable to my own life, but I realize that I was being close-minded to familiarity again. It's funny, most people want to be known or popular, but I wanted to be common. I eventually broke out of that ideal and became a pretty well-known figure on campus. I will take all that I have learned at Moeller and use it to help me succeed, and the hallowed hallways of Moeller have produced another man, John Medl.

2 ENTRY 2

THIS IS A LETTER I WROTE TO THE CINCINNATI-BASED NON-PROFIT ORGANIZATION, 1N5.org. Their mission is to stop the stigma surrounding mental illness through advocacy. They have fundraisers and share stories of people who are fighting the battle of mental illness. They have a website and can also be found all across social media.

To Whom It May Concern,

I hope that sharing my story helps others within your organization. I was first diagnosed with bipolar disorder with psychotic features in 2006. Since then, I have been diagnosed with panic disorder/generalized anxiety disorder, post traumatic stress disorder, obsessive-compulsive disorder, agoraphobia, and claustrophobia. I have dedicated my life to helping others, spreading awareness, and ending stigma. I have a social media page, for which I am the administrator named "Mental Health Awareness and Online Support". I am also a published poet at maverickmagazine.com. Both are free resources for anyone interested. I have written 3 books, with my newest book just published titled, "The Last Day of July: 13 Years of Madness". All 3 books are available online. Thanks for your time in reading my story.

Sincerely,
John E. Medl

3 ENTRY 3

THIS NEXT ENTRY WAS WHEN I WAS REFLECTING ON MY LIFE ON MY 38TH BIRTHDAY in October 2019.

38 things I've learned in the last 38 years:

1. Love is the most powerful force on Earth
2. Most things we worry about don't matter
3. Kindness is never the wrong thing to do
4. You don't have to be rich to be charitable and generous
5. Broad social change starts with an individual. (Thanks, Prof. Connelly)
6. Every day has the potential to be a good day
7. A loving family and good friends are priceless
8. The world is full of good people. If you can't find one, be one.
9. People who put you down don't like something about themselves
10. The world is changed by your example, not your opinion
11. Apologize whenever necessary
12. Everyone runs this race we call life at all different paces
13. Money can be a great thing, but don't let it run your life
14. Being positive and having a grateful heart really helps in tough situations

15. The world is full of suffering, but it is also full of people overcoming it
16. Recovery from tragedy is not linear
17. Perfection is not an option
18. There are many varieties of intelligence
19. If you tell the truth, you don't have to remember anything
20. Even the smartest person on the planet only knows a small amount of all there is to know
21. Dream big
22. Don't let mistakes define you
23. You don't get an award for being right. Sometimes, it's worth it to walk away from arguments.
24. Forgiveness is an attribute of the strong.
25. Sometimes a kick in the teeth is what you need at the time
26. Never give up; there is dignity in fighting
27. Integrity is doing the right thing even when no one is looking
28. Fix the cause. Not just the symptoms.
29. Practice your craft. You will statistically get better.
30. A career is a job. A vocation is a calling.
31. The thing people will remember most about you is how you treated them.
32. It is not any of our jobs to judge others
33. Everyone you meet is fighting a battle you know nothing about
34. You meet everyone for a reason
35. Not everyone you lose is a loss
36. Eat, drink, and be merry
37. Prayer never hurts
38. You only get so many birthdays

4 ENTRY 4

THIS NEXT ENTRY IS A LETTER I WROTE TO HOME BOUND SENIOR CITIZENS FOR Christmas.

Hello, I hope this card brightens your day and your holidays! My name is John, and I attended St. Saviour school for all 8 years, and then Moeller High School and The University of Dayton. I wanted to send you a Christmas card to let you know that there are so many people that care about you and are praying for you this Christmas season. I'm hoping for a white Christmas, but I don't have to travel. I hope you have plenty of loved ones to share the season with, and if you don't, this card is a reminder that people care about you, even people you have never met before. MERRY CHRISTMAS!

5 ENTRY 5

I WAS GIVEN A SIGNED BASEBALL BY THE COMMISSIONER OF MAJOR LEAGUE Baseball after I wrote him this letter.

Dear Commissioner Manfred,

I would like to request an autographed baseball from you. I'm not exactly sure if that is how it works. It seems very generous of you. I collect Cincinnati sports memorabilia, so that's why I am interested in an autographed baseball. I will include my address at the end of this letter. If you can't oblige, that's okay. I will just tell you a few of my thoughts about baseball. I was lucky to play on a little league team for ten years when I was a child. I am thirty-three years old now. Those were the best times of my life. My dad and I watch every Cincinnati Reds game that is available on TV/Cable. It's one of the only things we have always had in common.

I really like what you have done for the speed of the game. The games go much quicker, but not too fast. I know people get touchy when you start talking about changing in general, but the rules of baseball more so. I think you are doing a fantastic job with suspensions and penalties as well. Criminals, PEDs, and any form of cheating belittles the integrity of the game and should not be tolerated.

I would not be a good Reds fan (for my whole life) unless I give a mention to Pete Rose being allowed to be on the ballot for the Hall of Fame. I know you know that many players, former and current, have done much worse. I think the man has done his time for his crimes against baseball. Regardless, he is the greatest hitter of all time. No one can take that away from him. It would be nice if he took his rightful spot in the Hall with all the other greats.

There is a topic that is near and dear to my heart that I need to mention too. That's mental illness. I was diagnosed with bipolar disorder in 2006, and since then, Obsessive Compulsive Disorder, Panic Disorder, Generalized Anxiety Disorder, and agoraphobia have been added to my complete diagnosis. I have not seen a night in baseball in any stadium devoted to mental illness, and to the people who are suffering and the ones we have lost to suicide. I know it is not a happy topic, but it would be great if MLB could do something for one night in every stadium. A lime green ribbon is our symbol. The statistics are staggering for how common mental illness is. I believe that as many as one in three people have some type of mental illness. I volunteer my time every day to a social media page that I created for mental illness awareness. I am also a published author of my life story titled, "Millions Like Me: My Struggle with Mental Illness". I am a published poet at maverick-magazine.com as well. Thank you so much for your time and devotion to the betterment of the game.

Sincerely,
John E. Medl

6 ENTRY 6

MANY YEARS AGO, I HIT A PARKED CAR GOING ABOUT 10MPH. NOTHING BAD happened, but they took me by ambulance to the hospital to get checked out. I had about two beers and I took a hit or two off a joint. They did a blood test to check for drugs, and nothing significant showed up.

I was sitting there with two African-American police officers, and I kinda had the munchies, and I said, "Do you have anything to eat around here?"

One of the cops said, "We might have some juice or crackers".

So I said, "What did you call me?"

We all had a good laugh.

7 ENTRY 7

I HAVE TO SEE THE DOCTOR TODAY, WHICH IS USUALLY UNPLEASANT, BUT I FEEL pretty good today. I've been upset about this appointment for weeks. Luckily, I was able to still enjoy the holidays the best I could, although I'm not much of a festive person. I'm lucky that I have a doctor I like, and we are on a first name basis. He reminds me of a "bro"....maybe someone I would be friends with outside of the clinical setting. He is very proud of me, and he's very easygoing and easy to talk to. I have some good news to tell him today, but I also have a lot of questions about my progress. I am getting to the point where my anxiety when leaving the house is too much to bear, and I have extreme irritability on a fairly regular basis. I don't know how much I can expect from my brain and body, which really is the whole mystery about mental illness. It's a lot of trial and error, whether it be medication or cognitive therapy. There's no road map, and there's no magic pill. Some of the work has to be done by the patient (me). Right now, I have high anxiety when leaving the house and low energy, almost always. I want to see if that can be improved, either with a medicine change or other cognitive therapy. One thing is for sure: I have fought the whole time. It's one of my redeeming qualities. I hope when my life is over that being a fighter is one of the main things people remember about me, followed by how much I loved and gave to others.

8 ENTRY 8

I haven't done much journaling since I finished my last book in July 2019, which has been a nice break, but I wanted to share a few things today about my progress and mental illness in general. I have to see my doctor today, who simply wants me to call him Ben. Really awesome, younger guy. Very smart, kind, and approachable. I really like him as my doctor. It's going to be a great feeling when I hand him a copy of my new book. He was very impressed that I had written so much last time I saw him. It seemed like he was just generally impressed by the work I do, and my insight into my illness.

I'm glad the day of my appointment is finally here, so I know that it will all be over by this afternoon. I'm in better shape, anxiety-wise than usual, and overall, it is getting easier to see the doctor now that I am on a 3 month schedule rather than every month. Within the last few years, I used to have major anxiety and panic attacks at the doctor. My chest hurt and my head felt foggy every time I saw the doctor. I used to have to steady myself against the wall sometimes just to keep my balance.

One thing I want to say about mental illness is that there's no real clear cut objectives. No finish line or deadlines for improvement. Yes, things like taking a shower, driving, and socializing have gotten easier for me, and I guess that's because I kept trying. When I drove myself downtown the other day, that was a major accomplishment, but there's no guarantee that I can do it today or tomorrow. It's all so subjective and case-by-case. I know people with bipolar disorder that have full-time careers. That is not possible for me right now. If I was in proper shape, mentally and physically, I would try to apply for a career other than writing. It's just frustrating that there's no end game. Am I a success now? I would say yes. Is it possible that I could return to work eventually? Probably, but again, there's no guarantees. Just wanted to share my thoughts for a minute.

9 ENTRY 9

When I saw the doctor yesterday, I was totally ready to change my medications, as scary as that idea sounded. I talked to my doctor, and he was actually happy with my progress. He told me he took the time to read through my medical records (over 13 years' worth) and my books, and I really have come a long way. Like almost miraculous. I feel pretty good most of the time. It's at least tolerable. I don't expect to feel perfect all the time. I told him a lot of feelings and thoughts I have, and he basically pointed out that I overthink a lot of things, which I kinda already knew. He told me I have to find ways to turn my brain off, per se. Music, crossword puzzles, whatever works. Writing about all of this really helps me, and I know it helps others as well. Another part of shutting down my brain is taking time for myself to recharge my batteries before I do too much advocating. Everything I do doesn't have to be for a cause or to help others. The doctor was more concerned with my mood being stable and that I was getting enough sleep. He wasn't even concerned that I gained 12 pounds, but I am. I have to work on that. I'm still down 38 pounds overall, however, so I'm not starting from scratch. My BP was 138/88, which I have no idea what that means, but I know it's always high at the doctor's office. My pulse is always elevated, too. I had a brief panic attack when I got in my mom's van to go to the appointment, but I got out, and took some deep breaths, and I was able to keep the appointment. I'm really glad it's over until almost April. I found that riding in the back seat helps, for whatever reason. Maybe because I'm not right up on the dash or something. He recommended therapy (CBT) for my cognition, but I'm still thinking if I want to make that commitment. It was nice to be reminded that I have made so much progress, but I'm also looking forward to the challenge of improving little things in my life that might make a big difference.

10 ENTRY 10

THIS IS A LETTER I WROTE TO ELLEN DEGENERES, AND I INCLUDED A COPY OF MY first book. I think this was sometime around 2014.

Hi Ellen! (Ms. DeGeneres is probably more appropriate, but it doesn't feel right. I think of you as such a kind, humble person)

Here is a copy of my book. It's my life story, detailing my struggle with mental illness. I have been diagnosed with bipolar disorder with psychotic features, generalized anxiety disorder/panic disorder, post traumatic stress disorder, claustrophobia, and agoraphobia. I would be honored if you just gave it a read. I remember watching your sitcom as a younger adult, and it was hilarious. As I started watching your talk show, I saw again how funny you are, but I also saw such a humble, happy, and kind soul. Thanks for any time you give me.

Love and Best Wishes,
John Edward Medl
johnmedl7@gmail.com

11 ENTRY 11

I HOPE YOU FIND THIS AS FUNNY AS I DO.... THE DYNAMIC OF MY HOUSEHOLD goes like this—Mom pretty much controls the household and knows everything that's going on. My dad has veto power, but in a limited capacity. I am the low man on the totem pole, and I try to just mind my own business and keep to myself whenever possible. All of us get along fairly well, all things considered, UNTIL the balance of power is messed with. All of this leads me to the day when my dad said something so funny to my mom. My mom was trying to tell my dad what clothes to wear or that he needed a jacket or something, and my dad was just like, "I think I can do what I want". Wrong thing to say to Queen Bee! LOL

12 ENTRY 12

I HAVE BEEN TO MANY HOOKAHVILLES, STARTING AROUND 1998. HOOKAHVILLE IS a weekend-long music festival where the band Ekoostik Hookah is the main act. My last Hookahville was Spring 2006, or whichever one that was when Blues Traveler was there. I used to go to all kinds of concerts, but I was diagnosed with bipolar disorder and anxiety, so I don't leave my house much, and large crowds intimidate me. Well, I decided to step outside my comfort zone and go see my friends' band, The Summit, (with Ekoostik Hookah) around November of last year. My buddy, Mike Hennel, (drummer for The Summit), introduced me to Eric, the drummer for Hookah. I told Eric a little about my story and he asked if I had any requests. I honestly couldn't believe Eric was even asking me. When I was growing up, Hookah were some of my heroes. You never really think of ever meeting them or connecting with them on a personal level. The only songs I could think of were Ohio Grown and Loner. Sure enough, right as I was about to leave (early) for the night, Hookah played Loner! I like to believe it was for me :) Much love to you all! (Hookah later confirmed that the song Loner was, in fact, for me). What a great night.

13 ENTRY 13

Sometimes, it's our own bullshit that is holding us back. No one tries to trigger me or upset me. It just happens. It's hard to know how much I can actually control how I react. I have to train my mind to not worry and overthink so much, which is quite a battle. I have to work at it. The worst panic attack I've had in the last couple months was in the beginning of November 2019, and I was tempting the Fates. I drank coffee and didn't allow my medicine to work properly before getting in the car. I knew better. I don't know why I thought I could sneak something like that past my illness that day. Being successful takes extreme care, caution, maintenance, and constant attempts to improve.

14 ENTRY 14

I've been foolish lately, or perhaps just human. I have been getting caught up in the struggle and stress of daily life, and I have been forgetting how blessed I am. I can't believe my life has turned out the way it has. Thank you all to everyone who has supported me in any way. I don't really know anyone with a mental illness who has as much support as I do, not that it's a competition, obviously. I have everything and everyone that I need, but the more good people the merrier.

15 ENTRY 15

Fear is a part of anxiety, but I wouldn't say I'm always scared when I have anxiety. I bring this up because I need to drive and run some errands today. Not an emergency or anything. My mom will run them for me if I can't do it. I'm lucky in that regard. But driving is so difficult for me because there is definitely a fear present, but I also have physical symptoms like numbness in my arms, dizziness, and chest pains. It's really hard for me to understand because I used to drive for a living. I guess I'm scared to drive because I don't want to cause an accident. I don't know if that's a reasonable concern or if I'm just guilty of over-thinking again. For me to successfully run errands, I have to shut down my mind enough to drive without a ton of worry, and I have to make sure my body is ready for the trip so that I don't get symptomatic while I'm driving. It would be easy if I could predict when all this is going to happen. It's just kind of a confident feeling and I guess a leap of faith that my medicine will work enough to drive. When I get excited about driving somewhere successfully, it really is an accomplishment for me. Sometimes, I just don't think people understand how bad it can be, and also I don't want others to feel ashamed if they struggle with driving too.

16 ENTRY 16

I LEFT MY LAST DOCTOR'S APPOINTMENT A FEW WEEKS AGO WITH A LOT OF THINGS to work on and think about. My two main challenges right now are driving/leaving the house and over-thinking. I've started to put together a Lego set, filling in crosswords, and trying to read, both for pleasure and education of my illnesses. I'm trying to improve my mood and patience with others. I always wonder how much I can actually control my reaction to things. I have an open relationship with my parents where I can say things like, “Give me a minute. It's time for my medication.” and things of that nature. My weight has been a battle my whole life, so I'm always trying to improve my physical health, mainly through weight loss. I am doing a better job of that since the holidays have passed. I only weigh myself a few times a year, but I can tell by how my clothes fit. I would like to start walking in my neighborhood. Hopefully, I can get up the energy and motivation when it's warmer outside, but if it's cold and if it's time, I will walk in the cold. I am even smoking less and drinking less coffee. I have extreme OCD when it comes to my medication times, and I still refuse to take my medicine early, but I have relaxed and allowed to take them later than scheduled. It's a trick of mine to have more energy, but I would never skip a dose entirely, on purpose anyway. Journaling like this has always helped me cope, and I probably have enough material for another book, but I'm not planning on doing that. I might look for a writing job somewhere. "The medicine works" my doctor tells me, so I tell myself that when I don't feel great. It really is amazing how far I've come. I have a lot to work on, but I'm in a great position to do whatever I want to do with my life from here on out. I'm grateful and blessed in many ways.

17 ENTRY 17

I GOT A SMALL SHIPMENT OF MY OLDER TWO BOOKS TODAY. I WILL BE GETTING another shipment of my newest book on February 4, 2020. I always enjoy autographing them all. It's a personal touch, and I feel like a part of me goes with every copy. My super secret wish is that my signature would be worth money some day, and my friends could sell my books for a lot of money. I used to practice my signature in grade school because I dreamed of being a professional baseball player. I dreamed of signing baseballs and roaring fans in a packed stadium. I guess a writer is close enough haha. I just don't think I was meant to be rich because I don't love money enough. When I have money, the greatest joy I get is to share it. It's part of my desire to help others and make other people happy. There are downsides to having that kind of personality, but overall, it has worked out for me. I was able to drive my car again to give it some work with no real issues, and I had a nice dinner with my parents. I finished my Lego set I was working on, and I'm almost finished with my article for The Antioch Review that's due at the end of February. Just writing about some pleasant thoughts that I had this evening.

18 ENTRY 18

I BELIEVE THAT MENTAL ILLNESS IS MOSTLY A GENETIC PREDISPOSITION THAT COMES to the surface after a variety of environmental factors take place. It would be hard to pinpoint exactly what led to my diagnosis(es), but most of it had nothing to do with anything I did wrong morally or otherwise. I guess what I am getting at is that it doesn't help myself or anyone else to beat myself up for past behavior or feel sorry for myself. I try not to fall into that trap. I have work to do, and I can't accomplish treatment goals or help others if I am constantly looking back and wondering what I could have done differently. The past is over. There's very literally nothing I can do about it now, so I have to ask myself 'Now what?'. My medication helps calm my symptoms, but I have to do a lot of the work myself to gain progress. I am testing my anxiety every day, more and more, and I have had some great results. What did I have to lose? A panic attack? I've survived hundreds of those. Whenever I try to leave the house, most of the time every signal in my body is telling me “No, you can't do that”. My brain is sending fear signals. I guess at some point I made a leap of faith that my medication will work and the fear would go away. If you are stuck in your progress, ask yourself what you have to lose. My memory isn't very good, but in the past year, I have made a lot of progress, and I have gained so much. If you have severe anxiety or other mental illness, please keep trying. It can get better. I can't promise you anything, but it has gotten better for me. I don't know how to give away that resiliency that comes with not giving up. All I can do is try to be a good example and tell you what has worked for me and that my life has gotten better. I never quit on anyone.

19 ENTRY 19

Only a few people in my circle on social media talk about mental illness, and I only know them in a professional capacity. It helps me to talk about my illness because it helps others, which in turn, helps me. It makes me feel like my struggles are all worth it. So, I just want to mention that people "let themselves go" for a variety of reasons, but it tends to happen a lot with people with mental illness. Hygiene can be a big challenge, which includes things like taking a shower, weight control, and other personal cleanliness. I have lost over 50 pounds now, and of course I'm proud of myself, but I have a long ways to go before I really feel like I'm at a healthy weight. I think it's important to celebrate small successes along the way, but I try not to get too comfortable. I'm not really ready to declare victory over my illness, and I probably never will. I am always on high alert for triggers and red flags, which may sidetrack my progress. I fail sometimes, but I always try to put forth the best effort I can. I took a shower this morning and did some personal grooming. I also went out to lunch with my mom. All of these things are victories over my illness in that I both couldn't do them before, and that these tasks are still hard for me. I guess what I am getting at is that I'm starting to feel better mentally/psychologically, so I hope it will be easier for me to lose weight and take better care of myself physically. Just trying to hang tough, live right, and do the right thing.

20 ENTRY 20

I DROVE MYSELF DOWNTOWN AGAIN. I'M SO PROUD OF MYSELF AND JUST SO grateful and happy (not always). If some of you knew what I have bounced back from, you would be amazed. My recovery and recent success is really something special. The best gift that mental illness gave me was appreciating every little success along the way. This is a lifelong illness. There is no cure. I am going to have to manage it the rest of my life, but when I can enjoy life at the same time, the struggles don't seem so bad. I have made so much progress!

21 ENTRY 21

When I think of authors, I think about people like Stephen King and James Patterson, but not myself, for some reason. When I was a kid, authors of books that I read were just otherworldly or something. I never thought I would become one, especially three times over. I am lucky to know some amazing authors and writers, and they have taught me a lot. I always think that I couldn't be a writer for a living, but here I am, writing again. I've thought about getting my MA in Counseling or doing some public speaking too. This whole journey has been very surreal in a lot of ways.

When strangers meet me, a lot of the time, they say it seems like they have known me for years. I think I'm pretty transparent. What you see is what you get. Maybe it's good vibes or something. A lot of people confide in me, which is a compliment that people trust me so much with their life stories. I very rarely get overwhelmed with all of it. I just feel like this is what I am supposed to be doing right now. I haven't changed too much, and if I have, I would like to think I'm just a better version of my old self. I'm always trying to improve myself, and every day, I am getting better at coping with mental illness. I am surrounded by so many people that love me. It really helps me deal with life. It's also a pretty amazing feeling to think that I am helping others by simply telling my story, perhaps even saving lives. I've come so far.

22 ENTRY 22

I hope I have made a positive impact on your life in some capacity. You probably don't have to read my books to know a lot about my story. If you aren't feeling well mentally, please reach out. There's the crisis line, or even calling the police or an ambulance. You can reach out to me, but I can only help so much if you need medical attention. I've lost a few friends to suicide and drug overdoses, and I want it to stop. 10-20% of bipolar sufferers die by suicide, and 50% have attempted suicide. One in five people have a mental illness. These are staggering numbers when considered to scale of the general population. I know I can't save everyone, but no one is going to stop me from trying. I guess I am a little greedy in that I want to have an impact on more than one person because a lot of people say, "If I could just help one person..." I want to help a lot of people, and I hope my story is read and told for many years after I expire.

23 ENTRY 23

I will have 7 more copies of my newest book around September 24, 2019. Around that time, I will be shipping a variety of my books to NAMI (National Alliance for Mental Illness) in New Mexico, totaling around 10 copies. Thanks to my readers, friends, family, and even strangers who love and support me. It truly makes a difference. If I hear that I'm doing the right thing from others, it seems like life has been treating me well, which I take as a sign from the universe that I am doing the right thing. I am wise and humble enough to not declare victory just yet over my illness. It's going to be a lifelong battle. I hope I am up to the challenge. So far, so good I guess. Whatever mental illness has taken from me, I have gotten back exponentially, and I am grateful and blessed.

24 ENTRY 24

I'VE HAD 2 PANIC ATTACKS IN THE LAST TWO DAYS, AND SOME GENERAL ANXIETY. The panic attacks are less than a minute usually, but I was hyperventilating, which I haven't experienced in some time. General anxiety can last much longer. For me, it lasts until I eat a meal and take a nap. Mental illness is not fair, nor is life. I miss out on a lot of things to remain stable. If you think mental illness is "all in our heads", you are simply wrong and don't understand mental illness. I hope you never have to understand. It's physical, emotional, and psychological. It's a daily struggle to remain stable. I am physically sore and exhausted from the panic and anxiety. I had planned to go see my friends' band play today, but I simply don't feel up to it. I had been planning on it for months.

A panic attack that lasts a minute can bruise my ego and confidence. One minute is all it takes for me to be less confident about my progress. I am kind of a veteran of panic and anxiety, so I know I just have to build my confidence up again. I also know that a meal and a nap will take care of the problem. Just a little disappointed today, but I'm sure it will be better after I rest.

25 ENTRY 25

I don't know if this is a surprise to anyone, but I'm not that confident of a writer. Sometimes I think people are just being nice when they buy my books. Maybe they believe in supporting local artists. All of that is great, and I appreciate the support, but when you delve into my books, you will find more than a little valuable information about mental illness. My second book was a poetry book, which was more my creative side, but my first book is very clinical, and my third book is journal style, detailing life with mental illness. I say that my books have value because it's just an amazing story. Not a lot of people talk about mental illness, and a lot don't even survive for a variety of reasons. Then, for someone like me to have a clear enough mind to write about all of it. It's just a rare thing.

26 ENTRY 26

I FEEL RAGE SOMETIMES. IT'S NOT RATIONAL ANGER. IT'S NOT ME, BUT I CAN GET fixated on something I don't like about life, or I can feel rage for seemingly no reason at all. Usually, it is when my medicine hasn't started working yet. I feel awful when I am mean to my parents, but they know it's not me acting out. They know it's not in my character. I always apologize if I think I was being irrational too. I have some things in place that I do that help ease my anger/rage until it passes. I want to share because maybe these techniques will help you:

I go into a quiet room. If I feel like listening to music, I put on relaxing music, emphasis on relaxing. Sometimes, I close my eyes and just breathe in and out in silence. I roll my own cigarettes, so that monotonous action helps calm me and helps spend unnecessary anger energy. I sit on my porch and have a cigarette, and watch the traffic go by. I try to think of myself as separate from the race everyone is running. I might text a friend and ask that person how their day went. I might crack jokes on social media to help cheer me up. I might go out of my way to be kind to someone else.

I am basically trying to distract myself and my rage long enough for the medicine to work. Rage is rare for me, but it's a strong emotion that I have. I absolutely hate it because it's not in my character or personality. I have a hard time being mean to people that deserve it, much less for no reason. Also, journaling like this helps too.

27 ENTRY 27

FOR THE LONGEST TIME, I THOUGHT I WAS JEALOUS OF PEOPLE WHO CAN DRINK alcohol all the time, have a good time, and still function. That's not it. Alcohol and drugs have and always will be there for me if I choose. Stability, productivity, sanity, and peace of mind were gone from my life for a long time, and I have been fighting very hard to get it all back. These are the qualities that I lost and that I value so much. I don't value being fucked up anymore. I don't need to self-medicate because my medicine works most of the time. I have slip ups. I had 5 beers about a week ago, and I had a good time actually, but I'm playing with fire. Shit man, I'm playing with fire when I have something as harmless as coffee. Maybe I have more to lose now than I did before, because stability, sanity, and all those great qualities are priceless to me. I'm not willing to risk a night of drunkenness for everything I have fought for. Overall, I'm doing a pretty good job, all things considered.

28 ENTRY 28

Every so often, I like to thank my whole support team, which includes my readers, family, and friends. It makes a world of difference in my fight to stay positive and stable with my illness. Kindness matters. A few months ago, a woman at the grocery deli called me fat to someone she was talking to on her phone. I still think about it. It hurt a little bit emotionally, but I know I am doing the best I can to control my weight, and I also know I have been big my whole life. My point is that this woman probably had no idea the physical, emotional, and mental strength it took me to drive myself to the grocery. This was a time when driving for me was near impossible, and social interactions made me extremely anxious. She also didn't know that I had $5 to my name, and all I wanted was my favorite pasta salad to treat myself. Would she have cared had she known all of that? Maybe, but probably not. The world has gotten more unkind over the years, in my opinion. A lot of people have a psychological need to put others down to make themselves feel better about their own lives, which they are probably unsatisfied with, hence this psychological need to put others down. "In a world where you can be anything, be kind". Simple words from Dr. Seuss, but it can make a huge difference. I am lucky and blessed to have so many who support me and my writing. I care more about others being comforted by my story than any amount of money I make off my books. I donate them whenever I can. If you think my story is disturbing or outstanding or tragic or whatever, you should see some of the cases of people who have no support. So, a simple thank you to all of you. I would like to take credit individually for my successes, but I am not much of a success without all of your support. I think of myself as a humble servant or vessel just carrying out a mission.

29 ENTRY 29

My attitude has been pretty shitty off and on lately, and that's on me. It's a little more challenging to control my emotional reaction to things because of my illness, but I'm not the guy who likes excuses. I drove to the tobacco store today, which is only a few miles away, but I didn't have much anxiety. I was worried that I was relapsing or something, which would have been devastating to my confidence. I can't tell you how annoying it is for me to have to wait almost an hour to be calm enough to drive, BUT I'm thankful I have a car and that I can drive at all because I used to pretty much be confined to the house. With me, it's all about perspective and gratitude, and I lose sight of everything I'm blessed with sometimes. I'm a good person, and I know it, but I'm not perfect, and I know that too. No one is.

30 ENTRY 30

My illness has changed me in many ways, some for the better, and some for the worse. I would like to think more for the better. I have trouble relating to a lot of people because they just don't have an illness to contend with on a daily basis, so their priorities and outlook are different from mine. I really just want to make a difference through my books and otherwise, and be happy most of the time. Anything above that is great too. I've had more money than I could spend, and I was definitely happy. I bought a bunch of stuff I didn't need and went to bars and bought everyone drinks. I had a great time, but I didn't save a dime. I learned my lesson, I guess. I still have trouble budgeting money, but it's not like I have some kind of million dollar trust fund to work with. I know that the white picket fence idea is not for me, at least not for the time being. I guess I understand the draw to that kind of life, but I'm selfish with my time and energy, and I'm not willing to share it with anyone right now in a relationship kind of way. I have plenty of people who love me in a familial and friendly way to keep me busy with my love. I guess it's hard to explain, and I certainly don't owe anyone an explanation, but everything changed when I got sick.

31 ENTRY 31

My really good buddy called me out of the blue around midnight a few nights ago. He just felt the urge to give me a pep talk of sorts, which I didn't think I needed at the time, but I did. He told me that I have to let the things go that I've done that I'm not exactly proud of. He's right. I think my biggest regret is not what I've done or not done, it's how much energy and guilt I gave to my regrets, and how much I cared about what other people thought of me. All that really matters is who I am today, and I'm proud of that person. There's no need to beat myself for things that happened a long time ago. It's not fair to myself, and it's not productive if I want to help and love others. I think when we are young; we are taught to feel guilt and remorse for things we've done wrong, which is a good way to learn right from wrong, but at some point in our adult lives, we have to let it all go. I'm the only person I'm going to have to live with my whole life. I have to love and forgive myself, and I'm still learning.

32 ENTRY 32

My books and my writings about mental illness will never be popular or well circulated. There are many reasons for that. Most people simply don't care about mental illness at all. The ones who do care either have an illness or someone close to them has it. Even some people with loved ones who have mental illness don't care. Some people don't even believe in modern medicine to treat mental illness. But, oh don't people love to blame mental illness, especially mass shootings, since they somehow have become trendy and popular. Everyone is in denial that the US has a gun problem. People actually think that people like me want to take their guns. Most people, even in their right mind, aren't responsible enough to own guns. They are dangerous killing weapons. Some guns' sole purpose is to kill as many people in as short a time as possible. Oh, but it's the mentally ill that's the problem. It couldn't be the access to guns. Then you have people who suffer from mental illness who are ashamed to even talk about it. Gee, I wonder why. The mentally ill are demonized by most of society and pill shamed if they need to take medicine.

33 ENTRY 33

I TELL PEOPLE ALL THE TIME THAT THE BEST GIFT MENTAL ILLNESS HAS GIVEN TO me is an appreciation for the little things (which maybe are big things) and a general sense of gratitude. I was never a bad person. I just didn't fully appreciate how blessed I was, and I took life for granted. I use the word blessed instead of lucky or fortunate because I feel like blessed is a superlative word, and that's the degree to which I feel the gratitude, if that makes sense. When I use the word blessed, I am basically just describing the overwhelming sense of gratitude that I feel quite often now.

34 ENTRY 34

My good buddy told me at my birthday party, "Just be you". Such a simple statement. This good friend thought that me being myself was good enough for him. I think we complicate things sometimes by always striving to be better and obtain more "stuff". There's nothing wrong with trying to better yourself and move up the money ladder, of course, but sometimes we define ourselves by status symbols and whatever else society says makes us good enough. Being myself is good enough for my friends, and that's actually an amazing thing, and takes a lot of pressure off me. I know how to be me. I can do that. I just want my friends to be themselves too. I wouldn't keep them around if I didn't think they were good, solid people. If you are a good person with good intentions, just be you. The world doesn't need more successful people (again, nothing is wrong with that). The world needs more good, kind, and loving people.

35 ENTRY 35

I'M REALLY PROUD OF MYSELF. I FOUGHT HARD TODAY. TODAY WASN'T TERRIBLE, but it certainly wasn't easy. I had some anxiety and racing thoughts throughout the day, but I managed to do some housework, which helps calm me and also helps my mom. I shaved my face, which may seem very minor to most, but when I was first hospitalized in 2006, I had to earn the trust of the nurses to use a razor. Razors and sharp objects were only allowed by patients at the nurses' discretion for (hopefully) obvious reasons. I always think about the tiny drab community bathrooms and showers when I shave my face. Shaving my face is a reminder of the freedom I have earned in recovery, and it gives me a sense of pride every time I shave. I have traumatic memories from the hospital too, but shaving my face elicits mostly good feelings. I don't even take shaving my face for granted anymore. I am also budgeting money better this month and improving my general mood.

36 ENTRY 36

I USE SOCIAL MEDIA FOR A LOT OF THE SAME REASONS EVERYONE ELSE DOES—sharing memes and photos, random status updates, etc. I definitely like to make people laugh, but I also like to use social media for a purpose. I run my own page devoted to mental health awareness, and it's a great tool for a small time author like me to promote my books. Social media has also allowed me to stay in contact with so many people when I was super sick. I also like all the live music venue feeds because I can't always be there in person.

37 ENTRY 37

I'm sitting here looking at a pile of my books that I ordered, and it's just such a wild feeling that I turned out to be an author/writer. When I got a degree in psychology, I thought I was going to be a psychologist. Being a writer was something so far from my plans. You may as well told me I was going to be an astronaut. Weird how stuff works out sometimes when you think it isn't. I'm helping at least as many people as I would have had I become a psychologist. It's just such a weird feeling to look at a book and know that I wrote it. I'm not trying to toot my own horn or anything. Just being honest.

38 ENTRY 38

My anxiety got the best of me just now. I tried 3 times to get into my mom's car to go get my truck from having repairs, and I couldn't sit still, and I had chest pains from anxiety. The reason I had an anxiety attack or whatever it was, was because I had just taken my medicine and it hadn't kicked in yet (usually takes about an hour or so). Luckily, my awesome parents picked up my car for me, so now I don't have to worry about it. I can't stress enough how important it is to have support with mental illness. I am truly blessed with great friends and family who I know are always going to be there for me. Others are not as fortunate, which is one of the big reasons I try to be a good example by fighting this illness and trying to be there for others. Usually, the best cure for a panic attack like that is a good meal and a nap, so that's what I'm going to do.

39 ENTRY 39

It really freaked me out when I couldn't sit still from panic and ride in my mom's car yesterday. I had a doctor's appointment scheduled for tomorrow, and I had to reschedule. I contacted my case manager, and I told him I wasn't feeling well or confident enough to endure a doctor's appointment tomorrow. Props to my case manager for responding to my texts when he was out of the office. I told my parents I wasn't feeling well too. That's all I can do I think. I'm a little upset because I feel like some of my progress was taken away, but hopefully, I will be okay shortly. It's been a lot worse before.

40 ENTRY 40

THE REASON I WRITE ABOUT MY STRUGGLES AND TRIUMPHS IS TO INSPIRE OTHERS and make others feel like they are not alone. I'm not suffering. I struggle sometimes, and there's a big difference. I don't want anyone to feel sorry for me, but of course, I appreciate the support and prayers. I would rather you pray for people who are really suffering, but I guess there's enough to go around.

41 ENTRY 41

I'M NOT A BIG FAN OF DR. PHIL, BUT SOMETIMES MY DAD WATCHES HIS SHOW because it's on TV right before the local news. He was talking to a 28-year-old female drug addict today, and he said something very powerful. He said, "You are 28 years old. You might have another 60 years on this planet. If you get help now, this could all just be a bad memory." What a wonderful thought for anyone who wants to change or put their past behind them. Maybe parts of my life can just be bad memories too, and I can move on (if I haven't already).

42 ENTRY 42

I'm going to sell however many books, but I really just want people to be inspired by my story. Maybe I can open some eyes as to what it's like to live with mental illness and how severe it can be, and how it's such a wide spectrum. Bills are bills, and money is money, but it doesn't matter to me if we have a chat about mental illness or you read about it in one of my books. It's just the same to me.

43 ENTRY 43

My driving anxiety has come back in the last week or so, but today, I drove to the library to submit my second book, "Poems from a Bipolar Mind" for their catalog. This book should be on the shelves in the next month or so. No anxiety issues at all, really. I was a little nervous when I left the house, but I'm really glad I was able to drive and get a little exercise. Anxiety and panic are only a little bit logical, so there's only so much that therapy can do. Usually, it's just a baby steps process to get back where I was, which I totally hate, but it is what it is. Just thankful I was able to overcome my fears today.

44 ENTRY 44

I JUST WENT TO WHITE CASTLE, AND THEY WERE SHORT 2 WORKERS. THEY CALLED off. Happens all the time in food service. Knowing this, instead of choosing to be angry and frustrated, I chose to just be happy that I was getting food that I was cheating on my diet. I was making conversation with other people in line and smiling. I also gave the cashier a $5 bill and thanked her for showing up. We make lots of choices every day. Choose to be the bigger person and the exception to the rule. Maybe on another day, I would have been upset. I don't know. I just think today was the day to show compassion and humility to these human beings who were serving me food.

45 ENTRY 45

I HAVE A MEETING WITH MY CASE MANAGER TODAY. HE HELPS ME A LITTLE BIT with cognitive therapy, but mainly, he helps me fill out all the long, confusing paperwork associated with my illness. He was a Green Beret, which I think is cool, so I will have to wish him a belated Happy Veterans' Day. He was shot in the back in combat, and he's had back problems ever since. I think he fought around the time of the Vietnam War. I don't have to see the doctor until January 6th, so another "fun" thing I have to do is get my medication refills approved so that I have enough medication until I see the doctor.

You have no idea how many times I've wanted to say to my doctor, "Okay, I'm ready for the good shit" haha.

46 ENTRY 46

"THE ROBBED THAT SMILES STEALS SOMETHING FROM THE THIEF" IS A Shakespearean quote that I've always liked. I thought about going so far as to get it tattooed on me. I feel like when I have a positive attitude and sense of humor in the face of mental illness (The thief, if you will), I feel like I am getting something back that mental illness stole from me. Mental illness took everything I had at the time, and then it tried to take my life. I have survived over 13 years since those days many years ago. Looking back on my journey, a lot of people would call it a success story. I don't know about all that, but I'm definitely proud of how I have handled everything and how my life has turned out.

47 ENTRY 47

I'M ALWAYS LOOKING FOR NATURAL WAYS TO ALLEVIATE MY BIPOLAR AND ANXIETY symptoms, and I read that singing out loud can help anxiety. This might explain why I don't have many problems singing karaoke, but why I still have problems driving to the bar to get there. Sometimes, I sing around the house without even thinking about it. Just a fun and weird thing about anxiety. I should say MY anxiety because what works for one person might not work for another. That's why mental illness is so hard to treat, whether with cognitive therapy and/or medication. Everyone experiences mental illness differently.

48 ENTRY 48

Sometimes, life can be overwhelming, and I let it get to me, and other times, I laugh at the magnitude of it all and my very small part in all of it. I laugh at all the dumb jokes I know or, ironically, the daily tasks when they seem never-ending. Of all the atoms that could have formed anything, a tiny fraction made me and you. Yes, I know the science. The fertilized egg, yada yada yada. But there still had to be a pretty incredible happening to form your being. Don't waste it. Have something to offer to others. As far as I know and believe, we only get one shot at this thing, so make it memorable. I always keep love and kindness in my heart, which I think helps me deal with a lot of things. Oh yeah, and as much comedy as I can fit into a day without annoying others.

49 ENTRY 49

I THINK BY THE TIME YOU GET TO BE MY AGE; YOU HAVE EXPERIENCED SOME kind(s) of heartbreak and trauma that has left you a different person, if you are wise. I wish for myself that I have become a more grateful person, and a better all around person since I was first diagnosed. I lost everything—my house, my car, my mind, my reputation—literally everything. I have spent so much time trying to get my life back on track, with a lot of success. I never thought I would be an author and writer. I have touched many lives and helped many people, and that makes me happy and gives me purpose and the will to continue the journey. My mission in life has almost nothing to do with longevity, but rather making an impact. I'm not planning on going anywhere any time soon, but then again, no one really ever does. I want my life to be a celebration like the stupid birthday parties I have been throwing for about 10 years. I'm never going to be confident enough to say that I beat my illness, but it certainly didn't beat me.

50 ENTRY 50

My medicine is designed to keep my mood and behavior somewhere in the middle of the mood and behavioral spectrum, and it does for the most part, but it results in this murky indifference and numbness. If I ever feel emotions like sadness or happiness, they are usually to the extreme, and usually accompanied by anxiety. I absolutely hate being in a bad mood, and I try to do things that make me happy to get out of that mindset. I enjoy lots of things—reading, music, watching sports, talking with friends, acts of kindness, etc. etc. etc. Most of the time, these things help my bad mood, but I have a feeling I don't experience emotions like most people. There's no concrete way to know, but I know a lot of people, and they don't seem to have the same emotional spectrum as I do. Just something interesting I've observed about my illness.

51 ENTRY 51

I WILL SEE THE DOCTOR IN A FEW WEEKS. I'M STARTING TO THINK ABOUT WHAT I want to talk to him about, and it's frustrating. I feel like I should want to do things, but I'm not interested in a lot of things. My energy level is low, and I'm sore from being overweight and inactive for a few months. It looks like depression symptoms, but I'm not really sad. I had enough energy to write my third book, but I don't think it would take this long to recover. For a few months, I was going out and driving and really enjoying myself. When the time and weather changed, and I had a massive panic attack. It was like the rug got pulled out from under me again. It's so frustrating. I finally have enough money to do things and maybe take a trip somewhere, but I can barely drive up the street. Bipolar disorder is episodic, which is a hope I am holding onto right now, and that this is just another phase. I'm very grateful that I got out and drove places when I could. I always try to seize those moments when I feel well because lately I haven't been able to do much.

52 ENTRY 52

Even the best of us get fed up—I'm sick of all the paperwork that goes along with being on government assistance. I'm sick of doctor's appointments and medications. I'm sick of being sober because I'm so worried about everyone else's health, and if something happened when I was drinking, I would feel completely awful. I would lose so much progress, but again, I'm worried about how my actions affect others. I think that a night out with my friends would solve these frustrations, or maybe even just a nice meal and nap, but don't think that I don't get upset and angry about all of this. I've been compliant ever since I entered treatment, but it's not my nature at all. I just hope I can settle down enough to continue to be on every else's time and schedules. I try my best to not complain and be a good boy and comply, but trust me, I want to break free of everything sometimes.

53 ENTRY 53

Many years ago, when I was in an emergency situation, my instincts and survival mode kicked in. And some sort of amazing pain tolerance that I have no idea where that came from. I don't really see surviving the emergencies I've had as courageous. What took courage was facing the aftermath each time, and dealing with mental illness day after day, week after week, year after year. I may have given up if I didn't have some solid support from family, friends, and readers of my books. I mention this because a few people have stopped by lately just to see me, and one of my friends brought me some homemade food. I just want people to know that kindness and support like this matter to people with mental illness, and I would think anyone, really. So many people don't have this kind of support, and that makes a negative difference, too. I don't really know what my point is here. I guess I just want to say that the support I have has helped me greatly, and if you are able, be that support for others. It matters.

54 ENTRY 54

Here's my funny story for the day to make you laugh. My mom will probably kill me, but oh well, I'll just unfriend her on social media again haha. So....I've only been to the strip club as a patron a few times. Not really my thing. But when I was working as a pizza delivery driver in Dayton, Ohio, we delivered to 3 strip clubs in our area. One night, I got such a delivery to a place called Pizazz (lol). Not classy at all. As soon as I walked through the door, I was in the middle of everything. I bring a pizza over to these 3 businessmen type people, and they tell me to sit down and have a drink with them. First of all, I wasn't old enough to drink, and secondly, I was driving all night. When I turned down the drinks, they gave me a $10 tip and told me to sit down and called over a stripper. They explained to me that I was going to get a lap dance too, whether I liked it or not. They didn't have to twist my arm or anything, but I felt so awkward because I'm pretty shy about this kind of thing. To make it even more awkward, when the stripper is doing her thing, she says, "MMM, you smell like pizza" WTF? I have no idea what I'm supposed to say. 'Oh yeah baby, it's a meat lovers'. I can get you pizza all night long. LOL. Anyway, hope that made you laugh. True story, of course.

55 ENTRY 55

There was a courageous woman from my area who was diagnosed with a fatal brain injury. In her last days, all she wanted was letters of hope. Here is the letter I wrote to her. She played basketball for a college called Mount St. Joseph's, and scored a basket in one of her final days.

Dear Lauren,

There is so much I want to say to you. I wish I could just talk to you over coffee or something. I also hope you get this message. You are such a hero to so many people, including myself. I hope you realize how big of an impact your story has had on everyone, near and far. You have shown everyone how to face adversity with dignity and courage. You have turned a negative into a positive. Even that is such an understatement. Your story will be told for such a long time. That is something so special. Your impact is on the same level as famous authors, scientists, and dignitaries. My friends and family are praying for you, and we all wish you a Merry Christmas! Keep fighting!

Love,
John Edward Medl, Age 33 Cincinnati

56 ENTRY 56

Weird happenings on the porch this morning... A man stopped his car in front of my house and started walking towards the porch. I thought it was my overdue package, but it was a guy my age who lived in the neighborhood. He said he drives by every day, and he saw me sleeping one day, and he wanted to make sure I was okay. He said it had been bothering him for a week because he didn't know if I was okay. I explained to him that I fall asleep sometimes on the porch because I'm groggy from medication. I told him I had bipolar disorder, and I take medication for it. He said he had bipolar disorder, too. He also has anxiety, panic attacks, and PTSD from the military. Same as me, although I was never in the military. He was 38 years old. I will be 38 in 9 days. He was first diagnosed in 2006. Same as me. This was just some random, kindhearted stranger from the neighborhood checking on me. So cool of him to do. Just a very nice, weird thing that happened this morning.

57 ENTRY 57

Having a positive attitude doesn't mean I'm happy all the time. I get in bad moods. Some (parts) of my days are bad sometimes. Mental illness and depression are very real and powerful, but if you start out deciding you are going to have a positive attitude, it's hard to say that you are a failure. I get enjoyment out of making people laugh and smile. I am also very candid about my struggles and illness. At the end of the day, when I'm laying in bed at night, I look back on the day. If I can look back on the day and see that someone was happier or inspired because of my life, I won that day. It's a daily measuring stick that I use to decide if I was successful for the day. I may not have had a great day, but if someone else did because of me, everything I go through is worth it. I am winning at life, despite everything. This is just simply my philosophy of life. It's not something that can be measured. It's not logical like mathematics. I'm just telling you what helps me get through hard days. I know it works because I feel it and live it.

I think most people know that bipolar disorder is a disease of extremes, especially moods. I am somewhat stable most of the time. I don't like it. I like being manic, but it's not good for me. I think I'm so addicted to coffee because it makes me manic sometimes, even at my anxiety's expense. Conversely, I can be in a good mood one minute, and the next minute, it feels like someone punched me in the gut with depression. It's strange and fascinating. I try my best to describe it.

58 ENTRY 58

Here's another poem and commentary I found from 20 years ago, when I was a senior at Moeller High School. Some of these old writings of mine are really weird because you can almost see and feel my mental problems coming on. This was written in the year 2000. I wasn't officially diagnosed until 2006. I guess it just feels weird to me because I wrote it and I remember vaguely how I felt. Like I said before, I'm still the same guy, and maybe my life turned out exactly how it was supposed to. I just took a few detours.

Detached Observer

Don't want to ruin the mood,
I'd never think to intrude,
Upon such important matters dear to you.
I care about everyone else because of all I have felt,
I will emerge in the end,
To see the vision of mirth again.
Dissipate the groups I've come familiar with,
Take away the sanity, which fades to a myth.
Move me along the world with no trace of a journey,
For no trace for anyone to find myself.

COMMENTARY

This poem I wrote when I started to feel that my life was becoming too hectic and rapid for my own mind. I felt that I would be lost in the shuffle of adulthood, and everything is going to change now that I'm entering the real world. I guess I'm scared, but more anxious. I wasn't a very happy person when I wrote this because I feel the pain of other people, and I'm oversensitive to negative occurring in life. I think the world is coming down on me sometimes, and I wonder why I'm here. I think that I may have a mission on this Earth to just simply be funny and nice to others, and I think that's an important vocation. It seems rather simple, but I think I can help others a great deal in the field of psychology to help those who have struggled like myself.

59 ENTRY 59

Do you think that others naturally grow apart as everyone gets older? I always wonder if it's because of my illness that I have lost so many friends and acquaintances. I don't want to believe that my former friends forgot about me on purpose or for any other reason than everyone is busy and has families now and such. When I go out, which is hardly ever, I'm trying really hard to keep the conversation about my books and my illness to a minimum. I care less about being liked, and more about being too much for people or having the conversation get too heavy when people just want to have fun. I also need a break. I have to deal with my illness almost every second, and then I'm advocating on top of that. I don't want my illness and work to define me. I have a lot of substance to my personality.

60 ENTRY 60

I REMEMBER SITTING IN THE EMERGENCY WAITING ROOM. I WAS READING BIBLE verses to an older black woman. She didn't seem to mind. She was friendly. I remember that much. I went to use the bathroom, and my urine was bright orange, like orange soda. I'm pretty sure I was hallucinating. The doctors took me back into the treatment part of the building. I couldn't calm down. A doctor asked me a bunch of questions—if I knew who the president was and if I was on drugs. She asked me all the drugs I have done, and I had to answer with embarrassment in front of my parents. The nurses gave me a big shot of medicine in my right arm. Shortly after, I laid down in a bed in a room off to the side and slept peacefully for many hours.

61 ENTRY 61

And everything was about politics and war
And now it's always more
Until everything had been bought from every store.
No one wants to leave home
Safety in their gadgets
All the information in the world,
And no one uses it.
Where do we go now?
What's it all for?
Nothing is much use if you don't
Venture from your doors.
To explore everything that has always been there
Just waiting to be enjoyed
But people would rather argue and play with their toys.

JOHN MEDL

62 ENTRY 62

I know I'm a strong person, but I guess I doubt how strong I am going about this whole driving anxiety problem. There's a lot of moments in my life when I say to myself, "Wow. That took a lot of strength". = You are a strong person. I guess I just wonder if I'm being too cautious about driving. When I have physical symptoms of anxiety and panic—chest pains, dizziness, numbness in limbsI feel like I am a danger on the road. Not to mention these symptoms make it extremely difficult to drive.

63 ENTRY 63

I AM MANY THINGS. I'M A SON, BROTHER, AND UNCLE. I'M A ST. SAVIOUR Golden Bear, a Moeller Crusader, and a Dayton Flyer. I'm a good person and a good friend. Some days I feel like I have the magic in me, and some days I feel like I'm just fighting to survive. One thing I am not is a quitter, and no one can take that away from me.

64 ENTRY 64

My maternal grandmother passed away around 1998-1999. Within days of her passing, I started to self medicate with drugs and alcohol. I never thought I'd be a party person like that. I think I was looking for emotional pain relief. I was hurt badly to a point that I had rarely experienced, if ever. In 2006, I was first hospitalized and diagnosed with bipolar disorder. She was a wonderful person. I've never met anyone so devoted to God. If there's anything after this life, I like to think she's looking down on us all, and that I've made her proud. We have a lamp that flickers from old wiring, and my mom says it's my grandma saying hello. It just happened, so I thought I'd write something about her. She never drove a car, and loved getting her hair done. She liked a little wine, and she was a smoker, except for the last few years of her life. I guess it hurt so badly because I thought she'd always be there because she had always been there. I know this sounds like a sad post, but I'm actually reminiscing about her fondly before sleep.

A big problem I have is with confidence. In almost every sense of the word. With my mom breaking her wrist, I've had to do housework that she can't do. I don't know if I thought I couldn't take care of myself or what, but I'm learning that I can should I ever move out on my own. My mom has devoted most of her life to taking care of my dad and my siblings. With me doing some of the housework, it's a good reminder of how much my mom has done for all of us. I cooked dinner tonight for the most part. Laundry. Garbage. I don't take it for granted how much my mom does.

65 ENTRY 65

A BIG PROBLEM I HAVE IS WITH CONFIDENCE. IN ALMOST EVERY SENSE OF THE word. With my mom breaking her wrist, I've had to do housework that she can't do. I don't know if I thought I couldn't take care of myself or what, but I'm learning that I can should I ever move out on my own. My mom has devoted most of her life to taking care of my dad and my siblings. With me doing some of the housework, it's a good reminder of how much my mom has done for all of us. I cooked dinner tonight for the most part. Laundry. Garbage. I don't take it for granted how much my mom does.

66 ENTRY 66

I SEE STUFF ALL THE TIME ON SOCIAL MEDIA AND WHEREVER ELSE THAT TALK about people on disability or public assistance. It's almost always negative and judgemental. Yes, some people abuse the system and fake disability, but I don't believe that's usually the case. But guess what? It's not anyone's business. Yes, tax dollars pay for public assistance, but what about the people who become disabled who paid into Social Security for years? God forbid anything happens to you or your family where you need public assistance. Mr. or Mrs. Jones is allowed to have nice things even if they are food stamps. Maybe they bought their nice items before they became disabled. Maybe they have a rich uncle or something. You just never know. That's why being judgemental makes people look ignorant. Personally, it took me 7 years to get approved for disability. The whole process was ridiculous and nearly impossible. I had a lawyer, but I dumped every one finally, and I was losing hope. The way I got approved was my mother took all my records with a picture of me to the Social Security/Disability office, and shortly after, I was approved. It was a miracle for my family. I don't know where all these people are who are rich off the government, but it's not me. I would kill to be able to work a normal job. I would make a hell of a lot more money. My parents taught me the values of hard work, so I try to do what I can to feel like I am earning those disability payments and $38 a month in food assistance. I know not everyone is like that, but that's me. I don't worry about everyone else.

67 ENTRY 67

During this pandemic, I see people being kinder to each other, in general of course. I see people respecting the elderly again. I see musicians finding new ways to perform. I see people making art and enjoying the outdoors. I see parents cherishing lost time with their kids. Maybe we needed a break and the world to stop for a minute...(obviously I know all of this has come at a great cost to a lot of people)

68 ENTRY 68

I've been depressed for a few weeks off and on. It's always off and on because of the duality of bipolar disorder. I've thought about what I might say if I knew it was the last of my time on Earth. I've thought about what my eulogy might sound like. Thoughts about death and dying are common with anxiety, depression, and bipolar disorder. There's as high as a 20% suicide rate for bipolar disorder as well. If I ever get to that point, I have faith that I would tell someone. Or write about it as I'm doing now. I've thought about my parents aging, and the real possibility that they might not be around some day. As always, the reason I'm writing this is for the greater good. You are not alone. If my symptoms aren't too bad, you can talk to me. Please get help if you need it or find an outlet that gives you relief.

69 ENTRY 69

From a reader:

Dear Mr. Medl,

I am a freshman student at the University of Vermont, enrolled in a class to discuss mental health disorders.

I have just read your book Millions Like Me, so I know reading is difficult for you.

Perhaps you have someone to help you read, but if not, I will try to keep this email short and space it so hopefully, it's easier.

I just wanted to say thank you for your book.

I do not currently think I have any mental disorders (I just turned 18) but this book was incredibly helpful and insightful for me regardless.

I of course cannot begin to imagine the work you put into writing it, but it's so valuable to learn from.

Your poems, while tinted with sadness and isolation, are truly powerful and beautiful to read.

Again, thank you

70 ENTRY 70

There's nothing for me on the other side
And I'm fine with that
Even if it is just an eternal dirt nap
What if there's more?
I'm tired and sore
I'm tired of thinking
My thoughts have always been my enemy
I just want to live silently
Head down.
Put in my days.
I just want to feel the sun's rays.
But the rain has its place.
You might even see a smile on my face
I want to feel content enough to be kind
My mind has failed me
But I trust my heart
Even when I fell apart

71 ENTRY 71

I've been depressed for a few weeks off and on. It's always off and on because of the duality of bipolar disorder. I've thought about what I might say if I knew it was the last of my time on Earth. I've thought about what my eulogy might sound like. Thoughts about death and dying are common with anxiety, depression, and bipolar disorder. There's as high as a 20% suicide rate for bipolar disorder as well. If I ever get to that point, I have faith that I would tell someone. Or write about it as I'm doing now. I've thought about my parents aging, and the real possibility that they might not be around some day. As always, the reason I'm writing this is for the greater good. You are not alone. If my symptoms aren't too bad, you can talk to me. Please get help if you need it or find an outlet that gives you relief.

72 ENTRY 72

GOING THROUGH PSYCHOSIS AND BEING DELUSIONAL IS A STRANGE THING, especially when I snapped out of it and back to another reality. I remember a lot of the insane things I thought and acted upon, and it just hurts. I think because it's so embarrassing. Not to mention how painful it was to go through that trauma. People I've known for a very long time witnessed my insanity, and like I said, it's so embarrassing. I'm sure when some people think of me, they think of the insane things I did, and not the actual person who I really am. I am not my illness. I've had a lot of great times in my life, and it seems like good times are rare for me anymore. I get in moods where I get so agitated that not even my mother's voice is comforting. I think about how nice eternal silence is going to be. I don't really believe in complaining, but I still experience a lot of pain—physical, mental, and emotional. Some days, I think I'm ready to call it quits, or if my life ended, I would be fine with it. I've paid back society and done my time. This is what bipolar depression looks and sounds like. I'm lost as to what helps or what can help me bring me out of a funk like this. I can't even think straight except for negative and depressing thoughts. I hold on to the hopes that it will pass as it always does. It helps when I joke around and make people laugh, or when I feel like I really reached someone who is also struggling. I felt like I didn't really know what to do right now, so I wrote it down, and I feel a little better. I'm going to try to practice some self-care tonight and just take it easy. Find something relaxing to do. I haven't read a single page of any book in a while, and I have a lot of interesting books I want to read. Self care might mean taking a shower or watching something mindless on TV. I wish I could figure it out like a math problem, but depression is rarely logical.

73 ENTRY 73

I WAS SUPPOSED TO HAVE A PHONE CALL MEETING/ASSESSMENT WITH MY psychiatrist today, but he was out of the office. I was looking forward to it because I wanted to talk about some emotional issues I've been having lately. I got rescheduled for 10 days from now, so it's all good. As much as I've written, I don't think I've ever just flat out said that mental illness is really hard to deal with. Maybe a few times, but not often. I don't like talking about it, and I hate complaining and excuses. Mental illness and not having a properly functioning brain has BY FAR been the hardest thing I've ever had to deal with. The worst day of my life was when I was first hospitalized in 2006. Although I wasn't completely coherent, but I remember more than I should. I've tried to make the most of my situation and stay positive by writing and cracking jokes, etc., but it's really hard on me sometimes. I know a lot of you out there have to deal with all sorts of things that maybe you don't talk about. No matter what the ailment, you are not alone. I struggle a lot too. Like I said, I do a pretty good job of playing it off, but my mental illness can be unforgiving.

74 ENTRY 74

I had a meeting over the phone with my psychiatrist today. He's very positive. He reminded me of how far I have come and told me I am doing a good job. If I could only internalize what others see in me. I am an over-thinker and my own biggest critic and enemy. Even after all this time, I am still a work in progress. I don't know if I will ever be satisfied. My doctor even said that he wishes he could put me on payroll to talk to some of his other clients. I have been completely compliant, especially with medication, which is not my nature at all. I put my trust in the experts' hands, and they delivered. Before my diagnosis, I never even took Advil or Tylenol, much less psychotropic medications. Somewhere deep down, I know I am a success story. I know I inspire people. I know I am blessed, and I am grateful for everything I have and everything I've worked for. I have a sick brain that tells me lies and sometimes I can't convince myself that I'm actually doing pretty well compared to my mental health history. I guess it was nice to hear from my doctor. I've been humbled to the point of rock bottom, but I still believe there is something special about me. I've emptied the tank, so to speak, for so long and so many days trying to fight this illness. It's exhausting and frustrating, but I've never quit, which is something to hang my hat on. When I try to sleep at night, I remind myself that I am doing the best I can to provide some sort of mental comfort.

75 ENTRY 75

I conquered one of my biggest and longest lingering fears today. I saw a primary care doctor and had blood drawn. It had been about 10 years since both events. Everyone who gave me medical attention was great. My blood pressure was a little high, but not concerning. The blood work is the standard tests—kidney and liver functions, sugars, and metabolism. I guess you can't just be fat anymore haha. I have faith and hope in humanity, even if it is only temporary. What matters to me more is having faith and confidence in myself. It's a lot easier for me to help humanity when I feel good about myself. I can't help anyone if I don't believe in my abilities. I don't need faith in humanity. I've seen what it is—good and evil, ups and downs, lies and truth. It's always going to be that way. I just try to do my part, and I can't do that to my fullest ability without confidence, faith, and trust in myself.

76 ENTRY 76

There's noise coming from the magic box
As I roll up another cigarette
The actors have rehearsed their lines
Handed down to them by people
Who have never had to fight for anything
The brave warriors slave away
For a hundred dollars a day
If they're lucky
So the privileged can live in decadence
It's been this way for such a long time
When will this change like society has?
Fear and masks
All we know how to do is pray
I wonder if anyone is listening

77 ENTRY 77

Mania is a hallmark feature of bipolar disorder. When manic, a person can impulsively spend money or have trouble budgeting money. I have experienced this many times, and it's something I struggle with. Today, I was able to open my own checking account. For years, I have been sharing an account with my mom, and it has caused a lot of stress in my family. Glad to check another thing off the list, working towards more independence and responsibility.

78 ENTRY 78

ONE OF THE HARDEST LESSONS I'M STILL TRYING TO LEARN IS THAT NOT EVERYONE is going to like me. There's a saying that goes, "You could be the ripest, juiciest peach in the world, and there's still going to be people who don't like peaches". Honestly, it's their loss. I'm loyal to a fault, and I have a lot to offer, I would never screw anyone over intentionally, and I don't wish harm on anyone, not even the people who have done me wrong.

79 ENTRY 79

Sometimes, I think to myself, "Why does anyone care what I write about?", but then I think, "Why does anyone care what anyone writes about? Why not me?" I'm not some expert who is just writing about something I've read in books. I've lived the Hell that I write about. I think that's one of many reasons why people gravitate towards me and are interested in reading my books. If you read my books, you will find that I am brutally honest about my symptoms and my experiences. Just something to think about for any aspiring writers. I also hope that my honestly does not come off as complaining because sometimes I think there's nothing worse. It's a toxic trait that creates a negative environment. I try to be grateful and humble. It's a challenge. It's much harder to be grateful and courageous in the face of adversity than the alternative.

80 ENTRY 80

Yesterday, I had a meeting with my clinical diagnostician, and today with my case manager. Relatively painless stuff. We basically laid out a treatment plan for the year. I wish I didn't have to do stuff like this, but it's probably for my own good. I really just want to be free and left alone most of the time, but all my meetings are good reminders of my goals and progress I suppose.

81 ENTRY 81

My parents are sleeping, so y'all are going to have to deal with my rantings. Before I wrote this, the office chair broke, which is supposed to have an 800 pound capacity or something. This is like the third one that has broken on me. I'm not slim, but I'm not 800 pounds.

We had to have a new sump pump installed in the basement today, which is basically not my territory of business, but it's just something that happened today.

The Department of Education forgave the remaining balance of my student loans years ago, but they still send mail to check up on me to make sure I haven't become wealthy or gainfully employed. Not a huge deal, but stressful and annoying in some small way.

Here's the really annoying thing. I started a checking account with $40 a few weeks ago, and it was overdrawn this morning. Every time I made a transaction, I checked the banking app first to make sure the money was there. When I set up the account, I told the people to make sure that no purchases would be approved if the money wasn't there. When I went to bed last night, I had about a dollar in my account, which is fine because when I set up the account, I made sure there was no minimum balance requirement. I MADE SURE all of these things to safeguard against an over-withdrawal. When I woke up this morning, I had to deal with the stress of my account being way overdrawn, and not just by a little. No one at the bank wanted to take responsibility, and everyone around me just assumed it was my fault because I've had a few bouts of financial irresponsibility. I guess it's at least partially my fault because I was the one at the controls, but I was so careful. I was even keeping track with pen and paper because I felt like something wasn't right. Long story short, fuck today. Let's hope for a better tomorrow.

82 ENTRY 82

Panic attacks are shocking in a lot of ways. I'm not sure if that's the right word. I'm just always shocked at how painful they are and that I've survived so many. I just had a brief panic attack, and they are not for the weak. My entire body gets stiff, and my mind races in nonsensical words and phrases. I get dizzy and I get stomach cramps. I just took an Advil to try to kill some of the physical pain. Loud noises are almost unbearable to tolerate, but soft and familiar music sometimes helps me. I roll cigarettes to try to distract myself. I try to move around to make the body stiffness better. When my stomach settles, I'm going to eat dinner and rest. That's how I deal with them. It's over after that. Then the battle begins again. This doesn't happen to me often, and I've actually been making some good progress.

83 ENTRY 83

Some victories that I've had lately:

1. I opened my own checking account so that I could be financially independent
2. Some of my family members visited for dinner, so I got to see them. I had anxiety almost the whole time, but I got through it.
3. I successfully completed 3 meetings this week--- one with my clinical diagnostician, one with my case manager, and one with my psychiatrist. We laid out a treatment plan for the next year, and my medications are staying the same, but that may change. My doctor didn't want to change anything because he hasn't seen me in person for months. I've been on the same medication for about 8 years now.
4. I filled out some official paperwork regarding the forgiveness of my student loans
5. I drove myself to the store and to the bank. I have major driving anxiety, and sometimes I can't drive at all.

All of these things are hard for me. They are challenges, and considered victories when I complete them. I think I had too many things going on in one week, so that's probably why I have had increased anxiety and panic attacks.

84 ENTRY 84

WHENEVER I HAVE A VISIT WITH MY PSYCHIATRIST, HE ALWAYS ASKS THE SAME beginning questions...."Do you think you can fly or do you think you have superpowers?" and "Are you hearing voices?". These may seem like strange questions to the average person, but I have answered "yes" to these questions before. Quick example. When I was first hospitalized in 2006, I was convinced that I could jump off the balcony at the hospital and "fly" or land safely below. I have no idea what stopped me. I have a "loud brain", which basically means I have an active inner dialogue. Not everyone has that, so I've found out. It serves me well with writing, but it's extremely annoying and exhausting when I'm trying to rest. As long as the "voices" aren't directive (telling me to do a specific thing), then I'm considered stable enough, I guess. I've had problems with directive voices/psychosis before also. I can only explain psychosis as watching myself in a movie and someone or something else is at the controls. I've always had a loud brain, but I haven't had problems with psychosis or extreme grandeur in a long time.

Am I angry at life because of my mental illness? Not usually. I don't see how that's productive, and the world doesn't owe me anything. It could always be worse. Even when I don't have any money, I'm richer than a lot of people across the world. I wish I were a stronger person so that I acted as blessed as I feel, but I'm just human with limitations. I've tried not to use my illness as a crutch, but it is a good explanation for a lot of my behavior. For me, mental illness is frustrating, painful, and exhausting. I've prayed for death and thought about taking my own life. My best days are when I get some relief. It doesn't happen often, as my illness is mostly relentless. I've chosen to educate others through my books and volunteer my time to help others find some relief. So many positive things have come from my illness, and it helps me to focus on all the good things rather than feel sorry for myself.

85 ENTRY 85

June 9, 2020—In the middle of a global pandemic and racial protests

I don't feel guilty for being white. I didn't get to choose my skin color as much as anyone. But I do understand what white privilege means. As a white person, I'm more likely to have access to all kinds of resources and less likely to be harassed by the police. It doesn't mean that my life is easy. I know good cops. I've known them almost my whole life. But once you are mistreated by the police, how do you forget that? My former professor is Latino and he was brutalized and beaten by police in Minnesota. He won a lawsuit against them. I'm seeing a lot of positive changes in the form of diversity programs and funding for minority causes. It's very strange as a white person. I think I was so used to everyday racism that I was comfortable. Change is usually uncomfortable, and I want to be part of the solution, and I want to be on the right side of history. If racial equality is going to happen, white people need to help because we're still running the show.

86 ENTRY 86

I HAD A PRETTY GOOD DAY TODAY:

1. I took a shower. Embarrassingly, it had been a while
2. I balanced my checking account, and the balance is positive.
3. I drove myself to the doctor for a sore jaw. He prescribed me antibiotics for the infection. I'll probably have to see a dentist, barring some miracle, but still a victory for me.

87 ENTRY 87

I'VE GOT TO LEARN TO NOT BE SO HARD ON MYSELF

I'm a lucky, blessed man. Everyone is so kind to me, especially my mom, the rest of my family, and close friends. I know this sounds stupid, but I feel like if I remind myself of my blessings even in hard times, that I will somehow heal faster. In a way, it does help me heal faster. Reminding myself of my good fortune at the very least occupies my mind with positive thoughts. I'm a simple man. I don't need much to be happy.

88 ENTRY 88

Mania is often referred to as a "high", like a drug. It's like the highest you've ever been off drugs that are in your brain. No street drugs compare. That's how intense it is. I've heard, "Medication took my superpowers away." That high. Delusional and psychotic high.

89 ENTRY 89

I'VE HAD PROBABLY THOUSANDS OF PANIC ATTACKS, BUT I REMEMBER THIS ONE IN particular. I remember smoking 9 cigarettes in a row. I just couldn't calm down. It goes that way sometimes. I remember because I counted. It's an OCD thing. I also roll my cigarettes in even numbers because I smoke 2 in a row while I'm out on the porch. I will always contend that mental illness is the hardest thing I've ever had to endure. Every day I survive is a notch in my belt. I'm extremely proud of myself for never giving up.

90 ENTRY 90

I SHOULD HAVE KNOWN SOMETHING WAS WRONG IN COLLEGE, BUT THEN AGAIN, I showed symptoms in high school and childhood. We all just had no idea. In college, I engaged in risky behavior, but I had this delusion that lights turned off when I was around. Like street lamps. It seemed like it happened a lot. Then, I told my friends, and they noticed too, which reinforced my delusion. The logical explanation is that these lights were on timers, and it was coincidental that the lights would turn off. I thought it was some kind of supernatural thing, but I didn't take it very seriously and kind of brushed it off.

91 ENTRY 91

One of my best friends visited the other day. He's known me since high school. He visited me in the hospital and has bought all my books. I try not to talk about my illness in regular conversation, but it always seems to come up. It occurred to me that I never really asked about this friend's mental health.

So I simply asked, "Do you have depression or anxiety or anything?"

And he simply said, "No".

It kind of blew my mind because I thought about how nice it would be to not have anxiety or depression, but I do remember a long time ago when I didn't have to worry about my mental health. It's an incredible blessing to not have to deal with. However, my buddy has physical health problems that I don't have to deal with, so his life is far from being a walk in the park.

92 ENTRY 92

On July 31, 2020, I will celebrate being a 14 year survivor of mental illness from the first time I was hospitalized. Mental illness tried to take my life many times, but my spirit was not having any of it. I really hope I get a chance to talk to the students of Moeller HS about mental health. When I attended Moeller, there wasn't much talk about mental health. All the advocacy work I do makes me feel like I'm fulfilling my purpose. That somehow, some way, makes me feel I am exactly where I am supposed to be, and I'm doing exactly what I am supposed to be doing. It's a great feeling to feel like you are fulfilling your purpose in life. The fear of dying with unfinished business goes away. The age old question of "Have I done enough with my life?" goes away. Whatever I have sacrificed for stability (most of the time), I have gained in perspective and purpose. I am extremely grateful for my life and how it turned out. I wasn't always so optimistic. I had to work at it. I've lost plenty of battles, but I feel like I am winning the war. That's as close to beating mental illness as you can get, in my opinion.

I just want to talk about intelligence for a minute because it's on my mind. I am going to describe my family because there are 7 of us (my parents and 5 siblings) because I think it is a good example of the varieties of intelligence. You don't need a college degree to be smart, but I think it helps. I also know people who didn't graduate high school who are master musicians and carpenters.

I guess I will start with my dad. My dad has a two-year degree from The University of Cincinnati. He is an electrical engineer by trade. He must be good with money too because we don't have a whole lot of it, but we rarely go without necessities. My mom didn't finish college. It wasn't really a popular thing for women to do in the 1960s. However, she has raised 5 kids with good values and morals with not too many injuries haha. She is an extremely hard worker, which I think is a type of intelligence in a way. She is also very organized, which I think is another kind of intelligence. My oldest brother is a radar specialist for a government contractor out in Arizona. He has a Master's Degree. My next brother never finished college, but he is a master carpenter and very good at investing and money. My sister never finished college, but she is an office manager who oversees collecting invoices for a billboard company. My closest brother has a Master's Degree in Mathematics and is extremely book smart and computer smart. He's the brother we call when our computer screws up. Then there's me, the youngest of all of us. I consider myself intelligent, but like everyone else, I have my moments of dim bulbness. I just wanted to write about my family because I love them all, of course, but I think we are all intelligent in our own way. Some of us have degrees, and some don't. It doesn't have to be an either/or thing where you are smart if you have a degree, and dumb if you do not. All of this probably just relates to the fact that you shouldn't judge people, and it seems like it comes down to that a lot.

93 ENTRY 93

My spending was out of control this month, so I gave control of my finances to my brother. My checking account is closed, credit cards are frozen, and I don't have any way to move money with apps like Venmo and PayPal. I'm a little disappointed in myself, but I know it's for the best. I was borrowing money from a lot of people, mainly to gamble, and it had to stop to get this household's finances in order, and also to plan for the future. Gambling gave me hope that I could win a lot of money in a short time because I can't work a standard job. The writing job I was hoping for isn't going to work out either. On the bright side, I drove myself to the store, and I'm getting closer to finishing my fourth book each day. I'm just having a difficult time.

94 ENTRY 94

So here's a story that I've never told before. Damn, I remember it like it was yesterday. It was at least 10 years ago at Good Samaritan Hospital. I was being treated for psychosis and panic. One of the nurses gave me a pill and asked me how I felt. "Heavenly", I said. I was looking out into the sun-setting sky, and that's really how I felt. Several times. I've felt a supernatural force acting upon me, usually good, but sometimes evil feeling. I found out later that the pill was just for heartburn, but I think I answered in that way because that's what I thought the nurses wanted me to say. I'm not really sure. I do vaguely remember actually feeling that supernatural, heavenly way. I don't think anyone can truly understand psychosis and mania unless you have been through it. I don't care how many degrees you have. You have to feel it and experience it. Some people describe mania as a high, but that doesn't fully encompass the feeling. It's not like a let's smoke a blunt in high school high. It's like the best drug you have ever taken, combined with the worst hallucinogenic drug you have ever taken times a million. And psychosis is like watching yourself in a movie, with someone else at the controls.

95 ENTRY 95

When I was 618 pounds, I should have just hung it up and let nature take its course. I didn't. I don't use a scale, but I'm almost certain that I've lost over 100 pounds. Every time I was hospitalized, people would have understood if I quit. When I had to take medication, that made me feel absolutely awful, I should have given up. When I was lying on the couch in a medicinal haze, I should have just stayed down. I kept getting up and forcing myself to take showers when it felt impossible. When I had panic attacks while driving, people would have understood if I quit trying to drive. I wasn't raised that way. We (my siblings) weren't taught to quit. We were taught to fight. Our parents led by example in many ways, but the most impressive was that my mom and dad each beat cancer twice. My dad only has one kidney. In all honesty, I don't know how I survived a lot of things I have. I don't know why I didn't quit when I didn't know what I was doing. My mind was gone, and I still didn't quit. Now, I'm about to be an author for the fourth time. I'm going to be mentioned in the Fall Newsletter for my alma mater, Moeller High School. I'm also trying to get a mention from my college alma mater, The University of Dayton, but they have been unresponsive to my messages. I've worked with the Cincinnati-based non-profit 1N5.org on several projects. I'm the founder and administrator of a social media page devoted to mental illness and inspiration for 8 years now. We have almost

800 members. At times, I don't know how I've come this far, but I'm glad I did. Yes, I'm bragging about myself. I've earned it.

96 ENTRY 96

WELL, TODAY'S THE DAY. I SURVIVED ANOTHER YEAR. FOURTEEN YEARS AGO today (July 31, 2006), my life fell apart. I lost my house, car, job, girlfriend, and any reputation I had as a sane person. I was rushed to the hospital with what they call a psychotic first break of bipolar disorder. I stayed in a locked down psychiatric unit for 11 days. It was a nightmare, and I still have flash-backs sometimes, even after all these years. I am extremely proud of how I have handled all my diagnoses and what I have accomplished. I have made my family and friends proud. I have a grateful and loving heart. I appreciate life now more than I ever did before. I tell everyone that I am blessed. I have everything I need, which is more than a lot of people have. At some point in my recovery, I decided I wanted to do more than just survive and exist. I've made lemonade, as they say, and I've played the cards I have been dealt to the best of my abilities. I can't express enough my gratitude for all the support in every capacity. The love that has been shown to me, by all sorts of people, has been tremendous. I am just a humble servant trying to carry out a mission of kindness and awareness of mental health issues. Thank you for your support. For being there for me. It absolutely makes a difference.

97 ENTRY 97

I DON'T WANT TO BE YOUNG AGAIN, BUT IF I COULD GO BACK IN TIME FOR A weekend in high school, I think I would agree to that. Party all weekend without a care or responsibility. Barely sleep, except on Sunday to recover for the upcoming week of classes. No smart phones or every app imaginable. Not many people had cell phones, either. I can't remember if I did or not. I remember people having pagers, which I never had. No Netflix and the like or social media. We took pictures with disposable cameras and actually had to wait to get the pictures developed. Weekend long binges at music festivals with a bunch of mostly kindhearted strangers just camping and listening to music. I think of those days fondly, but I still would only want to go back for a weekend. I enjoy my life now as a writer and mental health advocate. I appreciate peace of mind and silence. I don't like party atmospheres anymore. I don't think I'm boring. I just lived the party lifestyle already, and I'm done with it all. I want to keep those fond memories just as memories, and thank my lucky stars that I survived. Now, at age 38, I feel like I don't know about so many things, and I was so confident, borderline cocky in high school, which is amazing, because I was incredibly stupid compared to now. But I would still go back for a weekend if I had the chance. Maybe I am just feeling nostalgic today.

98 ENTRY 98

I USED TO BELIEVE IN THE GOOD IN EVERYONE. THE WORLD HAS SHOWN ME THAT'S not true. I used to think that bad people were just good people who did bad and evil things. I think people either chose to be evil or they are born that way, or some combination. That's usually how it goes in psychology. Nothing is really ever black and white. On a psychology exam, the answer is rarely straightforward. The answer is usually all of the above, none of the above, or both A and C. Things like that. I studied out of a philosophy book that was titled, "Taking Sides", and if I remember correctly, it was all about how people don't have to always take a side on every topic. You can agree or disagree with some parts of one side or the other. I think people get trapped into thinking in black and white terms, so when they are confronted with conflicting evidence of their beliefs, they won't give an inch because they have chosen a side. It's very hard for people to change their minds once they are made up. I believe this is the spirit of cognitive dissonance.

I remember writing a whole term paper on rationalization. It was either a psychology or philosophy course. In many ways, those two subjects overlap and are related. Anyway, the thesis of my paper is that rationalization is extremely dangerous because you can rationalize almost anything. Right now, I am fighting a gambling addiction. I have been gambling half of my life. It turned from recreational to a maniacal addiction. I don't like to use bipolar disorder as an excuse, but it definitely is an explanation and played a role. I was so stressed out about my parents' finances and their health. Every time I gambled, I thought I was going to win. It's really hard to give up because I have won a lot of money gambling. It was getting to the point where I was borrowing money and losing control. It had to stop. Maybe one day, I can recreationally gamble again, but for now, I am sickened by the idea, and I am trying to find myself again and finish this book. Getting back to my point, I rationalized my gambling habit because I don't drink alcohol or do drugs. I thought my gambling was acceptable because I didn't have those other coping mechanisms that most people have. You can rationalize anything if you lie to yourself enough.

99 ENTRY 99

I don't even know where to start. Last night, I was extremely depressed. I was watching a poker tournament on my phone, and I was just thinking about how nice it would be to have the money to play. I've been in a poker club for about 10 years now, and the tournament entrants were my friends. We usually play in person, but because of the pandemic virus, everyone plays on an online computer application. I haven't been able to play in person for several years now, with the exception of one night, because it's hard for me to concentrate that long and sit still. The key to live poker is to be as unreadable (a la poker faced) as possible, and my anxiety gives me away every time. It's not even fun anymore.

My checking account is closed. All my credit cards are cut up and my credit is frozen. I have no access to any gambling sites on the computer. I have no access to money applications on my phone to move money around. All of this is for the betterment of myself and my situation, as well as lightening the worry and burden on my parents and siblings. I know that. I'm trying to accept that. I don't know if I need a night out with my friends or if I need someone to visit me, or what. Sometimes I just feel like running away and starting a new life. I think about living in a tiny place with few possessions by a body of water and just living there until I die without talking to anyone again. I feel stuck. I don't know if I should live here with my parents or go start a new life somewhere. I don't even know if I could handle living on my own or afford it for that matter. I don't want to abandon everyone, but I really do get that urge a lot. Maybe I'm just tired or anxious or otherwise symptomatic right now. I could barely sit still enough to write this entry.

Journaling is a coping mechanism for me, but it's also a force where I feel compelled to write like my brain needs to throw up, per se. Writing helps release the pressure in my mind of all my thoughts. I wonder if other writers or artists or musicians feel that creative force too.

I don't know if it's possible for the living to understand suicide, but I feel like I do. A long time ago, I was suicidal, but I never attempted it. I've had suicidal thoughts too. Mental illness and anguish is incredible pain, and my best guess is that it gets to be too great for some people. I don't think people who commit or attempt suicide are cowards. I think they're just humans who have had too much pain to bear. My writing and mental health advocacy have given me purpose, which helps me when my thoughts get dark. I don't really have suicidal thoughts anymore. I've had to call my case manager several times because I was in mental anguish, and I'm always confident that I will ask for help if I need it. I know the world is a better place with me in it. I know my family and friends would be sad, and I want to go down swinging with dignity. Even with all these great reasons to live, the dark thoughts still creep in sometimes. Mental illness is incredible pain, as I mentioned. Most of the time, I feel okay. I feel good about my life and my contribution to society. But the small amount of time when I am symptomatic is incredibly painful.

It is currently August of the year 2020. I live in Cincinnati, Ohio. There's a global pandemic ravaging through the world with staggering infection rates and fatalities. I don't know if life will ever be the same again. I'm hoping and praying that the pandemic eventually subsides, and a sense of normalcy returns.

100 ENTRY 100

THIS BOOK IS RANDOM IN A LOT OF WAYS, BUT I WANTED IT TO BE THAT WAY. Mental illness can be very fluid and different every day. I think the goal of any treatment and medication regimen is stability, but it doesn't always work that way. I can have a span of a month where every day is a different battle, but I can also have a span of a month or several that are stable and much easier to contend with. I can't tell you exactly when I wrote all of the entries in this book, but I think it represents the volatility of my illness and mental illness in general. When I decided to become a writer and mental health advocate, my main goal was to bring awareness to mental health issues and to make others feel like they are not alone. I hope I have done that in this book and all my books. Much love to you all.

MENTAL ILLNESS IS AN ACTUAL ILLNESS

THOUGHTS, STORIES, AND PHILOSOPHY OF LIFE FROM SOMEONE LIVING WITH MENTAL ILLNESS

1 LOG ENTRY #1

LOTS OF GREAT THINGS ARE HAPPENING FOR ME. I DON'T KNOW IF MY psychiatrist was kidding or not, but he said he wants me to Zoom conference with his other patients just to talk to them. Compared to the other patients at my clinic, I am probably a success story. I don't always feel like a success story, but I'm starting to believe in myself a little more. My high school alma mater, Moeller HS, is going to give me a mention in their Fall Newsletter. I'm working on getting a mention from my college alma mater, The University of Dayton. I am getting shout outs from all over the country regarding my books. I've been making some really great connections to my readers who struggle themselves with mental illness or it runs in their family, or both. It's a little surreal sometimes.

I can't emphasize enough how sick I was when I was first diagnosed with bipolar disorder with psychotic features in 2006. For months, maybe years, (it's foggy), all I could do was eat, sleep, and go to the bathroom. If I took a shower, it was a big accomplishment for the day or week. I was down on the mat several times. Well, I got up every time. That's the only way I know how to be.

2 LOG ENTRY #2

I'M REALLY DOWN ON MYSELF BECAUSE ALL I WANTED TO DO WAS DRIVE TO THE store, and I can't. I'm exhausted and anxious while driving. I feel so trapped and caged in my house. I love my house, but it would be nice to be able to come and go as I please, instead of it being a big ordeal. I actually have money for once because I have been saving, and I haven't gambled in 39 days or so.

I don't want to be one of those people who need to hear they are doing a good job all the time. My parents and my educational institutions raised me extremely tough, coupled with what I have survived. Of course, it's really nice to hear that people think I am a good person, but I more enjoy when people say they are enjoying my books or my writings. I don't do all this work for money or praise. I do it because there are men and women and their loved one's struggling with this beast called mental illness, and maybe I can bring them some hope and sunshine. Most of the time, I don't even hear much feedback, and I know I am helping people who don't even really know me. I'm just extremely frustrated right now, and it usually helps for me to write about it.

3 LOG ENTRY #3

I HAD A PRETTY COOL IDEA THIS MORNING. I THINK I'M GOING TO START donating books to libraries across the country so that anyone with a library card can read my story. I think I'm going to start with the really big cities first because that will hopefully result in the biggest reach.

I never thought I'd be an author, and furthermore, I never thought my books would be available in the Cincinnati Public Library. That's a pretty big deal to me. When I studied psychology in college, my plans were to go on and get a doctorate/Ph.D. I ran out of money and motivation, so I never accomplished that. I wish The University of Dayton would award me an honorary doctorate like several universities have done for many celebrities, including Bill Cosby, who turned out to be an unsavory character. Maybe I should just go back to school. Anyway, the whole point of this post is to remind people that many of your plans aren't going to work out, but maybe something even better will happen that you never even thought about. It feels good to give up control, and let the universe and the Fates guide your life. Trying to control everything creates a lot of stress, worry, and anxiety.

4 LOG ENTRY #4

THIS MIGHT BE LONG WINDED, BUT IT'S IMPORTANT. I HAVE RARELY HAD TO DO this, but I called my case manager for help today regarding my mental health. Part of self care is being self aware when I need help. I needed to talk to a professional today. I've had a lot of stress in the last few months, and a lot of major changes. I have been irritable, tired, sore, anxious, manic, and depressed more than usual. I can't stress enough how frustrating and exhausting the rollercoaster ride is. I called for help because I noticed my symptoms were more frequent and more severe than usual. I am asking you all to seek help if you aren't feeling mentally healthy, or even if you just feel a little off. You can always reach out to me at johnmedl7@gmail.com, or call the crisis line (even if you are not suicidal) at 1-800-273-8255 or text HOME to 741741. Don't be ashamed to ask for help, and don't ever let people make you feel like less of a person if you do need help. I am going to try to take it easy for the next few weeks, and I know I will get enjoyment from distributing my books and people visiting.

5 LOG ENTRY #5

THE OTHER DAY, A GUY WAS USING LEAVES FROM A TREE TO WIPE HIMSELF AND acting strangely. Just now, another guy was walking down the street yelling at cars and every other word was the N word. There's a bus stop near my house, and I can only assume both guys were from the bus stop. I had never seen them in the neighborhood before. I didn't call the cops just now, but I did the other day. I wasn't trying to get anyone in trouble, it's just that it appeared both these guys had mental issues. With my personal and professional experience, it's pretty easy to recognize someone who is mentally unstable. It just makes my heart hurt because I've been there. I also wanted to post about it so that my neighborhood friends on social media know. The first guy didn't seem dangerous, but the guy I just saw was very belligerent and agitated. If these guys are indeed mentally unstable, their behavior could get violent and unpredictable.

6 LOG ENTRY #6

I THINK MOST PEOPLE ARE JUST TRYING TO BE HAPPY. WITH THEIR JOBS, LOVE interest, financial situation, whatever. All that stuff is just a means to end. That end is happiness. I guess I just don't understand any other way to be. I've chosen to live a simple life. Some of that is out of necessity, and the cards I've been dealt. I practice gratitude frequently. Despite having bipolar depression, I'm happy more often times than not. I like my coffee and cigarette sessions on the porch, music, reading, sports, and a lot of other inexpensive things. Luxury makes me uncomfortable, but some people chase after that stuff. I can't speak for everyone else, but I'm just trying to be happy. I don't understand the point of all this otherwise.

7 LOG ENTRY #7

AT THE END OF THE DAY, I'M THE ONLY PERSON WHO HAS TO LIVE WITH ME THE rest of my life. I'm not here to please anyone who doesn't appreciate or understand why I do what I do. I listen to the people I am helping. I listen to their heartbreaking life experiences and fantastic triumphs, and every point in between. We all have unique journeys, mental illness or not. I can't fulfill my purpose if I am constantly living in fear of the "what ifs", and if I don't take care of myself first. I can't help others if I don't allow time for myself. This is one of the biggest things I'm always working on.

It's a little overwhelming, actually. My life wasn't supposed to turn out this way, but here we are. I never dreamed that I would be so satisfied with the work that I do. If you are struggling mentally, please reach out. If not to me, to a loved one, or a trusted friend. We all need help sometimes, and it's okay to not be okay. Much love always.

8 LOG ENTRY #8

> "To know even one life has breathed easier because you have lived. This is to have succeeded."
>
> RALPH WALDO EMERSON

I REALLY BELIEVE IN THIS QUOTE, AND IT HELPS ME THROUGH SOME OF MY hardest days. Do me a favor, and I know my close friends will do this for me. Don't let me get a big head about all the attention I get with my books and my work. I would consider that a failure to my purpose almost as much as if I gave up. There's a line that some people cross from confidence to arrogance when they think they are special and don't have to play by the rules anymore. I don't want to be like that. I am a humble servant and merely a vessel towards a purpose. I'm still going to enjoy my life and even be selfish sometimes, but it's not all about me.

SELF MEDICATING

I think my self medicating began after the death of my maternal grandmother. I was a sophomore or junior in high school. That would make the year 1998 or 1999. It may have been the first time I had ever felt an immense loss. Shortly after her passing, I took a whiskey bottle in my room and drank most of it. I had a few beers before, but this was the first time I had really gotten drunk. I remember crying while I was drinking the whiskey. I started drinking alcohol more frequently in high school, and I started to smoke marijuana very heavily. The pot smoking began as a sporadic event, but became a several times a day habit. I experimented with harder drugs, but I don't really think my heavier drug use was self medication.

My alcohol and marijuana use continued for well over a decade. I am sober 99% of the time now, but I still get the urge for a beer or two. I was stoned almost every second of every day for a very long time. I drove my car for a living, so I could only drink alcohol when I wasn't working or driving, although sometimes I would drive while intoxicated. I often smoked marijuana while I drove my car around. I don't know why I didn't care about the law. Maybe it's in the invincibility of youth or the grandeur of bipolar disorder.

I was first hospitalized with bipolar disorder with psychotic features in July 2006. I was 24 years old. Before my first hospitalization, no one really thought about the possibility that I may have mental illness. I was in and out of mania and psychosis for a few weeks prior to my hospitalization, but I wasn't self aware enough or even coherent enough to realize there was something terribly wrong with my behavior.

9 BLOG ENTRY #1

POLICE: HOW I SEE THEM

JOHN MEDL AND JULIE N. STRICKLAND
10/2020

INTRODUCTION (JULIE)

When John Medl offered to guest blog, I jumped at the chance. This website has never been about just Julian. That is, my goal is to help as many people as possible. John has been diagnosed with bipolar disorder and openly advocates for mental health. John was kind enough to write this and answer some follow-up questions, in the hopes of helping others. We are unified in our purpose.

You can read more about John in our previous blog (jnstrickland.com).

ARRESTED (JOHN)

I was arrested during a psychotic episode related to bipolar disorder (No one knew at the time) for trespassing and criminal damaging. I was following coded messages obtained from ordinary objects like lottery tickets and the US Mail to get my reward for uncovering a gang in my neighborhood. I opened the door to an unlocked car and got in the driver's seat. I tried to start the car with a screwdriver. I thought the car was my reward based on these delusional messages I was decoding. I thought I worked for / was helping the CIA, and that there were microphones placed by the government in my house.

I was placed in handcuffs, arrested, and put into the back of the police cruiser. I was non-violent and compliant, even though I was going through mania and psychosis. My conscious mind was gone, and I had no grasp on reality. I was placed in a holding cell with about a dozen other men when we arrived at the police station. Only after I threatened to throw my food tray was I given a phone call and a private cell. I was given a meal of hot dogs, sauerkraut, and white bread. I had to ask for a glass of water. I slept off the mania and psychosis.

I was released in the morning and referred to mental health court as opposed to criminal court. I had an amazing, educated, understanding judge who knew that I needed psychiatric help, and I was not a violent criminal. Because of (now deceased) Judge Stautberg, I have received mostly excellent care since 2006. The verdict in mental health court was not guilty by reason of insanity (NGRI).

I don't really know how much better the police could have handled my situation. I can't recall the officers drawing a weapon of any kind or threatening me. I assume their training told them that I was going to comply, and that I was non-violent, and they were correct. I think I even remember having light, friendly conversation with the officers on the way to the police station. I remember feeling like I was in a taxicab.

I was Caucasian/white, unarmed, friendly, and compliant. I doubt that many mentally unstable people are like this during an arrest. I should also add that I am a man of large stature, both in weight and height, and the police officers still knew I was not a threat. Did their training and education prepare them for a situation like mine? Were they just outstanding police officers? What if they had had a bad day? Would my situation and outcome have been different? The two arresting officers were African American. When you start adding variables to confrontations with the police (weapons, aggression, race, gender, etc.), the danger level rises for everyone involved. The idea is to serve, protect, and preserve life, and at the same time, protect the lives of police officers in deadly/lethal/violent situations. I imagine it's hard to tell the difference between an armed, sane person, and an armed insane person. Is there really a difference to the police officer? A weapon is a weapon, and violence is violence. The police officers have to protect themselves. It's no one's fault when mental health problems are present. It's such a slippery slope.

HOW DO YOU THINK YOUR EXPERIENCE WOULD HAVE BEEN DIFFERENT IF AN AMBULANCE HAD PICKED YOU UP INSTEAD OF THE POLICE?

Going through psychosis like I did is extremely terrifying. I'm not sure if it would have been any less terrifying if an ambulance had picked me up. I remember feeling safe with the police, but again, I had no idea what was going on. I think my experience with the police during psychosis went just about as smoothly as it could have. I know this is not always the case.

SHOULD POLICE BE RESPONSIBLE FOR PICKING UP PEOPLE WHO ARE EXPERIENCING PSYCHOSIS?

Only if they are breaking the law. Police officers' primary job is to enforce the law. If someone going through psychosis is not breaking the law, let's hope that person gets help on their own or has family members that will help him/her. I will say that I think there is an exception where if the person going through psychosis is demonstrating odd or dangerous behavior, then yes, I think it's up to the police to direct that person to the proper resources. This means that police officers need to be trained about mental illness and psychosis. I remember in my psychology classes watching plenty of videos of people with mental illness. Videos like those would help officers identify a nonviolent, mentally unstable person versus someone breaking the law out of his/her own choice.

WOULD HAVING A SOCIAL WORKER PRESENT HELP?

I'm not really sure. You are adding another life to the dangerous situation. I think social workers are trained well enough to handle people during psychosis, but I don't know how the logistics would play out. Would a social worker ride along with the police on every run? It just doesn't seem like it would work out. You might have a situation where a case worker is present during an armed robbery, for example. That doesn't seem very helpful or safe.

When I was hospitalized during mania and psychosis, I was given a very heavy sedative via syringe. I remember being terrified and surrounded by police officers and security guards. I think I remember about a dozen officers, all armed. It's a little blurry. I have no idea how I finally gave in and let the nurse administer the shot. Even in my psychosis, I think I realized I was outnumbered.

ALAN PEAN WAS SHOT WHILE AT A HOSPITAL IN HOUSTON, WHERE HE HAD CHECKED HIMSELF IN. WHAT ARE YOUR THOUGHTS WHEN READING ABOUT HIS EXPERIENCE?

https://www.nytimes.com/2016/02/14/us/hospital-guns-mental-health.html

I think there was definitely a mishandling in the case of Alan Pean. He could have been restrained more peacefully than being shot. Then, he could have received proper psychiatric care, which would probably include a sedative followed by close monitoring or a hospital stay. He showed all the signs of mental instability, and even stated so on several occasions. It was amazing that Alan Pean was self-aware enough to state that he was manic. If someone going through mania and psychosis knows what's going on, the police officers should have listened and taken less violent steps, as I stated previously.

SUMMARY (JULIE)

You are important. You matter.

Email: jules2620@gmail.com
IG: @julie.n.strickland
FB: The Walls Are Breathing (jnstrickland)
Twitter: @JulieNStrick
Website: jnstrickland.com
#CureStigma #NoStigma

10 LOG ENTRY #9

I don't remember much from my days on the couch after I was first released from the hospital. Almost 15 years ago now. All I could do was eat, sleep, and go to the bathroom. My mom would set out a towel and my clothes about once a week for me to take a shower. I took a shower last night. It felt great, and it wasn't really difficult like it used to be. I used to get dizzy and claustrophobic in the shower. It had been a few days.

Personal hygiene is often difficult for people with mental illness. Experts think it's because having a mental illness is just so exhausting that tasks like showering are just too much energy to exert. I can't remember too many visitors in those days on the couch. I can't even tell you how long I was confined to the couch. My mom tells me that she remembers the first joke I made after being released from the hospital. I vaguely remember that, too.

My parents, as much as any doctor, deserve credit for nursing me back to health. This is why and how I can say that I'm blessed. I remember those dark days. I remember those days in my worst days in the present. I don't know how I fought through it, to be honest. Maybe I was just sedated into indifference. When I tell people that I feel blessed, most don't understand how I can say that. Mental illness can be a blessing in disguise sometimes, but in general, it's a severe hindrance. There are all sorts of ranges of severity, but usually it's a major life obstacle. Often times, it is so severe that mental illness is labeled a disability, which is the case for me. Disability does not mean inability. I can do many things well, but I am not well enough to hold down a job or manage my own finances. Some days, I am still very symptomatic.

I just don't know any other way to be. From the way I was raised to my life experiences to all the people who have crossed my path. I'm extremely proud of myself for never giving up and the work that I do. When I help others, it helps me heal too.

11 LOG ENTRY #10

Positive thinking does not come naturally to a lot of us with anxiety and depression. There are times when I can't manage a single positive thought. However, I have been practicing positivity for a long time, like any craft, and I have gotten pretty good at it. But I had to practice. It started with me reading inspirational and motivational quotes. I had to stop watching most TV and the news. I have to take breaks from social media. I am sober almost always. I am 100% medicine compliant.

All of these things that I cut out of my life were feeding my anxiety and depression, like gasoline. I still drink a lot of coffee, which is terrible for my anxiety, but I'm between a rock and a hard place. I take sedatives to keep me calm, which in turn, makes me drowsy and tired. I want to be awake and lively, so I drink coffee to wake myself up. I get hyper only to be sedated again. This is called the vicious cycle of anxiety.

The point I want to make is that you have no chance surviving anxiety and depression if you feed it with triggers. Cut out as many triggers as you can so you have a fighting chance. Then, you can replace the triggers with positivity, gratitude, music, journaling, gardening, whatever gives you relief in a healthy way.

12 LOG ENTRY #11

Mental illness is a deceptive term because it implies that symptoms are only present "in our heads". Of course, mental illness is literally in our heads because that's where our brains are. On average, a person with bipolar disorder lives 9 years less than the average healthy person. Think about what kind of mental and physical trauma "mental illness" can do to the body to cause 9 whole years to be taken from someone's life. Some recurring physical symptoms I have are: stiff joints, chest pains, sweating, itching, and I can't sit still sometimes. These are just a few. Yes, I have mental symptoms like brain fog, repeating/negative thoughts, paranoia, and I've experienced psychosis, which is a total break from reality several times. I just want to point out that mental illness is not just a mental illness, if that makes sense.

13 LOG ENTRY #12

I'm feeling a little extra blessed today. I had to have a major truck repair, and I went without a car for almost two weeks. My truck is fixed now, and I drove myself, unmedicated, to the gas station. It was so nice. I am going to try to work on my driving skills so I can get out of my house more. I've gone 74 days now without gambling even a penny, so I actually have a little money in my pocket. I was able to read a few chapters in the book I'm reading for the first time in months. My symptoms have been fairly calm today, and I don't have to do any major work until I get my next shipment of books in about two weeks. I'm going to try to help around the house a little more and maybe cook dinner a night or two. My birthday is on October 22nd, and I'm looking forward to celebrating with a few friends and my family. Birthdays are a big deal to me ever since I got sick because I feel so lucky to still be alive. I thought I was a goner so many times. I also feel like it's a middle finger to my illness when I survive another year.

14 LOG ENTRY #13

It's a weird feeling to think that so many people are interested in my writings. Writing is second nature to me and also a coping mechanism for my illness, so it's almost like if people wanted to watch me breathe. I thought by now I would be a millionaire doing what millionaires do. Maybe real estate or something. I chased that dream for a long time, then one day, I realized I didn't want that lifestyle. I was literally killing myself, physically and mentally, to try to outdo other people and acquire wealth. I thought the whole point in life was to become rich.

Then I started doing advocacy work and writing books. It's more rewarding than I ever thought any career could be. I'm just not money motivated anymore. I'm not willing to risk my health and happiness for it. I guess I thought I couldn't be happy without a lot of money.

15 POEM ENTRY #1

I'm a dimly lit candle
Among the fires burning inside me.
I'm my biggest hero and harshest critic.
I commiserate with the sick
And plead to the cynics.
Everyone has made up their minds.
And I'm just an hourglass
Waiting for the sands of time.

16 LOG ENTRY #14

I HAD AN ENGLISH TEACHER IN HIGH SCHOOL NAMED MS. PHOEBUS. SHE USED TO call me Johnny Swagger. I always liked the nickname, although people usually just call me Medl, even to this day. I guess I could be cocky at times in high school. I have no idea what I had to be so cocky about. Looking back, I was such a fool, at least to compared to how much I have learned since then. I believe I'm a good person and a talented writer and many other great qualities, but I still lack confidence. Sometimes I wonder if this is why I have social anxiety sometimes, even around my closest of friends. My hunch is that is another chemical failure in my brain. I am looking for a more quiet confidence now, and I have to work on that. Some days, I think I want my high school swagger back, but then I remember how young and foolish I was. I guess I am looking for a confidence level somewhere between outrageously cocky and a nervous wreck.

17 LOG ENTRY #15

When I say that I'm blessed, I don't necessarily mean that in a religious way, although it doesn't bother me if someone interprets it that way. I mean it in a superlative way. I think the word blessed is just as about as complimentary as I can get with my life. Charmed is a little too dramatic for me, but it's the same idea. A lot of people, after hearing my story, don't understand how I can say that I'm blessed. First of all, I'm alive, which is amazing in itself, and secondly, I have everything I need. I also get to write and advocate for the sick for a living. It's very rewarding work. That's just how I feel about my life.

I want to show people that someone can have a mental illness and not be crazy, in the generic sense of the word. I actually hate that word and label, and I try to avoid using it whenever I can. My brain is sick, just like a person who has cancer or diabetes. I take medication for it. Most of the time, the pills work. Sometimes, the medication is not enough, and I have to rely on coping skills and experience. I'm not comparing hardships, but I'm trying to point out that mental illness is still an illness, even though it is mostly invisible. My symptoms can be very visible, and only my close friends and family have seen me symptomatic. Aside from professionals, of course.

18 LOG ENTRY #16

THINGS I FIND ANNOYING

1. Infatuation with politics and politicians. Do you really think most of them give a damn about common people? Some people act like politicians are their friends or family or something. Super annoying.
2. Most people don't think that people on disability or food assistance deserve it. A lot of people think it's some kind of free ride where everyone is living the high life on $38 a month (that's what I get in food stamps). It also took me 7 years to get approved for disability. The government doesn't just hand it out like free samples at the grocery.
3. Most people have no clue how painful mental illness is. Physically, mentally, emotionally, etc. I try to educate people the best I can, but only so many people read my books or social media posts. Only my parents see me curled up in bed in pain on a fairly regular basis. I don't talk about my struggles as much as my victories because I don't want sympathy. Save that for the hungry and homeless who are going to be sleeping outside this Winter.

19 LOG ENTRY #17

I HAD A LITTLE ROUGH PATCH TONIGHT. NOTHING TERRIBLE. ANXIETY AND mania. I always tell myself, "it wasn't that bad". But it is. It's hard for me to remember life and how I felt before symptoms and medication. And I know this sounds irrational, but I don't know if I would want to be cured if there was one. I've gained so much.

20 POEM ENTRY #2

11-4-2020

When the blissful moments
Are fleeting, hold on
With everything you have.
These are the moments
That make up our best memories.
Maybe the afterlife is just
Reliving precious moments over
And over again.
Or maybe we'll get another chance
To spin the wheel again
To correct the wrongs of the evil
And maybe good will prevails next time.

21 LOG ENTRY #18

Kindness helps me make sense of life. I would like to think I've always been kind, but my desire to be kind has gotten stronger since I have been ill. I think I like the way kindness makes me feel, and in a way, I'm just giving back to the universe for all the kindness I have been shown. Maybe I like the way my kindness makes others feel. It definitely benefits me in a therapeutic way.

22 LOG ENTRY #19

WHEN I HAVE A NEGATIVE EMOTION OR ADVERSE REACTION TO SOMETHING, I wonder if my emotions fall into the range of a normal, prudent person (because of my illness). I dislike the term normal, but I am only using it here to differentiate from abnormal. I think feelings and reactions are always on a spectrum. I could have irritability or anxiety or intense sadness, and many other emotions that come along with having mental illness. Am I being irrotational? Are my feelings still valid even though they are fueled by an abnormal brain? I think my feelings are valid even when I am being irrational because those are the emotions I am feeling in reality. Most of the time, an explanation and apology diffuse any tension between myself and other people. When I am very upset, I try to isolate myself so that I do not bring others down into my upset mood. This is not always possible. Being open and honest about my emotions really helps. I think the key is recognizing when I may be irritated or depressed or anxious. When I am self-aware, I can deal with emotional situations in a more reasonable manner. It's frustrating to realize that it's me who is the offender in an emotional situation. I guess everyone wants to be perfect. Maybe I have high standards, or maybe I know, deep down, that I am a kind. loving person. My illness makes me act out of character. I am not my illness. I know this because I act a certain way when I am stable, which is the majority of the time. Since emotional outbursts are sporadic, I know that it is my illness taking over and causing me to act in a negative way.

23 LOG ENTRY #20

THE OTHER DAY I SAID TO MY CASE MANAGER, "MY PARENTS RAISED A MONSTER". Probably unsettling to hear as a case manager from someone who has had problems with delusions and grandiosity. All I meant is that my parents put high standards on me, and showed by example, never to quit. I've quit things before, but I was referring to my life and recovery. Quitting is not going to happen. It's not an option at all. I've endured some of the most horrible pain that a human can bear. I'm not quitting now when life isn't so bad for me. I didn't endure everything I did to not enjoy the sunshine on the other side.

24 LOG ENTRY #21

MONTH 11 OF THE PANDEMIC YEAR 2020

I'M STARTING TO FEEL BAD FOR PEOPLE WHO AREN'T USED TO ISOLATION LIKE I am. Aside from employment issues. I'm just referring to having a social life and traveling and basically "normal" people being able to come and go freely. My anxiety has isolated me for a long time, and it's just weird to see normally functioning people getting a taste of my life. I wouldn't wish it on anyone.

25 LOG ENTRY #22

Time is a weird thing. In my younger years, I would go on weekend long party binges that seemed to only last a few minutes. I felt like I had all the time in the world, and it's up for debate whether it was wasted time. Then, I'd do it all over again the next weekend. Now, I get symptomatic, and minutes and seconds feel like hours. I value time more now, and I think that comes with maturity and gratitude.

26 LOG ENTRY #23

Human beings are a lot like computers. What you put in is what you get out. If you are surrounded by negativity and stress, you aren't going to have a positive outcome. It's impossible to eliminate every bit of negativity in life, so it's almost like damage control. When you surround yourself with negativity and digest it and other stressors, you have no chance against anxiety, depression, and other mental illness.

27 LOG ENTRY #24

THESE WERE REAL FEELINGS I HAD LAST NIGHT....I WAS VERY DEPRESSED, negative, and stressed out. The local and national news were on the TV almost all day in my house, and I skipped a meal. Are these feelings valid or was I symptomatic, or both? Here was my social media post from last night.

NOVEMBER 20, 2020

I'm not feeling like my normal happy self. Please pray for me. It doesn't pay to be kind. I've been beaten and tortured and I've taken it with a fucking smile, no less. People treat me like shit and don't respect my work because they know I won't fight back.

28 LOG ENTRY #25

Weird day today. I just can't stay awake. Aside from being sober 99% of the time, my method to stay somewhat stable is my medication and sleep schedule. It's completely out of whack today, but I'm stable and in a good mood. I think I finally hit a wall where I just need to rest. I thought I was going to have some time off, but more books are coming Friday. Oh well, good problem to have, and I have more good days than bad, so I don't think I can ask for more. I treated myself to some really expensive coffee, so I'm just enjoying that and a cold, rainy day in Ohio.

29 POEM ENTRY #3

The smoke and ash
Fill my lungs
And that seems to help for some reason
Until next time.
I'm in a hurry to go nowhere
And I don't know what to do
With my shivering body.
More smoke and ash.
And everyone wants money
But I don't really care
I watch a cloud come from my lips
And fill the air
I hope people hate me for who I am
Because they don't occupy my thoughts
Not even for a minute
I have more important things to do
But for right now, I will eat
And rest again
So I can continue at a later time.

12-2-2020

30 LOG ENTRY #26

THIS WAS AROUND 2004. THE YEAR I GRADUATED FROM COLLEGE. I WAS WORKING at a pizza place, but I also had a third shift job at a gas station near my apartment. I heard there was a meeting for potential candidates to be manager the next day about a 45 minute drive away. I had made my mind up I was going to be a great manager at this gas station. I had run out of plans, money, and energy for going to graduate school, and I had no idea what to do with a degree in psychology. I worked a full third shift and drove myself to the meeting for potential managers. I had to fight to stay awake both while I was driving and at the meeting. At the meeting, I was standing up straight and drinking coffee to stay awake. I was just determined to be a manager at this gas station. It didn't end up working out, but I put a lot of effort into this idea I had. That's how I've always been. If I believe in something, I give 110% with no regard for my health or psychological well-being.

This is why I display my degree in my bedroom almost 20 years later. The amount of effort I put into getting my degree while fighting a psychotic breakdown is really something to be admired. I'm extremely proud of myself for graduating.

31 LOG ENTRY #27

THE TITLE OF MY PREVIOUS BOOK IS "THE ENTROPY OF BIPOLAR DISORDER". AN Internet troll accused me of using the word entropy because I was trying to sound smarter than I am. Anyone who has taken a basic science course knows what entropy means. I just always think of it as randomness, like how atoms move around in a cell. I used the word entropy because at first, mental illness symptoms can feel very random, and also my book was just a collection of random thoughts and entries, so I thought the word entropy was appropriate. In one of my previous books, I remember saying to my readers, "Be prepared to feel weird sometimes". The symptoms of mental illness and the subsequent medications are not perfect solutions. The ultimate goal is stability as an overall condition, but it just doesn't always work out that way. I am probably considered stable by my doctor, but I still have to fight through symptoms sometimes. These symptoms can be mental or physical. Eventually, you have a mental list of symptoms that you just get used to. So when you have these familiar symptoms, you don't panic or worry anymore. It's just par for the course. I've learned that my symptoms virtually disappear after a nap, so I know if I can bear it long enough to sleep, I will get relief. (My sleep schedule is also closely related to my medication times, so I know the medication does its job as well.)

32 POEM ENTRY #4

With quivering hands
I jot down a few words
Unwavering strength
And goodness of heart
"I have not yet begun to fight"
Another restless night
But yet I still hope and dream
With optimism and enthusiasm
A life charmed in many ways
I have surpassed my predicted days
I don't have another life left
In my old, cold bones
I don't have the luxury of tomorrow
My joy overpowers the sorrow
Another day in the books
Another notch in my belt
What a wonderful victory it will be.

12-10-20

33 LOG ENTRY #28

I just drove myself to get some gas for my truck. It felt like such an accomplishment, and it is for me. I was just thinking back to how bad I've felt in the past. When I had my psychotic breakdown in 2006, it felt like I was going to die, (although I didn't really know what was going on at the time). Before I knew what a panic attack felt like, it felt like I was going to die when I had one. I was so overweight that I couldn't even stand at the stove and cook myself food. My feet were so swollen that I couldn't wear gym shoes. I have absolutely earned the right to be grateful for all the little things and all the small victories I accomplish, like just driving a short distance to get gas for my truck. Being grateful for otherwise small things to other people not only feels good psychologically, but it's the best solution I could come up with from dealing with extreme symptoms and difficulties. It's not my nature to give up or feel sorry for myself, but I had to discover that on my journey. So many good things in my life would have never happened if I had given up.

34 LOG ENTRY #29

I LIVE FOR THE HIGHS AND DREAD THE LOWS. I'M TIRED AT NOON AND WIDE awake at midnight. I have to give myself a pep talk to get out of bed. Intense anger, and then apathy and indifference. Different feelings and emotions at unpredictable, differing times of day. I handle it well with medication and support. Sometimes I can drive a car, and sometimes I can't, and I still haven't figured out what it depends on. It seems like I've tried everything. It's hard for me to imagine life any other way. Still fighting almost 15 years later.

35 LOG ENTRY #30

I'M NOT MONEY MOTIVATED. A COMFORTABLE, TEN YEAR OLD JACKET IS JUST AS good to me as a brand new one. I don't care about status, and I know that life isn't about acquiring as much "stuff" as possible. The only reason I buy "stuff" is because it brings me joy and happiness, which is way more important to me than the actual "stuff", if that makes sense.

I used to practice my signature/autograph in grade school because I thought I might be a professional baseball player some day. I think a lot of kids probably did that. I never thought I would be signing books. I wouldn't mind being famous for my writing because I've worked so hard and been through so much, but money is low on my list of things that are important to me.

I don't have the luxury of tomorrow. I don't even understand what tomorrow means anymore. I write as much as I can because I don't know if there will be a tomorrow. It's almost an act of desperation that has diminished over time since I was first hospitalized. It's getting better. I think about the future a lot more often than I used to.

36 LOG ENTRY #31

In the morning, sometimes coffee is not enough to wake me up, and other times, I cook a few meals for my family for the week. Maybe bake some cookies or brownies. Some days, it feels like the best day of my life, a gift from above. I have a song or two repeating in my head that's been playing for at least a month. I have to lie down in the dark and play games on my phone or listen to other songs. Maybe roll some cigarettes or look through my sports card collection. I go from being fatigued to wound tight with a lot of energy throughout the day. I try to adjust my work and activities accordingly. At night, I'm so happy to be alone and have a nice bedroom all to myself, and then I feel fear and loneliness that no one is with me. I think of all the people I miss. Then I read or watch a sporting event. Eventually, I drift off to sleep, and it starts all over again. I don't have any regrets, and I don't want to be anyone else. Not even for a day. This is my life, and I'm proud of it. Imperfections, struggles, and all.

37 LOG ENTRY #32

I REMEMBER A LONG TIME AGO GETTING FINISHED WITH WORKING A LONG DAY, and that amazing feeling of collapsing on the couch and cracking open a nice cold beer. I still chase that feeling because I don't work a traditional job anymore. The difference between working at a pizza place and helping people with mental health is that now, I have no set hours and my work seems to never be finished. That part about what I do is frustrating, but it's very rewarding. It took me 7 years to get approved for disability, and I am grateful for it, but I also feel like I should work for it somehow. That's just how I was raised. Major credit to my mom for helping me get approved for disability because I wanted to quit trying many times. It was a lot to handle with all the red tape and lawyers and such.

One day, my mom took my entire case files with all my medical records with a picture of me to the disability office. She physically drove herself there, and hand delivered all my information. Shortly after, I was approved. It was a miracle for myself and my family. There were times when I wasn't an author and advocate, and I couldn't do much to work for my disability payments. I am able to put in some very rewarding work now, and I'm not going to stop talking about mental health and trying to help others. The only thing I need to watch out for, which I fail at sometimes, is setting limits to relax to protect my own mental health. I don't have all the answers, but I have some. I am struggling along with my readers and others who need help at the same time.

38 LOG ENTRY #33

I don't know if I will ever get used to being a writer and author. The idea that people are paying hard earned money for my words and experiences is surreal to me. The more surreal part is that none of this was planned. Probably a teachable moment here. I took some writing classes in college, but I was supposed to be a Doctor of Psychology, not a writer. When I was first hospitalized in 2006, I couldn't have even dreamed that my life would turn out this way. I didn't even know if I was going to survive, much less make anything significant out of my future. I have such a grateful attitude now, but it developed. I wasn't born with it. I had to struggle to obtain it. Of course, my nature allows me to feel extremes, and I guess I just feel extremely grateful sometimes, which isn't such a bad thing.

39 LOG ENTRY #34

I WANT TO BE LIKE ANDY DUFRESNE PLAYED BY TIM ROBBINS IN THE Shawshank Redemption. The scene I am thinking of is when Andy negotiates with the prison guards to do their taxes in exchange for some cold beers for his friends on a hot day while they are putting hot tar on a roof. I know from my brother that this is a very difficult, hot job. How awesome of a gesture is that? Andy doesn't even drink a beer for himself. He just sits there basking in the glory of generosity and kindness. What a feeling.

40 LOG ENTRY #35

3 THINGS

1. Count your blessings when you feel terrible. This will make you shift your mind to the positive things in your life and help you endure the pain.
2. The world won't treat you better because you're a good person. Accepting this fact will help you deal with unfortunate situations better.
3. Almost always be kind! Not only does it make you feel better emotionally, it makes others feel good, too. Being kind can relieve symptoms of depression and even lower your blood pressure!

41 LOG ENTRY #36

Less news. More positive vibes. What do I know? I just have a degree in psychology and 15 years experience living with anxiety and depression. Wrote 4 books about it. I don't know why this is so hard for people to understand. If you ingest negativity, it's really hard to be happy, healthy, and positive.

42 LOG ENTRY #37

I'VE TRIED TO EXPLAIN THIS BEFORE, BUT I'LL TRY AGAIN. I HAD A VERY SIMPLE task to do. Clean the kitchen. It ended up taking me 5 minutes in the end, but psychologically, it seemed like an impossible task because my symptoms are wearing me out today. MENTAL ILLNESS IS EXHAUSTING. Another classic example is taking a shower and personal hygiene type things. I feel like I conquered a mountain after cleaning the kitchen.

43 LOG ENTRY #38

This was a social media post directed at my friends....

Some of you have seen me at almost every stage of my illness—manic, depressed, anxious, intoxicated, reckless, etc. I wouldn't trade my wild days for anything. I'm glad I lived wildly while I could. Those memories help me get through the hardest of days. We were lucky to have survived, first of all, but we were luckier to have each other and understand friendship love at an early age. It's embarrassing for me for my friends to see me when I'm unwell. It's embarrassing that I can't control my mind and body sometimes. I'm less embarrassed around my family, who have supported me the whole way. I do weird things like having to lay in my bed during gatherings, and I just baked cookies at 2am because I was so hyper. It's nothing super weird, I guess. It's just that I have to filter my energy into something productive rather than vices and self medicating.

44 LOG ENTRY #39

I had a weird experience today. I haven't been sleeping well, and I think it finally caught up to me. I was exhausted, and even the smallest task felt overwhelming. I think that's one reason why my illness is a disability. I had to completely pause my life to simply rest. It wouldn't have mattered if I had work to do or something super fun. I had to rest. Disability does not mean inability, however. I do many things well and at a high level. It's just that somewhat frequently, my illness tells me to slow down, whether it be exhaustion or anxiety or a panic attack.

45 LOG ENTRY #40

Maybe I did have a drinking and smoking problem. Maybe I still do. I think about it every day. I also think about the hospital every day almost 15 years later. Maybe I just think too much, and my medication has wired my brain differently. Maybe I changed. If I had a few drinks and a smoke, nothing bad would probably happen. Maybe I don't want to risk the small chance that I have a panic attack or something of that nature. I could get away with it. Everyone who loves me would understand and forgive me. Maybe I'm content with my life now. No additives needed anymore.

46 LOG ENTRY #41

Social media can be a very valuable resource for mental health. I think it's great when people say, "Hey, I'm depressed. Show me some happy pictures." Or "Hey, I could use some encouragement today." Depression is complicated. Sometimes, it seems like there's nothing I can do to cheer up. We've all seen that depression and mental illness can be so painful that people are desperate to end the pain, and they do so in a variety of ways. I founded and created a support page that has about 900 members from all over the world. I try to make at least one post a day. I've been doing this for about 9 years now. Conversely, social media can be detrimental to mental health, but I wanted to talk about the positives for now. You are not alone. I'm struggling right along with you some days, even though it's been 15 years since I was diagnosed. If you needed a sign to keep fighting, this is it.

47 LOG ENTRY #42

I gush about my mom sometimes, and if I talk about my dad, it's usually something weird or annoying. I really do appreciate my dad and all his hard work. He has always been the provider and disciplinarian. Emotions and conversations are not his strengths. I'm developing more patience with my parents. We're almost 2 generations apart, after all. All 3 of us have our own way of doing things. I just don't want to give off the wrong impression about my feelings towards my dad. I love both my parents with my whole heart, and I do my best to make sure they're happy and enjoying their Golden Years.

48 LOG ENTRY #43

I was irritable at times today, and I don't know if my parents even noticed because I try to avoid people as much as possible when I am like that. It's very frustrating because I consider myself a very loving person.

49 LOG ENTRY #44

WHEN I WAS YOUNGER, MY DAD USED TO MAKE ME BREAKFAST BEFORE MASS. That's how it was for a long time. Times were so much simpler. It seems like everyone was happier, too. A part of me misses those days, but I would never go back. On a certain Sunday morning when I was about 15 years old, I refused to get out of bed to go to Mass. I think I was just burned out. I had been going to Mass my whole life, plus Catholic schooling. I'd like to attend Mass one of these days. I am too weak and anxious to go right now. I'm not big on organized religion, but it's comforting to be in a place of prayer.

50 LOG ENTRY #45

IN THE MIDDLE OF THE GLOBAL PANDEMIC. JANUARY 29,2021....

One positive thing about the pandemic is that the general population is realizing how important mental health is. I wish it didn't have to happen this way, but any publicity is good publicity, as they say. Mental health can affect so many things—sleep disturbances, general mood, drug and alcohol abuse, other risky behavior, impulsive and compulsive behavior, and suicide as a final consequence.

51 LOG ENTRY #46

My life has been a lot like riding a rollercoaster, and I don't necessarily mean in the generic, cliché way of the ups and downs of bipolar disorder and anxiety. When I was younger, I was full of excitement and ambition, like when you are waiting in line for a rollercoaster. Then, I started the ride, and I felt the thrill and terror of the first hill. I think of that as my first psychotic break in 2006. During the ride, eventually, you get tired of being jostled around and just want the ride to stop. You are satisfied with the short amount of excitement, and now you are ready to calm down and talk about how much fun you had. But bipolar disorder and anxiety is a rollercoaster that never really stops. Bipolar disorder is a genetic, lifelong illness. I will die with it, unless there's a cure in the future. Sometimes, I wonder if I would even take the cure if it was available. Bipolar disorder does not define who I am, but it is certainly a part of my personality.

52 POEM ENTRY #5

The phone is ringing off the hook,
The television is spouting the same bad news.
So I step outside to enjoy my coffee and a smoke.
I'm not thinking about much
Except how beautiful the snow is on
Another gray day in Ohio.
The closeness of Spring is keeping me going.
I can't wait to feel the warmth and sunshine.
Better days are coming.

53 LOG ENTRY #47

I'VE BEEN IRRITABLE MORE THAN USUAL THE LAST FEW WEEKS, AND I DON'T KNOW if it's from being so isolated or the nature of bipolar disorder, or both. In psychology, the answer is usually both or all of the above. I wonder how much my parents notice since I live with them. All that aside, today has been pretty good. I had some trouble sleeping last night, but I rested a lot today. I have a few offers for people to help me dictate my books into audiobooks. I am very close to reaching a deal with someone, and I'm excited about how that new medium is going to work out. My hopes are always to reach as many people as possible.

54 LOG ENTRY #48

I'm not a religious person, and I rarely pray, but I prayed today. I hadn't planned on it. It just felt like the right thing to do. It was a prayer of thanks for everything I have, and a prayer of hope for better tomorrows. If only for a few moments, I felt a sense of calm. I would never claim to know if everything's going to be okay, but in those few moments, it felt like it.

55 LOG ENTRY #49

I completed my first podcast interview the other day, right about this time of day. I didn't tell the host this, but it was exactly when I was due for my 4:30 PM medication. For audio reasons, I couldn't talk on my phone with speaker phone so I had to hold the phone up to my ear. I was pretty wound up because my medicine hadn't started working yet, so I stood almost the whole hour duration of the interview. We spoke about a lot of painful things for me to remember. I know it seems like I talk about everything, but there's some things I don't mention very often, and I would rather forget. When the interview was finished, I felt like I had just been through a boxing match, and I had to lay down. The interview should be available soon, and hopefully I can sell some books and further help more people.

56 LOG ENTRY #50

I have some very fond memories of Dayton, Ohio. I miss my friends I made there. I miss the comforting campus of The University of Dayton. Maybe it was just a better time in my life, although I'm pretty content now. There was a bar called Tailgators near my apartment, where I started to sing karaoke as soon as I was old enough to drink in a bar. I've been singing ever since. I always tell people to sing even if they think they suck at it. It's therapeutic and builds confidence.

57 LOG ENTRY #51

Here are some things I've been thinking about. I'm just going to let it fly. Due to the nature of bipolar disorder, I feel extreme highs and extreme lows. The highs can feel euphoric (amazing) or dysphoric (agitated), and eventually, there is a depressing crash. Every time. I'm laying in bed in a relaxed state thinking about how much I love to watch it snow with a cup of coffee and a smoke. I'm thinking about how lucky I am to be alive. I'm wondering why I'm still here. I've done enough work. I've never done anyone wrong intentionally, and if I have, I think I've made up for it. I'm at peace with my past, and I'm at peace with what I've contributed to society. Mental illness will probably always need advocacy, unless experts start discovering cures. I imagine scientists are more concerned with diseases like cancer. I don't have to worry about necessities or caring for my children. I've always believed that I survived because I had a mission and purpose, so I guess the higher forces aren't finished with me yet. I think what I'm trying to say is that my spirit is at peace for when my work is finished. I'm good. I'm lucky to be alive, and I'm blessed.

58 LOG ENTRY #52

Almost every day, I promote my books. One way I do this is making an ad in author support groups and mental illness groups. I offer my books for free in an email with the hope that people will donate to my Venmo, cash app, etc. Yesterday I made such a post, and almost 700 people responded. I only made $35 in donations. It's just a little frustrating. I've had much better luck on other days. I keep sending emails because I always think of the people who are struggling who might not be able to afford my books or have access. Just because I can't save everyone doesn't mean I shouldn't try.

59 LOG ENTRY #53

I have a new psychiatrist, and our first appointment was today. He's very professional and thorough. Not very friendly, and he kept interrupting me. Not terrible though. I'm learning that it's easier to write out my thoughts than verbalize them. He's putting me on a new medication called gabapentin. It helps treat chronic pain, anxiety, and seizures. I'm excited to try something new as I have been on the same cocktail for almost 10 years. I figured out that my irritability comes from being in physical pain, so I hope this new medication helps. The other 3 medications I take are Invega, Trileptal, and Klonopin. I ended up discontinuing the Gabapenten because it was making me tired and depressed. I take Naproxen 3 times a day now for pain, and it's working.

60 LOG ENTRY #54

My college experience was different from most students at The University of Dayton. My freshmen year, I lived in the dorms, and I didn't need to have an outside job. Starting sophomore year, I decided to have my own apartment off campus and work full time while attending classes full time. I had an almost around-the-clock schedule until I graduated in 2004. I have always had an uncanny ability to retain information the first time, and it has always served me well. I used to wear my work uniform to class when I did attend class to save time. Many of my professors were lenient with my physical attendance, which I truly appreciate. I don't think I'm smarter or better than anyone else, but I worked my tail off to earn my degree, and I'm a proud graduate.

61 LOG ENTRY #55

One thing I've always found interesting about being diagnosed with a mental illness is the delineation between personality and my disorders. Where does my personality begin and where does my disorder begin? In the end, it doesn't matter because the end result is the person I am. However, there are things I can try to do to help alleviate my symptoms, which may change my personality. They are far from mutually exclusive. Hopefully, that makes sense. Someone who is in pain all the time may not always have a sunny disposition.

I started a medication a few days ago called Gabapenten, also known as Neurotin. Its primary purpose is to relieve nerve pain, but also has qualities of reliving anxiety. I am noticing a small difference in my pain level, which has affected my disposition from irritated frequently to irritated slightly. It's not a perfect solution, and there are no magic pills, but I think I will continue this medication.

I'm a believer in science and mental illness. I've experienced a wide range of symptoms for almost 15 years now.

When I was first diagnosed, I was the most depressed I've ever been in my life. I was a zombie from the sedatives. It was a few years before I could even think about trying to function again. I started by reading inspirational, motivational, spiritual, and philosophical quotes and sayings. I started to feel a little better. I started to gradually incorporate chores and "normal" daily activities into my life. I was even able to return to work full time. I try to keep a positive attitude now above almost anything else. It's important to me. The reason I'm mentioning this is I want to tell people that you may have more choice to be happy than you think. There's an amazing quote that talks about having no chance to be happy if you surround yourself with negativity. It's absolutely true. It's just hard to figure out if it's clinical depression/chemical imbalance, or something that can be solved with positive action.

62 LOG ENTRY #56

I WAS TALKING TO MY MOM ABOUT GETTING OLDER. I'M GOING TO BE 40 YEARS old in October, which is shocking to a lot of people besides myself. The neighborhood and friends of my family have watched me grow up. I was telling my mom about the fun my friends and I used to have, mainly at music festivals. Those were some good times. A lot of us were wannabe hippies, but maybe we were all just old souls. By my age, a lot of people have families of their own, and I don't see that happening for me. Times were so much different when I was a teenager. No social media. Not many people had cell phones. You had to buy a disposable camera and have pictures developed. The music scene was some of the best times of my life. When I'm having a rough day, I try to remember all the good times we had, and it helps. Anyway, I hope the next generation still has some old souls and doesn't let the world get to them too much.

63 LOG ENTRY #57

FEBRUARY 23, 2021

IN THE MIDDLE OF A GLOBAL PANDEMIC. APPROXIMATELY 11% OF THE POPULATION IS VACCINATED.

I've been fighting this brain illness officially for almost 15 years. Even still, I have to go back to the basics of what got me to this point in my recovery. I just had an episode where I was anxious and physically sore to the point where I had to lie down and let my medication work. I managed to shave my face and send some emails. That might be all I can do today, and even now, the day will have been a success. I have to protect and take care of myself even though I'm high functioning. If I forget to take care of myself, my brain and body remind me. I'm hoping I feel better after lunch and a nap. Having symptomatic episodes is always very humbling. And yes, a little discouraging and depressing, but I'm still here fighting and the sun is out. I'm taking a break for a few hours, and hopefully I will have recovered.

64 LOG ENTRY #58

Yesterday was one of the worst days I've had in a very long time. My whole body hurt, including my chest from anxiety, which is very unsettling if you've ever experienced it. I was symptomatic nearly all day, and I went 18 hours without a bite to eat. So much pain. Resiliency matters, and I wish I could bottle it up. I have no idea how I have gotten this far. My mind was racing out of control, and I felt like I might lose my mind. But I didn't, and the sun still rose this morning, just like every day. Almost everyone is experiencing trauma right now and getting a taste of what mental illness and isolation are like. I'm asking you to go to that place in your heart where you usually don't go because it's terrifying, and fight like Hell. We need as many good people in good health as possible right now and in the future. I have to protect my own mental health, but you can reach out to me if you are struggling, and I will do my best to help you. Whatever you do with your life, don't forget love and do it with love.

65 LOG ENTRY #59

I FEEL PRETTY STABLE TODAY FOR THE FIRST TIME IN A FEW DAYS. I THINK THE NEW medication I tried is out of my system. I had high hopes that Neurotin was going to solve all my problems, so I'm a little disappointed. It was the first new medication for me in about 9 years. I don't really like my new psychiatrist, but we've only had one appointment, and I'm not giving up on him yet.

I think what happened was I got off schedule a few days ago, and I was in physical pain from anxiety. If I get off schedule, my OCD runs wild and causes extreme anxiety to the point of physical pain.

I hate structure, but I need it to stay stable. I take it very seriously. Stable is not fun. Mania is fun. Getting wasted is fun. Even a small deviation can cause all sorts of problems, from mania to depression to anxiety to physical pain. I have to monitor my meal times, how much I eat, medication times, and times when I need to rest. I even monitor how much coffee I drink. It seems like when I'm not as careful about monitoring my illness is when I struggle the most, which seems obvious, but having structure in my life is not enjoyable. I don't feel like a free person sometimes. Not being able to drive when and where I want compounds that.

I was overwhelmed with things I wanted to improve in my life. I had one bad day, and I was questioning everything I've ever done. A spiral (mostly downward) is definitely a good representation of how mental illness can take hold of a person. I'm so worried about improving that I don't stop to enjoy everything I've accomplished.

I used to worry what people will think of me after I leave the Earth, but I'm starting to care less and less. Not because I don't really care, but because I've proven myself, time and time again. If people don't think of me in a positive light by now, I don't know what else I could possibly do.

AFTERWORD

In conclusion, it's important to remember all the great things your brain can do when you are symptomatic, or at least after the symptoms have gone away. I love so many people with a deep love that I don't know if other people feel love so deeply. I'm intelligent. My brain can hold incredible amounts of information, and I like to think of myself as a deep thinker, capable of complex emotions. Unfortunately, overthinking is a by-product of having a complex brain. I've shared my story with everyone who will listen, and I know I have inspired people. Probably saved a few lives. There's no better feeling for me than helping others to that degree. It makes me feel like I have a higher purpose, and maybe my life and my own desires are smaller than the picture I have painted. If you have mental illness, build yourself up every chance you get because mental illness will beat you down. It's not bragging at that point. It's self-preservation.

MAKING BIPOLAR LEMONADE

RANDOM OBSERVATIONS FROM MY BIPOLAR LIFE

1 ENTRY 1

Bipolar disorder is a disease of extremes. It's a genetic magnifying glass. I feel joy and depression intensely, and I'm lucky that I'm more likely to be manic than depressed, but mania is extremely dangerous too. I also have noticed that I'm more likely to have euphoric mania as opposed to dysphoric mania, the former extremely enjoyable, and the latter as extremely unenjoyable. Before I was hospitalized and diagnosed in 2006, I didn't have the appreciation for simpler things that I do now. I'm not going to go so far as to say that I took life for granted, but I was rather reckless at times. Perhaps the invincibility of youth, but magnified exponentially. Moderation was not my thing, and now it is the primary goal for my treatment plan. Call it stability if you want, but my treatment goal is to keep my mood and subsequent behavior somewhere in the middle on the spectrum of emotions and behavior. I've gotten used to being stable, and actually appreciate the peace of mind, but sometimes I think it borders indifference, which I think there's nothing worse. Any time I put any kind of substances in my body, I'm trying to derail the system. Even something as seemingly harmless as coffee. Even if just for a few hours, I want to feel that rush of not being stable. In the same way that bipolar disorder magnifies my emotions, my appreciation for life has been magnified after surviving everything so far. I've lived a pretty full and interesting life, and I haven't even turned 40 years old yet. Of course, I hope to live to be 80 years old like my dad, but I don't take the time I've been given so far for granted at all. It's very rare when I'm not self-aware of my illness because it is mostly a full-time job. I think it's hard for people without mental illness to understand, by no fault of their own, so just realize I've been blatantly truthful in all of my books. I have tried not to exaggerate or belittle the experience of living with mental illness.

2 ENTRY 2

INTERVIEW WITH MICHELE LANDE CLARK

I was diagnosed with bipolar disorder one with psychotic features in 2006. I was hospitalized in a locked down ward for 11 days until I was stable enough to be released into the general public. I have had a few hospitalizations since then, but none for 10 years or so. I also have Generalized Anxiety Disorder with panic attacks, Obsessive Compulsive Disorder, Post Traumatic Stress Disorder, and agoraphobia and claustrophobia.

I wrote books because I wanted my story to be told to last long after I am gone. Maybe I felt like I had to defend my name after I lost my reputation as a sane person. I also lost nearly all my possessions along with stable employment and a lot of relationships that I had to rebuild. I also found out that I was helping people when I talked about my illness. That's my main motivation now. Helping others. When I wrote my first book, "Millions Like Me: My Struggle with Mental Illness", around 2012 or 2014, it was almost an act of desperation. I was very sick, and I frankly didn't know how much longer I was going to survive. My first book is very rough--- it's only about 75 pages long, and the type print is very small. I didn't really know what I was doing. I was learning as I went. All my books are self-published because a friend of the family recommended a free service where I could publish my books. I certainly didn't have any kind of money to put into my books.

My second book, "Poems from a Bipolar Mind", is the odd man out. It's simply a book of poems that I had written through the years pre- and post-diagnosis. I give explanations after every poem of what I was thinking at the time or what the poems are about. You will find that my poetry is very raw and emotional.

My third book, "The Last Day of July: 13 Years of Madness", reads like a journal because it was designed that way. I literally wrote almost every day for 8 months. Each entry is dated. I write about any symptoms I may have experienced that day, along with general life experiences. All of my books have my pre- and post-diagnosis philosophy of life sprinkled in.

My fourth book, "The Entropy of Bipolar Disorder", is exactly what it is titled. Random. It kind of reads like a journal, but the entries are about many different situations, experiences, and generally trying to cope with my illness.

3 ENTRY 3

I DON'T KNOW WHAT MORE I HAVE TO SAY ABOUT JULY 31, FIFTEEN YEARS AGO. I've written my heart out, five books worth. Writing has always been therapeutic for me, and it turned into a career. I was diagnosed with bipolar disorder with psychotic features on July 31, 2006, and I was hospitalized, locked up, for the first time for 11 days in the psychiatric unit. Along the way, I would be diagnosed with several anxiety disorders, including panic attacks, and also a few short hospital stays as a result. My story has reached and helped people all around the globe. I'm extremely proud of myself for never giving up, and so are my friends and family. I've missed one dose of medicine in those fifteen years, which I credit to my success, and also the support of my loved ones and medical professionals. Every single day is a battle, but luckily, some days are easier than others. The impact I've made has been impressive and a little overwhelming to think about sometimes. I'm just a regular guy with a somewhat incredible story and journey. I do my best and try to have a kind heart, and I let life sort out everything else. There is dignity in fighting, not to mention the satisfaction of victory, no matter how small. I could go on forever about how this day changed my life, but I'll defer to my books and interviews and such. Fight on.

4 ENTRY 4

MAN, I DON'T EVEN KNOW WHAT TO SAY, AND I'M ALMOST HESITANT TO POST THIS because I don't want to jinx anything. I started a new medication a few months ago called Buspar. From what I understand, it is a booster of sorts of the medication that is already in my system. I am responding well. My loved ones, who spend the most time with me, are noticing. I'm able to be happy and content without being manic, and upset without being full of rage and irritability. I'm able to handle more responsibilities. It's a long list of improvements. Since day 1, I've put my trust in the doctors and professionals, and I'm glad I did. There isn't a cure for my condition, but I'm managing it pretty well. I appreciate all the support through the years, whether it be reading my story in my books or just simply giving me a compliment when I achieve a small goal. I'm lucky in a lot of ways. On Saturday, I am a fifteen year survivor of my first hospitalization, and I'm just so grateful that I was given so many chances. My main hope is that I have left a positive mark on your life in some way. I've withstood many storms, and now it's time for me to enjoy the sunshine. Much love and best wishes always. Again, many thanks!

5 ENTRY 5

I HAD A PHONE CONVERSATION WITH THE WOMAN WHO VOICED MY AUDIOBOOKS yesterday. She was very friendly, and she's a health coach who studies the mind-body connection. The conversation was about an hour long. It's much harder for me to speak about what I've been through rather than writing about it. I think both take courage, but I've never even read my books as a reader if that tells you anything. There's something different about mustering up the breath to speak the words and then to hear them coming out of my mouth. That is a different level of courage. Because of my writing and the attention I get from that, I find myself speaking about my trauma probably more than other people who have experienced trauma. It really takes the energy out of me. I felt so drained after our conversation. Sometimes, I even have a mini hyperventilation, almost like a punch to the gut. It's just really painful stuff for me to verbally speak about no matter how much time has passed. The podcast interviews I've done are difficult for the same reason. I don't necessarily like talking about myself, but the topic always seems to come up when I'm around other people. It's not that I even mind talking about my life. Just difficult.

6 ENTRY 6

INTERVIEW

GUMONMYSHOE.COM, JUNE 2021

I WAS INTERVIEWED BY AUTHOR MARTIN BAKER = MB. I'M THE JM IN THIS interview.

MB: Hello John, could you tell us a little about yourself?

JM: I'm an author and mental health advocate from Cincinnati, Ohio USA. I was diagnosed with bipolar disorder with psychotic features in 2006, and I have general anxiety and panic attacks. I will be forty years old in October.

MB: When did you start writing?

JM: I've been writing since high school, but my first book wasn't published until 2014. That first book was out of desperation. I didn't know if I was going to survive. I wanted to tell my story in case anything happened to me.

MB: That's a powerful motivation. How many books have you written?

JM: Five altogether. The first was *Millions Like Me: My Struggle with Mental Illness*, followed by *Poems From a Bipolar Mind, The Last Day of July: 13 Years of Madness, The Entropy of Bipolar Disorder*, and *Mental Illness Is An Actual Illness*. They are all available online in paperback, for ebook, and as audiobooks.

MB: I listened to the audiobook previews and I have to say I was really impressed. How did they come about?

JM: Reading is difficult for me, and I jumped on the chance to produce audiobooks.

MB: You used the same reader for each book, I think?

JM: Yes, because she was so good. I didn't know how a female voice would work, but I like it.

MB: Me too. I wonder if I could ask about your poetry. In our book, *High Tide, Low Tide,* we describe how Fran was inspired to write poetry for the very first time during a period of mania, shortly after we met in 2011. She wrote incessantly for months, but her poetry stopped when she fell into depression. When she finally emerged, she began writing again, but the new poems were very different from her mania ones. Would you say the style of your poetry is influenced by the different phases of bipolar disorder and your mental health in general?

JM: Most of my poetry was written during mania when I felt more energetic and creative. However, some poems were written while I was more sedated. The poems were written both before and after I was diagnosed and medicated.

MB: Where can people hear more about your story?

JM: I've recorded podcast interviews on *The Mark Howard Show, Screaming Chuy Show,* and *Tindel's Razor* talking about my books and my life.

MB: Fran and I have recorded a few podcasts and always enjoyed doing them. How did yours come about?

JM: Mark Howard saw that I was giving away free books in a writers' group, and asked me to do a podcast interview with him. The other two podcast interviews were referrals from friends or colleagues.

MB: Are you on social media, if people would like to connect with you?

JM: I am on Twitter, Instagram, and Facebook. I also run a Facebook page called Mental Health Awareness and Support.

MB: Thanks. I will include links for all these and your books, of course. What are your plans for the future? Do you have any more books in the pipeline?

JM: I finished my fifth book a few months ago, so I'm enjoying a little free time now. It was a goal of mine to convert my books into audiobooks too, and I've accomplished that. I've started painting and cooking as hobbies because I was too involved with my advocacy work. I was getting burned out. To answer your question, I'm in a little bit of a limbo right now, but I don't plan on writing any more books.

MB: If there was one thing you'd like to share with others about what it means to live with mental illness, what would it be?

JM: So much to say! It took me five books to say everything I wanted to. Having mental illness is difficult and a lot of work, but happiness and contentment are possible. There are going to be people who don't believe you, or even believe in mental illness. People are going to judge you for taking medication. I think the most important thing is honesty. Be honest with health professionals and yourself. Sometimes, it takes a few attempts to get the correct medications. There's no magic pill either. Mental illness can feel a lot like work sometimes. My doctor told me once that he was there to help me, not hurt me, and that comforted me.

MB: Thank you so much, John. It's been great to chat with you. Good luck with all you do.

My books are not best sellers. They probably never will be. That's not why I wrote them. Money and fame were not my top priorities. Firstly, I had a lot to say about life in general, and I think I have an interesting life story. Most importantly, I wanted people who are struggling with their mental health to know they are not alone. I'm lucky and blessed to have a large, loving support system, but this is not always the case. If my books have helped even one person feel comfort and continue the fight, my books and my life have served their purpose. Be kind. Everyone you know is fighting battles you know nothing about. Much love and fight on!

7 ENTRY 7

7-28-21

I look out from underneath the bill of my hat,
And I feel as fierce as a Texas thunderstorm.
The smoke is pouring from my mouth
Like a volcano from somewhere far away.
You can see fire in my eyes like a man possessed
And I wonder if I'm supposed to feel so charged
Anything is better than indifference, I think to myself
Why do I feel so well? It's only Wednesday afternoon and I only have ten dollars
Am I really this content?
I feel so strange for being so simple
Is this really what I've been searching for
For four decades?
I was making life so complicated
And this is the answer?
Watching cars pass by, sipping coffee, and smoking cigarettes?

8 ENTRY 8

I don't know how this is going to sound. If you haven't been diagnosed with bipolar disorder, you probably don't have it, statistically speaking. Only 3% of the population has it. Out of that 3%, 1 in 5 complete suicide. This disease is no joke. It's a disease of extremes, and can be destructive even when treated well. I urge you to follow Julie A. Fast. She's an expert on bipolar disorder and an author. I always offer my books for free if anyone thinks they will help their or their loved ones' understanding.

9 ENTRY 9

7-25-21

I took my shot
My wings were melted
I'll never be that high again.
Chasing dollars
Still fifteen years later
I wonder if I'm better off at all.
I took a chance
I took a gamble
And I crashed hard
But it was worth it.
At least I know I tried.
Happiness is fleeting
But soon I'll feel better again.
Over and over, all the time
I never imagined all the sorrow
My innocence was ruined.
But I'm okay most of the time
I remember when things were simple
It helps me pass the time.
A road I've paved with tears and laughter

I never thought I'd come to this.
But I am thankful
Usually grateful
I wake up every day
And sometimes I think that's a miracle.

10 ENTRY 10

7-19-21

Nothing feels the same anymore
The sky is not as blue,
And the sun is not as bright.
I don't feel love like I used to
I don't feel much at all
I'm here though, I guess.
I'm supposed to be grateful
I tell myself I'm blessed.
I don't know who or what to believe anymore
Everything has a shade of gray
Like a storm cloud
That follows me around
I'm still grieving the loss of myself.

11 ENTRY 11

I didn't want to go to college. I wanted to work for Italianette, buy a house in Deer Park, and live out my days. I've always been a simple man, more so now. My parents urged me strongly to go to college, and I graduated somehow, and the rest is history. I should say that I don't think there's anything wrong with skipping college and working. I really don't care what other people do with their lives in general.

I highly doubt I would have gotten help for my mental illness if it had not been an emergency situation. But I did, and again, the rest is history. I think before judging someone, you should consider what their options were at the time. It's really hard for me to understand some people, but it's not my place to judge. I don't enjoy taking medication, but I've seen the alternative choice. Options.

12 ENTRY 12

JUST A QUICK UPDATE. I HAD A PHONE CALL WITH MY PSYCHIATRIST TODAY AS scheduled. The only change is a small increase in one of my medications to help manage my anxiety during daytime hours, because that's when my anxiety is the worst. My psychiatrist wants me to have a physical checkup with my primary care doctor just as a standard practice. Just trying to be cautious. Nothing to be alarmed about. Since starting a new medication called Buspar in April, I have had less anxiety, panic attacks, depression, and more energy, but not to the point of mania or hypomania, which is really good news. I'm more alert and interested in hobbies, such as cooking and painting. I'm sleeping less during the day, and I'm slightly less fatigued in general. So, anyway, pretty much good news. If you've read my story or talked to me about how far I've come and where I've been, it's pretty remarkable. I'm looking forward to celebrating being a 15 year survivor of my first hospitalization on July 31st.

13 ENTRY 13

Many years ago, I made the conscious decision to be positive, grateful, and happy. Depression is very real sometimes, but generally, I'm in good spirits. There's no time for anything else.

Showing kindness to strangers is a great way to boost your own mood and maybe make someone else's day. I went to the store and a random woman, who seemed very shy, said she liked my shirt. I thanked her and it made me feel good. Then, a woman parked next to me, and I asked her if I was parked too closely because I have a large truck. I was well within the parking lines. I was just being polite and kind. I swear on everything that seemingly small interactions like these are actually a big deal to a lot of people. Sometimes people need just one person to be kind to them to give them hope and let them know that the world is full of good people. Not vice versa.

25 days I will be a 15 year survivor of my first hospitalization for bipolar disorder with psychotic features. Every year is special, but this year is a little sweeter. I reflect on all the hard work and struggling that has gotten me to this point, and I'm beyond proud of myself. I know a lot of you are proud of me, too. Thanks for the support because a lot of people with mental illness don't have it. When the curtain closes, I have no regrets, and I've given more than I've taken.

14 ENTRY 14

I GUESS I'LL TOOT MY HORN FOR A MINUTE. THIS TIME OF YEAR, I REFLECT ON how I'm contributing to the mental health community. On July 31, I'll be a 15 year survivor of my first hospitalization for bipolar disorder with psychotic features. It's a lifelong genetic illness. Five books, podcast interviews, fundraising, guest blogs, countless emails and book donations. I'm giving this illness everything I have, and I don't know how I could have handled it better. If you're struggling with your mental health, please reach out to myself or professionals. You are not alone. Not even close.

15 ENTRY 15

One weird thing about me is that I've never read any of my books as a reader. Just editing and proofreading. It's kind of triggering for me to relive everything. I'm sure I've written about this. Anyway, my family who still lives in town gets together on holidays and birthdays for dinner and to visit each other. I don't know when it started, but I get so anxious at these gatherings. My brother is having my family over for one of these gatherings today in Loveland. I just couldn't do it. I don't know if I feel guilty or if it's frustration or what. I have no problem with anyone in my family, and they're very understanding. I think it's just one of those things that I think shouldn't be so difficult. There's a few things in my life that are difficult for me that other people probably don't even give a second thought to. Maybe that's why I'm so passionate in trying to explain myself. I think I'm going to FaceTime my family for some sense of normalcy. It's just so frustrating and almost annoying.

16 ENTRY 16

2-9-21

The grips of death
Is the closest taste of freedom
I'll ever have.
I used to think it was road trips
Of hundreds of miles
Or drug fueled dancing
In open, muddy fields
In the cold rain.
But it was the terror
Of my life ending
That angered me
Enough to fight on.

17 ENTRY 17

Props to my mom for giving me a writing entry for tonight. I kept talking about how I couldn't go #2, which I do all the time. It's part of my OCD, but poop talk is generally funny. She says, "I wish there were hidden microphones in this house ". Well, if you don't know my story, this will be new information. When I was first hospitalized, one of my psychotic delusions and hallucinations was that there were hidden microphones in my house. I thought the CIA was listening. I was also getting hidden messages from the TV, mail, and everyday objects like lottery tickets and soda cans. When I'm telling you I've come a long way, it's no joke. I remember the tense energy and terror I felt all those years ago.

One weird thing about me is that I've never read any of my books as a reader. Just editing and proofreading. It's kind of triggering for me to relive everything. I'm sure I've written about this. Anyway, my family who still lives in town gets together on holidays and birthdays for dinner and to visit each other. I don't know when it started, but I get so anxious at these gatherings. My brother is having my family over for one of these gatherings today in Loveland. I just couldn't do it. I don't know if I feel guilty or if it's frustration or what. I have no problem with anyone in my family, and they're very understanding. I think it's just one of those things that I think shouldn't be so difficult. There's a few things in my life that are difficult for me that other people probably don't even give a second thought to. Maybe that's why I'm so passionate in trying to explain myself. I think I'm going to FaceTime my family for some sense of normalcy. It's just so frustrating and almost annoying.

18 ENTRY 18

I STARTED A NEW MEDICATION FOR ANXIETY ABOUT 6 WEEKS AGO, AND I'VE shown a lot of progress. I'm eating less, sleeping better, drinking less coffee, and even smoking less. Unfortunately, I think I'm getting depressed. I'm losing my appetite, but I'm not really happy or sad either. I'm bored and exhausted at the same time. I feel like I should get a job or go back to school. At the very least, pick up some hobbies. Nothing seems interesting and I have trouble focusing often. I reached out to my case manager, and we're going to talk tomorrow. Blah.

19 ENTRY 19

I HAVEN'T WRITTEN ANYTHING IN A BIT, AND I MISS IT A LITTLE. YOU MIGHT notice that mental health and mental illness are being talked about now, perhaps more than ever. If I've contributed to that in the smallest way, I'm mighty proud and it's all been worth it. My books are being distributed around the world, and they're available in the library for anyone who has a library card. I've donated hundreds of books to people who may need help. I've written to everyone I can think of, along with blog posts and podcast interviews. And the list goes on. It's a pretty unbelievable and inspiring story if you knew how sick I've been. Everyone tells you to tone it down, and winning doesn't matter. I don't believe that. Be an absolute monster. Much love. You are not alone.

During the pandemic, my mom usually watches Mass virtually on her phone on Sundays. I told her I always pray for vengeance upon my enemies haha, which is totally not true. I don't know if I have any enemies, and that's probably a bad thing. This is in my books, but I don't know where I'd be without a sense of humor. I try to keep my parents happy and laughing just like how I run my Facebook stuff, for the most part anyway.

20 ENTRY 20

So much to say.... lots of people have asked me why I've told my story and why I often donate copies instead of making money off every single reader. My goal is to reach as many people as possible. That's it. Whatever it takes. I'm bringing families together, and helping suicidal people through the days and nights. Some things are priceless and cannot be bought. I let love guide me, not money.

21 ENTRY 21

I'VE HAD ENOUGH. THIS IS WHAT I'M GOING TO TALK TO MY PSYCHIATRIST ABOUT:

I think we got off on the wrong foot because it seemed like you were more concerned with my physical body weight than with my mental health. You questioned what size water cup I use, which seemed pretty insignificant against my overall picture of health. I realize that mental and physical health are intertwined, but I have lost 144 pounds on my own before, and I can do it again when I am ready. My mania and anxiety have increased gradually, and I need some relief. Maybe it is just a matter of adjusting my medication positions and timing. The Gabapentin you prescribed helped my anxiety, but I had unbearable stomach cramps and racing thoughts. I am not willing to compromise my health and safety to return to the clinic for in-person treatment. I can barely drive a car, and I get physically ill when I ride in a car. I am not a drug addict or alcoholic, and I haven't been hospitalized in over 10 years. The people at the clinic are severely ill, and I don't belong there. Even if you think I belong there, I can't tell you how many times I thought I was going to pass out from anxiety on the car ride to the clinic or while I was there. It's just simply something I'm not willing to do anymore. I'm almost certain you have to accommodate me according to the Americans with Disabilities Act. If you will not accommodate me, I will find services elsewhere. I have done everything I have been asked to do, and this is one thing I am not willing to do.

22 ENTRY 22

There's a certain way I like to interact on social media. I don't like to be depressing or controversial or dramatic. Basically, I don't like to be negative. I think there's enough of that out there. Writing and cracking jokes are 2 ways I cope with my illness. I don't want sympathy. I want people to read my work and think. Helping others is my calling and purpose. The more people I impact positively, the more my life has meaning and value. My life isn't always happy, but I do have some choices in this regard. I try to surround myself with positivity and cut out things that don't bring me joy and satisfaction. Some things are unavoidable and inevitable, but I try to stay self aware so that I can live my best life while at the same time fulfilling my purpose. I have a loving heart, but I'm trying to fight a relentless illness at the same time. It's exhausting, frustrating, and maddening.

23 ENTRY 23

I don't do nice things for people because I expect something in return. Truly kind people are the same way. I've seen the positive vibes that kindness can bring. I'm lucky that my friends and family don't expect anything in return from me also. A single act of kindness can set off a positive chain of events that can really bring about change. Kindness absolutely matters!

24 ENTRY 24

I've written 5 books about living with mental illness now. Maybe I thought it would go away if I talked about it enough. It's never going away, although some days are better than others. I don't have much trouble writing about my experiences, but talking about it makes me really emotional. It may seem like I handle it well, but I'm extremely angry. This is not how life is supposed to be. I've experienced terror that I wouldn't wish on my worst enemy. I could go on forever, but it's also very embarrassing to lose control of one's mind. I feel like such an idiot sometimes. I don't even have control of my own finances, and I'm almost 40 years old.

25 ENTRY 25

3-11-21

All I have to offer
Is a small silent prayer.
For all my loved ones everywhere.
If I could buy the world,
I'd give it all to you.
I don't want to ever lose
The wonder I feel
Looking at the stars
And the mountains
And the oceans.
I wish I could give it all to you,
But until then,
May love and goodness prevail.

26 ENTRY 26

Thank you from the bottom of my heart for all your support. I wouldn't have been able to make it this far without a lot of love and support. If you have read about how sick I was, you were probably thinking, "No way". I thought the same thing all those years ago. It's really hard to believe how far I've come sometimes. I'm not a rich man, but I'm making an impact far beyond what I could have hoped for, and I'm generally happy. All of this was never in my plans, but I did always know that I wanted to be happy in whatever I chose to do, and I always knew that I wanted my name to be well known. Much love. Be kind and enjoy yourselves.

27 ENTRY 27

3-1-21

The church bell tolls
8 o' clock again
And I'm my only friend.
I'm a dimly lit candle
Among the fires burning inside me.
I'm my biggest hero and harshest critic.
I commiserate with the sick
And plead to the cynics.
Everyone has made up their minds.
And I'm just an hourglass
Waiting for the sands of time.

28 ENTRY 28

Yesterday was one of the worst days I've had in a very long time. My whole body hurt, including my chest from anxiety, which is very unsettling if you've ever experienced it. I was symptomatic nearly all day, and I went 18 hours without a bite to eat. So much pain. Resiliency matters, and I wish I could bottle it up and give it away. I have no idea how I have gotten this far. My mind was racing out of control, and I felt like I might lose my mind. But I didn't, and the sun still rose this morning, just like every day. Almost everyone is experiencing trauma right now, and getting a taste of what mental illness and isolation are like. I'm asking you to go to that place in your heart where you usually don't go because it's terrifying, and fight like Hell. We need as many good people in good health as possible right now and in the future. I have to protect my own mental health, but you can reach out to me if you are struggling, and I will do my best to help you. Whatever you do with your life, don't forget love and do it with love.

29 ENTRY 29

I WAS TALKING TO MY MOM ABOUT GETTING OLDER. I'M GOING TO BE 40 YEARS old in October, which is shocking to a lot of people besides myself. The neighborhood and friends of my family have watched me grow up. I was telling my mom about the fun my friends and me used to have, mainly at music festivals. Those were some good times. A lot of us were wannabe hippies, but maybe we were all just old souls. By my age, a lot of people have families of their own, and I don't see that happening for me. Times were so much different when I was a teenager. No social media. Not many people had cell phones. You had to buy a disposable camera and have pictures developed. The music scene was some of the best times of my life. When I'm having a rough day, I try to remember all the good times we had, and it helps. Anyway, I hope the next generation still has some old souls and doesn't let the world get to them too much.

30 ENTRY 30

One thing I've always found interesting about being diagnosed with a mental illness is the delineation between personality and my disorders. Where does my personality begin and where does my disorder begin? In the end, it doesn't matter because the end result is the person I am. However, there are things I can try to do to help alleviate my symptoms, which may change my personality. They are far from mutually exclusive. Hopefully, that makes sense. Someone who is in pain all the time may not always have a sunny disposition.

I started a medication a few days ago called Gabapenten, also known as Neurotin. Its primary purpose is to relieve nerve pain, but also has qualities of relieving anxiety. I am noticing a small difference in my pain level, which has affected my disposition from irritated frequently to irritated slightly. It's not a perfect solution, and there are no magic pills, but I think I will continue this medication.

31 ENTRY 31

Here are some things I've been thinking about. I'm just going to let it fly. Due to the nature of bipolar disorder, I feel extreme highs and extreme lows. The highs can feel euphoric (amazing) or dysphoric (agitated), and eventually, there is a depressing crash. Every time. I'm laying in bed in a relaxed state thinking about how much I love to watch it snow with a cup of coffee and a smoke. I'm thinking about how lucky I am to be alive. I'm wondering why I'm still here. I've done enough work. I've never done anyone wrong intentionally, and if I have, I think I've made up for it. I'm at peace with my past, and I'm at peace with what I've contributed to society. Mental illness will probably always need advocacy, unless experts start discovering cures. I imagine scientists are more concerned with diseases like cancer. I don't have to worry about necessities or caring for my children. I've always believed that I survived because I had a mission and purpose, so I guess the higher forces aren't finished with me yet. I think what I'm trying to say is that my spirit is at peace for when my work is finished. I'm good. I'm lucky to be alive, and I'm blessed.

32 ENTRY 32

Almost every day, I promote my books. One way I do this is making an ad in author support groups and mental illness groups. I offer my books for free in an email with the hope that people will donate to my Venmo, cash app, etc. Yesterday I made such a post, and almost 700 people responded. I only made $35 in donations. It's just a little frustrating. I've had much better luck on other days. I keep sending emails because I always think of the people who are struggling who might not be able to afford my books or have access. Just because I can't save everyone, doesn't mean I shouldn't try.

33 ENTRY 33

SELLING PAPERBACK COPIES OF MY BOOKS IS A PRETTY HARD SELL IN THESE TIMES, but I seem to know a lot of people who read. I think it's a cool thing to do with free time. I think once people start reading my story, they'll hopefully be interested enough to continue reading. It's a pretty inspirational story. I've gone from basically a sedated vegetable to the person you know today. I don't know why I haven't quit. If you knew me 15 years ago, you would understand if I had quit. The funny thing is I'm still the same person at the core, illness and medication, and all. Of course I've changed. Hopefully, for the better.

Here's an interesting thought. My buddy and I used to get stoned and munch out at a fast-food restaurant near me. We thought it was hilarious to zone out and not focus on a single conversation in the restaurant. It sounded like nonsensical music almost, and we thought it was hilarious. Fast forward to now, I can't handle loud crowded rooms very well. Not funny at all. It's sensory overload, and like nails on a chalkboard to me.

34 ENTRY 34

I had a job at the sandwich place, Jimmy John's, many years ago. I was a delivery driver, and I became a shift manager. I did such a good job that I was supposed to go to Chicago to be trained as an Assistant General Manager and then eventually a General Manager. The owner was great, and we're still friends to this day. This was around 2010. He used to bring me gifts for my hard work and pay me the manager rate per hour to deliver, which meant tips, too. It would have been great money, and a pretty good life. When I first started, we used to use these styrofoam cups for fountain drinks. I used to write the names of famous people with bipolar disorder on these cups. A few people I can remember are Edgar Allen Poe, Vincent Van Gogh, Drew Carey, and Jim Carrey. It was a way to motivate and inspire me to keep going. I don't know if I really looked up to these people exactly, but they gave me hope that one could be successful with this illness. I was working long hours in an extremely fast-paced environment, partying all the time, and barely sleeping. I started to be paranoid at work and having panic attacks. Eventually, I could no longer work. It took me 7 years to get approved for disability, and I did everything I could to avoid that situation.

35 ENTRY 35

If there is a God or gods, may they bless my mother. For a lot of reasons. She's the person most responsible for my success who isn't a professional. She's been by my side the whole time, as I survive into year sixteen. When I was bedridden, she used to buy me greeting cards and tell me she was proud of me. I was barely surviving. She used to set out fresh towels and clothes for me so that I could save energy when I needed a shower. When I was heavily sedated, a shower was probably my biggest accomplishment in my life at the time. My mom told me there was a preacher who made her upset because he was very negative, and talking about fire and brimstone and all that bullshit. I'm going to tell you right now, if my mom doesn't go to heaven, I have no chance, and that goes for most everyone else. However, this entry is not about my awesome mom. At some point, I'm going to have to take credit for some of my success. I am as humble and modest as I can be, but I've fought so hard for everything I've achieved. All of this leads me to being symptomatic this morning. I slept longer than usual, which you would think is a good thing. Professionals talk about the importance of good sleep for everyone, but especially people with bipolar disorder. I had my usual morning coffee and took my medication on time, just like every day, and my body was literally, physically buzzing with energy. It was almost a vibration. My thoughts were not intrusive or negative, but extremely rapid. The thoughts were about my writing and a lot of random knowledge I have. It didn't stop for at least 3 hours. I didn't do anything "wrong". This isn't a punishment. It's a genetic brain malfunction. My guess is that I've been working too much. I'm having great career success, but this disorder doesn't care about all the great things I'm doing. It can be cruel and ruthless. I don't feel like I failed. I'm not going to beat myself up. I didn't shed a single tear. I'm trying to have an "it is what it is" mentality. Besides the rapid thoughts, I had severe muscle tension and pain. The toll that this illness takes goes beyond psychological. It's hard for most people to understand, and mental illness is almost a misnomer. Anyway, I'm going to try to take it easy for a bit and recover. After I slept off my symptoms this morning, I woke up feeling brand new. It's been this way for a while. Perhaps knowing the symptoms are temporary keeps me fighting. I know that if I can just calm down enough to fall asleep, my slate will be wiped clean. Sometimes I really have no idea how I've survived this long. Again, I have to take some credit, but it's also how I was raised, and I'm inspired by how so many people have rallied around me. Your love and support absolutely make a difference. Fight on.

36 ENTRY 36

So here's my hypothesis. Feel free to chime in. I had a hard time dealing with my feelings regarding my survivor anniversary date and the death of my neighbor, so I started working nonstop as a trauma response. It came to a head/crescendo yesterday morning, and I had pretty severe mania. Not bad for an imitation therapist, eh? An underlying stressor that I really don't talk to anyone about is that my parents are getting older. My dad is about to turn 80 years old, and my mom is two years younger. It's hard watching them get older every day because I share a household with them. I'm trying not to worry about things out of my control, but my anxiety is making it extremely difficult. I just want to tie them to chairs so they don't hurt themselves doing chores or gardening in the yard. I imagine it's the same feeling a parent gets when his/her child is getting older. You just want to freeze time. It really does fly by.

I think one of the most important things is to believe in yourself and be confident. I really struggle with this. This may be surprising to people who know me. It also helps to have a few good friends and family members believe in you, too. I think my confidence comes and goes. It's really hard on me when I make a mistake, and I have a terrible guilt complex. I'm my own biggest critic too. None of this negativity and self-doubt is productive. Most of the time, I can snap myself out of it with positive affirmations like positive self talk, but sometimes, my liar of my brain gets the best of me. You'd be amazed if I kept track of how often my brain tells me I'm a failure, despite overwhelming concrete evidence to the contrary. Perfection isn't even an option or viable possibility, so why do I expect that of myself? The mind is a terrible thing sometimes.

37 ENTRY 37

I don't know when it happened, but I was called to serve. A job versus a vocation, or calling, are two different things sometimes, but in my case, I guess they're the same thing. I offer my books for free to anyone who shows interest, and people pay me because they want to support me as a writer and mental health advocate. I'm not going to act like I don't try to make money, but it's not my top priority. It's ironic that when I stopped worrying about making money, I had the biggest sales month this month in 7 years of being a published author. I know it doesn't always work out that way, but I'm very fortunate and blessed.

Unfortunately, The University of Dayton library (Roesch) is not accepting pieces of mail to be cautious about the spread of the virus. I'm going to stuff an envelope and address it anyway, as a symbol of hope that the virus will be contained as soon as possible. I need little pieces of hope to keep me happy and motivated. If you've ever interacted with me, you know that I have a lot of hopeful sayings from authors, writers, and philosophers. People will no passion might think these little sayings are foolish. I'll tell you that reading inspirational quotes was the beginning of pulling myself out of a deep, sedated depression. I was so sedated and depressed that I really didn't see the difference whether I lived or died.

38 ENTRY 38

8-16-21

A young girl
In a green dress
Approached me
With the biggest smile
But I knew she
Wasn't really there.
She hugged me
Without a word
And all I felt was love
I had never met this girl
Nor do I know
Why she chose me.
It was nice to be awake and dreaming.

39 ENTRY 39

IT WAS REALLY NICE HAVING ALL MY SIBLINGS TOGETHER. ONE THING I'VE realized as I've gotten older is that my parents aren't superheroes. They never were. When they were raising me and all my siblings, they were just regular people trying the best they could. I never felt like my parents were just going through the motions. I always felt loved and cared for. It's more special to me that they didn't have superpowers. My siblings and I weren't raised with a lot of money for extra-type things, but we always had a bed, food, clothes, and questionable haircuts. It's hard seeing my parents' age. It's bittersweet, but they're still alive and healthy, which is more than some people I know. I've really learned to appreciate my parents. I'm sure they feel like they made mistakes at some point, but my siblings and I turned out to be pretty good people. Most of the time, we just do the best we can, too.

40 ENTRY 40

I don't have the exact research on hand, but I think I remember hearing that one of the things suicidal people have said is that they just wanted to be seen and heard. It would have made all the difference to them in those hard times. Give someone 5 minutes of your time. Smile and wave at strangers. Ask how people are doing. Like I've said before, kindness matters. It really does.

41 ENTRY 41

Stability is a grind, day after day. It's like sticking to a diet. I have to stick to a pretty strict schedule, including meals, medication times, and sleep. I didn't sleep at all last night, and I skipped lunch. I paid for it. I was depressed all day after being manic for weeks. I'm finally starting to feel better after my night medication, and my parents going to bed. I just need to be alone sometimes. I need space, and I don't want to blow up on anyone. I'm a very loving, kind person, but I have triggers that can make me have rage, irritability, mania, and depression. Today was a roller coaster on fire.

42 ENTRY 42

I've talked to a few people who were very depressed. Very close to being suicidal. I don't claim to have all the answers, but I told them it's an "all hands on deck" situation. Survival mode. A life or death situation. If you need to eat a gallon of ice cream to give you an ounce of joy to keep fighting, do it. If you need to pet your animals for 8 hours straight, do it. I think you get the idea. I wouldn't recommend destructive behaviors. Sometimes, people just want to get wasted to numb themselves and forget about life for a while. It's only a temporary solution. A lot of people get wasted to escape life, and many people can continue living that way. Borderline suicidal people are a whole different ball of wax. Their very existence is fragile, and can depend on how their day(s) goes. Sometimes, something negative happens, and it's what sends someone over the edge. That's why it's important to be easy on yourself, practice self care, and indulge in something non-destructive if that's what's going to keep someone alive another day. Just because you had a bad day today doesn't mean that tomorrow will be bad. Keep fighting and at least give yourself a chance.

43 ENTRY 43

I used to think if I didn't have to work, I'd be happier. Now, I have to remind myself to take breaks. I really believe in what I do and sharing my story. I'm very lucky, fortunate, and blessed that people have supported me to a high degree. I almost have to pinch myself sometimes. Please understand that I thought I was dead over 15 years ago. I had the will to live, apparently, but I really didn't see the point. I wasn't suicidal. I was just barely breathing. All the good that has happened from my misfortune was never expected. Not like this. I've gotten more than 2 chances, and I'm just trying to make the most of it. I'm starting to believe in my abilities again. If you're familiar with my story, it's almost hard to believe. At least that's how I feel.

44 ENTRY 44

5 STAR REVIEW OF MY SECOND BOOK!

Beautiful Poetry

Reviewed in the United States on August 24, 2021

A wonderful collection of beautifully written poems.

John is clearly a poet and wonderful with prose. I've found that people with a mental illness, have absolutely wonderful minds. My mom also has bipolar, and her writing is wonderful, when she can put the discipline to sit down and do it. She's no poet, but her eulogy for grandma was absolutely heartfelt, as several other small pieces she's actually written.

John's poems are clear, concise, and a promising insight into the mind of bipolar. They're beautiful, and I hope he continues to write them.

Another 5 star review of my newest book!

Mental Health is Read. Bipolar is Real.

Reviewed in the United States on August 24, 2021

John has done it again. Another fantastic book in his collection on mental illness. John gets it. John lives it. It's great to get additional insight on bipolar from John in this more recent collection, as well as a few of his interviews where he answered questions about his illness, concerns on mental illness, and police and show they interact with mental illness.

His narrator for the audio book has gotten better. She always had a good voice for it, but the earlier books of his she did, the audio quality wasn't there. She's come a long way, and the audio book is well done.

45 ENTRY 45

THIS BOOK IS NOT MEANT TO BE SCIENTIFIC, BUT I'M GOING TO GIVE IT MY BEST shot here. I've incorporated stretching as a way to relieve muscle tension in my legs, back, and neck. So, why do my muscles get tense? I have a couple of ideas. The obvious answer is that I'm overweight and get a little strenuous exercise. However, mentally ill people, and especially anxious people, get muscle tension. Mental illness has physical symptoms. I think the reason is because an anxious person's nervous system/"fight or flight" response misfires constantly. My brain sends signals to my muscles that there's danger, and prepares my muscles for a fight or flight, when there is no danger. Long story short, stretching really helps relieve the tension caused by my brain misfiring.

46 ENTRY 46

Dark falls and the shadows creep
Madness comes and goes
A terrible story filled with friends and foes.
Visions that make the Night Man weep
Until fatigue claims its sleep.
The insides of a man covered in tears
Held back for so many years.
The pressure of life pushing down tight
But the Night Man presses on.
And so will He forever and always
Through so many nights and days.
He will be paid back with a grim satisfaction
But sometimes, the night disobeys.

47 ENTRY 47

I found something I've never written about! I've done this for a very long time. If I'm symptomatic, and it's medication time, I always think if I took the correct combination of pills. Especially if the medication doesn't absorb immediately, which it never does. It can take 30-45 minutes before my symptoms are relieved. I always have this repetitive thought where I say to myself, "it's like peanut butter for my brain". What I think I mean by that is that my mind just runs smoother—slower and clearer thoughts mainly. It just feels like when you're spreading peanut butter, except for my brain/mind. So there's another super weird thing about me, if you're keeping track.

48 ENTRY 48

Positive self talk is very important for everyone, but especially people who have a tendency to be depressed. I think a form of positive self talk is called a mantra. A mantra is a positive word or phrase someone can repeat to themselves when they feel depressed and hopeless. I always say to myself, "Maybe something good will happen today." I say this to myself several times a day, as many times as needed. Do you give yourself pep talks? It really helps me stay positive.

49 ENTRY 49

It seems like there's this common theme among humans that we replay our mistakes over and over, especially when we're trying to sleep or relax. I'm learning to beat myself up less and less for mistakes I've made. I can't do anything about it now, for one. I'm only human. I'm going to keep making mistakes. I know I've always been a good person. People who have known me for any length of time would probably agree. It's time for me to let go and focus on all the great things about me. I would highly recommend thinking deeply about what you're accomplishing by dwelling on past mistakes.

50 ENTRY 50

5 STAR REVIEW OF MY NEWEST BOOK, "MENTAL ILLNESS IS AN ACTUAL ILLNESS "

Reviewed in the United States on August 30, 2021

John's book is a thoughtful account of his struggles. Likely helpful to others experiencing mental illness, conveying to them that they are not alone.

5 star review of my first book, "Millions Like Me: My Struggle with Mental Illness "

John has serious talent

Reviewed in the United States on August 31, 2021

John has so much talent and is doing everything he can to break the stigma that mentally ill people can't function like the rest of society. Overcoming every obstacle thrown at him he has made it his mission to spread awareness of how one can recover and adapt to being productive. I enjoyed his book so much that I bought 2 copies of all five of his books. One to stock one to share.

5 star review of my third book, "The Last Day of July: 13 Years of Madness "

Honest, raw, inspiring

Reviewed in the United States on August 30, 2021

As other reviewers have noted, this is a truly honest and raw account of the author's experiences. Medl shares his insights into how he's coped with mental illness in hopes that others might benefit from his experience

51 ENTRY 51

I'M PROUD OF MYSELF. I DROVE MYSELF TO THE GAS STATION THIS MORNING WITH no issues after a long night of rest. I really needed some sleep. I'm also proud of myself for standing up for myself. People have been disrespecting me as long as I can remember, and I tolerated it. Not yesterday. I feel a little remorse because it came out as anger and rage, but I had enough. I don't care if you love me or hate me, but I'm not going to allow people to treat me like dirt. I'm an awesome person. I work very hard. I've accomplished a lot despite my condition. I bend over backwards for people, and even donate to charity when I'm able. It's a long list. I'll be damned if someone is going to treat me like less of a person, and I mean anyone. Much love to everyone who supports and respects me.

Before I was a mental health advocate, and then an author, the only identity I really had was that I was sick with mental illness. From 2006-2011, I was sick off and on, and working off and on. When I could no longer work a traditional job, I started a free social media page devoted to mental health and inspiration. There are about 900 members from at least 15 countries, the last time I checked. My first book was published in 2014, but I still really didn't consider myself anyone but a sick person. Now it's 2021 and I have 5 books written, with a sixth on the way. I really feel like I made something of myself. I identify as a writer, author, and mental health advocate, even though I have a genetic, lifelong illness. I just never expected anything like this could happen to me. I've said this before, but I was down on the mat. Barely moving or breathing. Well, I got up, and here we are. I've made my friends and family proud, but I've also shown strength and courage that I didn't know I possessed. My confidence is coming back too. Since I am so proud of my body of work, I have something to gush about to other people. I don't have the usual things of an almost 40-year-old—wife, kids, pets, etc, but I've really produced something that will outlive me and my illness. You have no idea how good it feels after what I have been through. I am blessed and just a humble servant trying to leave my mark on this world.

52 ENTRY 52

9-9-21

If you heal me,
I promise to be a better person.
I'm doing everything I can,
And it's never enough.
I only have a few friends left.
I'm tired of being sick too.
I've shouldered more than my share
Over and over
With no regard for my health
I wouldn't have it any other way.
I stood up to everything and everyone
In my way.
I will not be stopped
Except for when I get called home.

53 ENTRY 53

I HAVE A LOT TO SAY THIS MORNING, AND THIS IS GOING TO BE THE CONCLUSION of my sixth book. As my friend suggested, I will have page numbers in this book. Again, thank you to everyone who supports my writing career. It's been an amazing journey, and my books are distributed worldwide. I've done video interviews, guest blogs, and podcast interviews. I think I've done a good job of getting the word out about mental illness.

I was feeling nostalgic this morning, just thinking about all the great memories I have, from childhood to little league sports to high school and beyond. I really am blessed. I'm not mad at the world, nor do I have hate in my heart for anyone. There's simply no room for that in my life. I don't feel like I got a raw deal, and the world doesn't owe me anything. It took me a long time to believe that I deserve the attention and success. Confidence is a tricky thing. I think it's an intrinsic value that one has to discover and cultivate over time. I still wouldn't say I'm a confident person, but it's higher than it was yesterday.

Some of my friends have passed away recently and over the years at young ages, and it's hard to deal with. I think one way to deal with it is to keep living and carry on and fight. I know that's what my loved ones would want me to do. That's what I intend to continue to do. Going into year sixteen of my recovery, and fortieth year of life, I hope to continue my mission and purpose through working for a nonprofit organization to help distribute funds to worthy charities and causes. It doesn't feel real right now, but I'm hoping my friend and colleague is granted federal funding. If I've inspired one person or made someone keep fighting through adversity, it's all been worth it.

BIPOLAR RISING

A MAN'S VICTORY OVER MENTAL HEALTH

1 ENTRY 1

THE LAST GIRL I DATED WAS ABOUT 10-11 YEARS AGO. SHE'S THE REASON I AM happily single. I want to thank her and her mother for calling me lazy. This was while I was basically caring for their daughter because she had MS. I'm dealing with mental illness, and I have to give injections to my ex for her MS. I'm not going to throw anyone under the bus because I'm better than that. Maybe my ex's mom was right. Doesn't matter now. I think I shattered that hypothesis. I've shown amazing strength and courage. Super proud of myself. I ask not for a lighter burden, but for broader shoulders.

2 ENTRY 2

I FIND MYSELF CRYING FOR "NO REASON", BUT I HAVE ACTUALLY VERY GOOD reason. I'm getting better, and things are falling into place. Yes, I have bipolar disorder, so I'm going to be emotional anyway, but this is different. These are tears of joy and relief. I've fought so hard. Could you imagine being sick for over 15 years, and then getting better dramatically? It's overwhelming, and I just can't hold it in. Much love y'all.

3 ENTRY 3

Please fact check me if I am wrong, but I am just speaking from experience here. I've been taking Tylenol Arthritis for a few months as directed, and it's really helping with muscle tension. I have also been stretching when I am anxious, which is usually near my medication times. Maybe that's why massages and yoga are so good for people with anxiety. Most people don't realize that mental illness and anxiety have physical symptoms, and there are many. I just want to focus on muscle tension and bone soreness for right now. I've also lost 60-70 pounds, so I know that helps too. The way I stretch is I bend myself over at the back over a countertop or railing and put my feet behind me to stretch out my back and calves. Man, it feels so good. By the time I'm done stretching, and the Tylenol and psych meds kick in, my tension and soreness are almost completely gone. I'm sure someone recommended this at some point in my recovery, but I tend to be forgetful. Just a pro tip that I learned recently. Also, it seems like at the end of my tension, I can crack my neck for even more relief.

4 ENTRY 4

When I'm upset, I write. I'm not super upset, but just want to mention something. I guess I'm just tired in general. People who I thought were close to me have been pushing me around and disrespecting me. My real people know who they are. I've been pushed to my limits. I've had all I can take. I've done everything I can in every sense of the word. My recovery is making a lot of people uncomfortable. I've been sick for so long that everyone could count on me and my life to make themselves feel better about theirs. I'm just going to keep doing me. Sorry, not sorry. People get stuck in a long line at Starbucks, and can't even get their shit together.

5 ENTRY 5

Long post alert, but I promise it's super interesting. First, I just want to say that I self-published all 6 of my books. The only entity that gets a piece is the online retailer. Totally free, but they take a bite. I do better than most self-published authors because I know tons of awesome people and they're generous. I also put a lot of time and effort into promoting myself. Anyway, I wanted to explain that I have something called anticipation anxiety, which I think is part of my OCD. There's 5 types of OCD, and my kind is called obsessional, specifically numbers. Anything related to numbers, I'm a bit freakish. It's sometimes really helpful, but it can be debilitating. I obsess about future appointments and deadlines to the point of exhaustion, which is also part of my anticipation anxiety. It all ties together. My point is that is self-published because I could do everything at my own pace. I'm usually spontaneous because it's easier on my mind. Quick weird thing about me. When I was very young, I used to practice my numbers obsessionally. Like 12 hours straight. Probably not even 5 years old. The Count on Sesame Street was my favorite of course. If you want to know more, check out my books! I have a pretty interesting, inspirational story.

6 ENTRY 6

No one changes unless they want to. It doesn't matter how rational you are or how much you love them. Nothing else matters except their own efforts. I stopped trying to change people and lowered my expectations. I'm more at peace.

7 ENTRY 7

A FEW MONTHS AGO, I SENT MY BOOKS TO A WOMAN WHO RUNS THE SUICIDE outreach program at Deer Park HS. Tonight she told me the library might order my books because they don't have any mental health books. Pretty cool. Not the reason for this post though. I was reflecting over my last 11 years of being first an advocate, then an author. It was a lot of work! I don't really talk about it much or really even realize it sometimes. I've had a lot of ups and downs in those 11 years, but I could always focus enough to help people. I'm not super religious, but I just tell people I'm a humble servant. If I think of myself as any more than that, it's hard for my mind to comprehend. I break down crying all the time because it's overwhelming and I feel so fortunate. It's no wonder I need medication and I'm not even trying to be funny. I'm just going to keep working and see what happens. Thanks to everyone who supports me and believes in me. And it all started because someone called me lazy.

8 ENTRY 8

The last few days have been a struggle for me. I've gone through full-blown mania a few times and maybe even psychosis. I should have reached out, but I didn't. I'm a mental health advocate and I didn't follow my own advice. I've shown incredible grit and courage the last 15 plus years, but I'm still human. I share this stuff about my mental health because I'm a writer, advocate, and friend to many. I'm incredibly blessed. I don't have demons. I have a lifelong genetic mental illness, and it's hard on me sometimes. I never really ask for help, even though I write about it all the time. My mission the last 11 years has been to be open and honest so that people who don't speak up or reach out will be comforted that they're not alone. A lot of people confide in me, and that stuff is private absolutely, and I consider that a high compliment. I try to be available to pretty much anyone. Like I said, I'm human, even though I try to be strong for everyone. Just please learn something from my work. That's been my goal and mission the whole time for 11 years. Much love y'all you are not alone

9 ENTRY 9

HAD A GREAT TIME WATCHING THE BENGALS VICTORY WITH MY VERY LONG-TIME friend Elliot Koop! We have a million great memories together, and we talked about a lot of things. He's my tribe and always has been. When we were younger, we had so much fun, and we were surrounded by so many solid people. In that way, we were more mature than our ages. We just liked to party and have fun. Things are different now, but also the same as it's always been. If you weren't a solid person back in the day, you moved on to take advantage of another friend group. When all my old friends started to disperse and grow into men and women, we encountered the real world. I can only speak for myself, but some people didn't have the same values we did. None of my old friends are perfect and neither am I, but we're solid people almost all the time. I'm talking about people I knew when I was a kid, and I have to really go deep into my memory bank to think of a single instance when these people have wronged me. It's just an amazing support system to have. I 100% trust a lot of people. Pretty cool. Reds won too, woo!

10 ENTRY 10

ANOTHER ONE OF MY BOOKS GOT CHECKED OUT OF THE PUBLIC LIBRARY. PLEASE take advantage of that if you want to read my work. The greatest satisfaction I get is when people read my books, above anything. My newest and sixth book will be available, eventually. I also have free promo codes for my audiobooks for my first 5 books. I haven't converted my newest book yet. Paperback copies will be available soon, and I can email my books to you as well. Some people make a donation to my Venmo or cash app, but it's not required. Everyone is struggling right now. Just trying to help.

11 ENTRY 11

I'M TRYING TO BE MORE HONEST WITH MY PARENTS AND MYSELF ABOUT MY illness. It's work, and it requires maintenance. Sometimes it's medication. Sometimes it's coping skills. Sometimes it's just resting peacefully. I'm stable most of the time, but it's a real battle and struggle sometimes. My friends and family have seen me when I'm symptomatic. It's a little embarrassing, but I'm not embarrassed or ashamed if that makes sense. Much love y'all

12 ENTRY 12

Long post alert! September was super busy and rough at times, but I'm looking forward to October (birthday month). I'm excited to meet my new friend today, who happens to be Gerry Faust's niece. Bengals won. Never a doubt ask Evan Vomacka. Bills are paid. I went out to get cigarettes last night, and an attractive young woman helped me, who didn't know anything about cigarette brands, which was funny because she was so nice about it. I'm surprised I didn't hold her hostage in conversation with my life story and career. I restrained myself because I even had business cards in my pocket. I ramble to strangers about my career, mainly because I'm super proud of myself. I'm actually not trying to sell anything. I donate plenty of books and I have a lot of free resources. Not everyone shares my enthusiasm. My out-of-town brother is coming for dinner. I guess I'm just glad I survived September, but it was still only like 10% weird.

13 ENTRY 13

It's hard for me to understand a lot of things about life and the world because of what I've been through. I know I think differently than most other people, but I'm not going to apologize and I don't feel bad. People can think what they want about me, but my intentions are always good. When I tell people what I think and feel, it's almost surprising because I was quiet for so long. I've had people tell me I was getting upset when I was simply being passionate. I get excited really easily because honestly, I'm glad to be alive. I try not to forget what I've learned from my experiences, complemented by coping with mental illness for probably my whole life. If you've read my books or talked to me personally, my views actually make a lot of sense when I tell you what I've experienced. I'm not concerned if it's right or wrong. There's no such thing, to some extent. I finally got a good rest last night, and I love writing thoughtful things, so that's the reason for this writing this morning. I wish the best for everyone. I could go on forever, but I have to stop at some point haha. Last thing I'll write is that one of the most satisfying things in my life is when people are interested in my story and enjoy my writing. I'm extremely proud of myself, and I know a lot of you are proud of me, too. Much love y'all.

14 ENTRY 14

All I really needed to do was go to the gas station to get cigarettes, and I was craving a cherry Coke. I know the women cashiers who work there. I was determined to be kind and funny. I actually do this a lot because people. Anyway, one of the managers was apologizing for not having as many cigarettes I wanted of my usual brand. She was talking about stress and hospital leave and stuff and I was trying not to laugh. I gave her a big smile and said, "I'm good. Thanks so much! Good to see you all. Have a great day." I must have looked beat up too because the women and I were talking and laughing about how small of an issue that really is. At the end of the visit, we were all laughing and smiling, and I was just like, "you either get it or you don't." We were having fun at this point because they all knew what I was talking about. Much love y'all.

15 ENTRY 15

I didn't gamble for a 13 month stretch after racking up $2k in a debt to friends and family. It's extremely embarrassing that I lost control, but I paid everyone back in those 13 months. It's probably the ugliest addiction/habit I have. I could tell you all the times I've won, and I could probably justify and rationalize it a million ways instead of just humbling myself and admitting I have a problem. "The worst thing to happen to a gambler is that he wins". I've borrowed money from a lot of people that I consider friends and family, and I've caused damage. I only owe 2 people money at this moment and they're very close to me and understanding and forgiving. I had to dig myself out again over the last month. I don't know what else to say. I want to say that I feel like I should be able to spend my money the way I want, but when I'm borrowing money, that's not what I'm doing. I truly believe I'm going to win every time, which is obviously irrational. I dream of winning a bunch of money only to share it with other people and live comfortably. I have the best intentions, but it's not rational and I've crossed a line with a lot of my friends when I borrow money. Another way it doesn't make sense is that I'm not a money motivated person. If I ever have more than I need, I donate it and give it away. I'm really sorry if I made my loved ones feel like ATMs for my habit. There's no excuse for that. Maybe when I have a lot of income, I can gamble recreationally, but from what I know about addiction, that probably won't be possible. I just don't know what to do this second except to apologize. I had a pretty emotional day yesterday. I was in a stress induced fog. There's a lot of reasons why I'm stressed out, but that's for another entry. I've shared almost everything about my life, but this is my worst vice. Only my family and close friends know until now. As always, I have a million more things to write about, but this is a good start. I really hate talking about it actually, but I need to put this into my journal because unfortunately, it's a struggle that I've had a long time. I don't know what else to say right now, except to simply confess and apologize without trying to rationalize it.

16 ENTRY 16

Sometimes I forget that I have mental illness, which is cool in some ways, but the result lately has been that I haven't been resting or putting myself first. I'm a giver to the extreme, so it's really hard to say no to people and admit I need to rest. It's annoying to me because I'm a very hard worker, and I remember the college years when I'd go to class in the morning and work all night with hardly any sleep. I was manic, so that's where the energy was coming from. I was clueless. I was self medicating with alcohol and marijuana, and those substances were in my life a long time. I try to stay sober now because I enjoy stability and peace of mind now more than ever. My life was chaotic for a long time, so when my mind and body are at peace, it feels like a miracle to me. It's my belief that if I were unmediated, I'd still be self medicating. There's a stigma attached to taking pills, but they saved my life. Everyone copes in different ways. If I take my medication on time, stay sober, reduce stress and triggers, I'm stable almost all the time. That's why I forget sometimes that I need to rest. I have forgotten lately, but my illness will always remind me. I feel a little dumb for taking my illness for granted. I swore I'd never forget some really hard times I've had, and I swore I'd never claim victory, metaphorically speaking. I just want to live my life, but part of that is taking care of myself and respecting the fact that I have mental illness. I'm very high functioning, so that's why it's easy for me to forget to rest. Maybe I'll talk about my anxiety disorders some other time.

17 ENTRY 17

When I was released from the hospital in 2006 after having a bipolar psychotic first break, I was heavily sedated and depressed. Seems so long ago, but I remember. My mom was the main person who took care of me, but my whole family and close friends helped too. When someone is that depressed, I call it an all hands on deck situation. You have to find the smallest bit of joy and hope just to survive another day. Weird example, but if eating a whole container of ice cream is going to keep you fighting and surviving until tomorrow, just do it. I think it's obvious you can't eat a gallon of ice cream every day, but it's survival mode. Hopefully, you can find something harmless to keep you fighting and surviving to prevent you from giving up or harming yourself.

18 ENTRY 18

I FEEL LIKE I WOKE UP TODAY OR FINALLY SNAPPED OUT OF THE SOCIAL MEDIA addiction. I wish the best for everyone reading this, but most of you don't really matter to me at the end of the day, and vice versa. I don't know why I took it upon myself to try to fix everyone, and I don't know who I'm trying to impress. If I really love you or care for you, I've told you directly. I like to think I'm pretty good at showing and telling people I care. I never thought I'd be so shallow.

19 ENTRY 19

I'VE HAD SOME PRIVATE CONVERSATIONS WITH LOVED ONES RECENTLY, AND THAT'S just about the only thing I don't share. I'm learning a few things that I haven't thought about recently.

Not everyone wants to talk about their feelings every single second of the day. My mental health is a huge part of my life, but it's not everyone's main concern. We all have different priorities and things that are important to us. Sometimes we share the same interests, struggles, etc. and sometimes we don't. If I want people to listen to what I care about, I have to give them the same courtesy.

I talked to another friend and he basically said he does what he has to do to be happy in his world. Another shocking moment for me. I rarely put myself first because I genuinely care about a lot of people and their comfort, joy, and happiness. I don't know why I feel like I'm doing something wrong by putting myself first. In the middle of writing this, my dad needed help with something unimportant to me, but it's important to him. Catch my drift? Patience really is a virtue. I've always said I'm a work in progress, no matter how much work I've done or how much I've achieved. Patience is a daily thing. You can read about how hard of a life I've supposedly had, but lots of people have way more to worry about than I do, but hardships are not comparable. Academics were fairly easy for me, but there's people who worked way harder who didn't make the grades I did. I could give hundreds of examples, but hopefully I've explained myself good enough.

20 ENTRY 20

THERE'S A WORLDWIDE? MOVEMENT CALLED #PAYITFORWARDCHALLENGE I DID this a few months ago, and I finally got around to doing it again. I just paint hearts on rocks and hide them. Some people put links or inspirational messages on the back. I always think it'd be cool to find if I were a kid, but there's been stories of grown adults finding these and it made their whole day, and maybe stopped them from harming themselves. It reminds me of the movie called Pay It Forward, where a young child sets off a chain of kindness that goes viral, for lack of a better term. I think it's just a very easy, cheap gesture of kindness. Let people wonder and be amazed again. My last batch was scattered at Chamberlain Park near the playground and railroad tracks. Creative Arts and Crafts Therapy for Mental Health

21 ENTRY 21

I'M A WRITER. I WRITE. IT'S WHAT I DO. IT'S AS NATURAL AS BREATHING TO ME. I'm finally saying that with confidence this morning. I had a very emotional day yesterday. I have more thoughts as I reflect on my day. I'm also a deep thinker. Probably too much, but I also say that with confidence. Generally, I'm not a confident person. I think I used to be. When doctors and everyone else tell you that you're mentally ill, it was humbling, but a huge confidence drainer, even though it was also a relief because I finally had an explanation for a lot of things. Not excuses. Explanations. I look back on my life so far, and a lot of it makes more sense to me. Conversely, I am not my illness, and it doesn't define me, and it's not who I am. I realized how lucky I was to still have my parents and have a good relationship with them. I get so caught up with life that I lose sight of what's important. I feel incredibly stupid, but I think it's part of the journey and learning. People say I'm so smart. I actually am aware that I'm smart, which doesn't really mean much, and I'm also incredibly hard on myself. When I'm stable, I'm self aware, and a lot of great things. I know. When I'm not stable, my brain lies to put it simply. In my heart of hearts, I know these lies aren't true, but they're strong feelings and emotions. No one likes me anymore. I'm a burden. I'm a failure. It's a long list of falsities. When I'm symptomatic, and in the heat of the moment, I can't think clearly or rationally sometimes. I don't think this is hard to understand for most people, mental illness or not. I could probably write a book about this (haha), but I'm feeling better and more clear-headed this morning. It's not really a matter of effort for me. It's more mindfulness of the fact that I have to take care of myself, maybe more than other people. Obviously, not a competition. Thanks for the support and for taking an interest in my story. It's the best thing about my journey. That people care about me and love me, flaws and all.

22 ENTRY 22

Any insight is appreciated. This happens to me every weekend. I feel like I should be doing something, but I really just enjoy relaxing most of the time. But it's hard for me to enjoy relaxing because I feel like I should be doing something. I started a new medication in March, and I've shown dramatic improvement, but a lot of things changed. I think it's my OCD that's acting up. My meal times and sleeping schedule changed. Bathroom habits. I have a much smaller appetite. I know this seems like minor stuff, but it leaves me confused and conflicted. Maybe I'm just content. I guess it's because change is hard for me, even if it's positive.

23 ENTRY 23

More things I feel like I'm learning for the first time. I need to sleep or at least rest undisturbed, probably more than the average person. Battling mental illness coupled with daily life can simply be exhausting and overwhelming. I was symptomatic last night and this morning, and I really just needed to rest and sleep. I don't know why I can't seem to understand this. Work ethic is one thing, but working to the point of being exhausted and symptomatic is another. My body hurt. I was paranoid. I was angry. I was having brain fog. I had to try really hard to think clearly. I've been symptomatic off and on for days. Looking back on the last few days, I feel like an idiot because the answer was so simple and like textbook stuff to people who know about mental illness. I need to start writing things down like a playbook for when I'm symptomatic and can't think clearly, among other things.

24 ENTRY 24

Once again, I feel like an idiot. I came up with a solution to be less available. Sometimes I need to be alone, and it's absolutely nothing personal to anyone, including my parents who I live with. The back porch/backyard! I have to walk through the whole house to get to the front porch, and I get overstimulated sometimes. Also, if I don't want to be available by phone, I have to turn it off. I'm actually fairly logical when I can think clearly. It's a great option for me because I don't have to drive anywhere and it's a simple solution to have another option and a change of scenery. Duh!

25 ENTRY 25

RANDOM THOUGHTS AND OBSERVATIONS AS I GET SETTLED FOR THE NIGHT. I really appreciate honesty for a lot of reasons. One reason is that it takes out any kind of guessing games. There's a way to be honest without being mean, condescending, etc. I think it's a form of love. However, so is not being brutally honest. You care about someone else's feelings, so you don't want to be blunt. I'm not an exception to anything I write about btw. I actually enjoy working on myself and improving myself because that's self-love, in my opinion. On a less serious note, I made a chicken wild rice casserole for dinner tomorrow because my mom usually makes dinner every night, and it saves her the work and it's important to her. I'll pretty much eat anything if I'm hungry.

26 ENTRY 26

I FEEL LIKE I'VE HAD SOME BREAKTHROUGHS, SO I JUST WANT TO SHARE. I HAVE A loud brain, which is exactly what it sounds like. Racing thoughts about pretty much anything, but examples are random facts, song lyrics, whatever my brain decides to whip up. This is what I mean by symptomatic. I'm stable most of the time, but I decided I needed to make a list to help me focus when I'm not stable. A playbook of sorts. I'll let you know if it works. Right now, it's just an idea/theory. Some of the things are not always possible in real time/reality. Side note—I've never read my own books. I'd like to do that.

When I'm not stable, I'm in no particular order. I'll keep adding to the list as needed.

1. Humor
2. Go to the back porch if overstimulated
3. Turn off phone if necessary
4. Rest when needed
5. Do what you have to do to be happy within reason
6. Enjoy coffee, but proceed with caution
7. Brains lie.
8. Stay occupied without overworking
9. It always passes. Success rate is 100%

10. My health is a priority
11. Identify triggers
12. Speak up if something is bothering me
13. Focus as in using grounding techniques
14. Avoid purchases or anything related to money

27 ENTRY 27

MORE THINGS I'M REALIZING... I'M BASICALLY ON A THIRD SHIFT SLEEP schedule, which is why I struggle mostly during daytime hours. It's like the middle of the night for me. Most of the world is on a first shift schedule. It's really hard for me to deal with anything during the day, and then I try to drink coffee to try to wake up, when I should just relax until I know I'm on my working schedule. The struggle is real.

28 ENTRY 28

When I'm symptomatic and unstable, lately I've been having trouble focusing. I'm starting to write things down for reference, so that I'm not trying to remember everything, if that makes sense. The first list I've been working on is for when I'm symptomatic to help me focus, and I think it's just basically a grounding technique, which is a technique used for anxiety to help people feel less disassociated. I just wanted to share in case anyone could benefit. It's also a working list, which means it might change over time or I might add or subtract bullet points as needed.

1. Humor
2. Go out on back porch if overstimulated
3. Rest
4. Do what you have to do to be happy within reason
5. Turn off phone
6. Enjoy coffee, but proceed with caution
7. Brains lie
8. Stay occupied without overworking
9. It will pass. Success rate is 100%
10. My health is a priority
11. Identify triggers
12. Speak up

13. Try to focus/grounding techniques
14. Avoid purchases
15. Get up and move around
16. Instagram is less stimulating
17. Keep it simple
18. One thing at a time
19. Sleep resets symptoms
20. Breathe
21. Work can wait sometimes
22. Options are good
23. It's okay to avoid triggers
24. Be aware of obsessive thoughts
25. Fun distractions
26. It's ok to be private
27. Being organized helps
28. Cold drinks
29. Fresh air
30. Medication can take an hour to work
31. Avoid social media

29 ENTRY 29

WHEN I WAS FIRST HOSPITALIZED AND DIAGNOSED WITH BIPOLAR DISORDER WITH psychotic features in 2006, I felt a lot of emotions, of course, but times were a lot different, even though it was only 15 years ago. What I'm getting at is in the present time, almost everyone is struggling with their mental health or otherwise. It's just a hard concept for me to grasp because, for a long time, I felt like I was the only one struggling. I don't even feel like anyone understands where I'm coming from. I've been struggling with my mental health a long time, and now it's pretty much everyone. It's so strange for me to experience. It's hard to even describe.

30 ENTRY 30

When I was in college, I was organized in the traditional sense because I had assignments due, work schedule, bills, etc., but 2 years after I graduated, I got sick. I remember taking my alarm clock and land line phone out of my room. I was no longer a part of the daily grind. I was in survival and recovery mode. Fast forward to present day, I'm having to relearn how to be organized with lists and many other things. Through no fault of my own, my life was paused for many years. I really enjoy cleaning and being organized and making to-do lists now when I have the energy. I guess it makes me feel like a functioning adult who's part of the real world, which means something different to everyone.

31 ENTRY 31

I told my mom I was going to find a 150-year-old person to tell her how young she is every time she talks about being old. I get no sympathy for about to be turning 40.

Mom, "I don't even feel old."

Me, "I do! Adulthood is straight up the worst hood I've ever lived in."

32 ENTRY 32

Moments of clarity are pretty rare for me. The only sound right now is familiar music. I baked cookies, made coffee for the morning, loaded the dishwasher. Typical stuff. I just remembered it's Friday night. I remember when I used to wait all week for Friday night. Long days in a factory. Long days and nights in school. I'm not on that kind of schedule anymore. Not for a long time. I think I'm content, bordering on happiness. Everything is icy calm right now. I won't remember this tomorrow until I review my notes and messages. I'm in a writing zone. I'll snap out of it just like always, but for now, I'm not thinking about much of anything except my next typed letter. We're all more similar than different, I think. We get hung up on the small parts that are different for some reason. I always forget that everything's small, really. Such is life and humanity. I'm torn between enjoying being alone in silence and trying to help everyone. I'm enjoying the peace and quiet right now, but tomorrow will be different. Balance and moderation. I've never been good at either.

33 ENTRY 33

Life is funny and painful and complicated sometimes and a million things, but almost all the time, keeping it simple is most effective. I think the technical term is parsimony, but who cares? Life isn't a psychology exam. Two simple analogies that apply to a lot of things. The more common one is to play the hand you're dealt. Simple. The other is we are not all in the same boat. We're in the same ocean. Some of us have yachts. Some of us have basic effective boats. Some of us have to build our own boats. Simple to understand, hopefully. Not to be morbid, but some of us drown.

34 ENTRY 34

Reconnected with another former classmate and current teacher at Moeller HS. They want to emphasize mental health in the curriculum, and he's interested in my books and story as a teaching tool. Any way I can help my alma mater is really cool. I'm not sure how much they need my physical presence, but we discussed some sort of way to speak to the students, whether it be a zoom meeting or actually visiting campus. #beremarkable

35 ENTRY 35

My writings are meant to be generalizations. I'm sure I'm guilty of every single thing I write about at some time or another. I really enjoy observing people and patterns of behavior and stuff like that. It's always been interesting to me, which is probably why I majored in psychology. I thought of a funny analogy from my life that applies to a lot of situations. I used to go to bars and get drunk like a lot haha.(I'm sure my getting drunk in a bar days aren't over haha). I really enjoyed it at the time, and I just don't anymore. Anyway, I always thought it was weird that people got into bar fights. I always thought to myself, "I can be upset for free. Why would I go to a bar and fight people?" There are many reasons why I've never been in a fist fight, mostly because of my personality, but also my size is a pretty nice deterrent, haha. There's also lots of reasons why people do get into bar fights. Just speaking from my own personal experience here. Why would you fight the biggest dude in the bar, right? Haha. Bar fights remind me a lot about daily life. If (big if) you have a choice, why would you choose to be upset? It applies to social media for some. It applies to the news for me. When I freely choose to put something into my mind, why would I choose to be upset? Yes, I know things are unavoidable. Obviously, everyone is different, but there are patterns and similarities. That's basically what psychology is. My hope is that everyone will get a good chuckle out of this post because I believe it's pretty true.

36 ENTRY 36

I never know where to start. It's really funny to me that I've never read my own books except for proofreading. It's hard for me to focus to read, but also, the subject matter is triggering. The best times of my life have been when I wasn't thinking, and I lost track of time. It seems like I should be finished writing about my life, but I really enjoy it. It seems like every day I think about something worth writing about. It's as much therapy for me as the people who can relate. I can really zone out when I write. I'm starting to have moments of clarity where nothing matters at the moment except what I'm writing, like now. Believe it or not, I'm not thinking much when I write. Everything is much easier when I'm stable, which is most of the time now. I guess some days are easier than others. I'll write an entry like this and then read it later like "Wow! This is pretty good." Haha. I'm a total space cadet sometimes, and it's wonderful. I never thought that thinking would be so annoying. Do people really think I'm smart? I can barely focus enough to make coffee sometimes. It's extremely quiet and peaceful this morning. Not thinking about much at all right now. Sometimes I prefer silence, and sometimes I need busyness. I don't know why I was in denial that I was a writer for so long. Probably my lack of confidence. It comes and goes, but usually not very confident. I was today years old when I figured out I could use my phone to write and make notes. I'm not the best with technology, but I get by, I guess. Once I write something, it's out of my mind, which is great, but my mind is pretty much a wild party most of the time. My mind races very quickly most of the time. Medication definitely helps and saves my life. I have a few written lists I'm going to transfer to my phone. I try to save writings in several places. I don't really need hard copies of anything anymore, but I think it's good to have, for sentimental reasons at the very least. I was writing while making soup just now. Again, today years old. I'll be 40 years old in 4 days. Every day, I try to be thankful, but my actual birthday hits me differently. More emotional mainly. I like rereading journal entries like this. Kinda like a pleasant stroll down memory lane. Nostalgia is a nice feeling.

37 ENTRY 37

Working lists I've been working on to be more organized:

DAILY REMINDERS

1. Most people are working during the day. More people are available on the weekends.
2. We all have different priorities and to do lists.
3. Patience
4. Drive somewhere/try something new
5. Everything always works out. Don't obsess over money.
6. Limit phone usage when possible. Try only using it when absolutely necessary.
7. Make time for fun and enjoyable things.
8. Moderation

WHEN NOT STABLE...

1. humor
2. Back porch if overstimulated
3. Turn off/silent phone

4. Rest
5. Be happy actively
6. Be aware of coffee
7. Brains lie
8. Stay occupied without overworking
9. It will pass. Success rate is 100%
10. My health is a priority
11. Identify triggers
12. Speak up communication
13. Grounding focus
14. Avoid purchases money
15. Avoid gambling
16. Instagram is less stimulating
17. Keep it simple
18. One thing at a time
19. Sleep resets everything
20. Breathe
21. Work can wait sometimes
22. Options are good
23. Avoid triggers if possible
24. Focus on something else if obsessive thoughts
25. Fun distractions
26. It's okay to be private
27. Being organized helps
28. Music
29. Cold drink
30. Fresh air
31. Avoid social media
32. Medication can take an hour to work
33. Look at sports collection
34. Symptoms delusional paranoia
35. Write
36. Limit messages

TO DO LIST NOT URGENT

1. Read your books or any books

2. Phish flag
3. Find a job and move out, eventually
4. Look into Stash
5. 1st and 6th book to public library
6. Moeller, Ursuline, DPHS libraries
7. Moeller campus visit
8. Hide heart rocks

MEDS

- 4am 9mg invega
- Buspar
- 1 mg klonopin
- 1030am Trileptal
- 1mg klonopin
- 3pm buspar
- 430pm Trileptal
- 1mg klonopin
- 930pm Trileptal
- Buspar
- 1mg klonopin

38 ENTRY 38

Everyone makes mistakes. Literally everyone. I don't know a perfect person, and neither do you. Having high standards for myself/yourself is really awesome, except mistakes are brutal on our psyches. I'm learning to be easier on myself, but I still put a lot of pressure on myself to be above average (to put it lightly) all the time. When you love someone, you don't want these people to make the same mistakes you made, which is a loving gesture. The problem is that personal failure is a great teacher, so you're actually depriving your loved ones to learn from these mistakes (hopefully) by themselves. Success hasn't taught me nearly as much.

39 ENTRY 39

The reason I don't need to read my own books is because I lived it. I may not know the exact words, but close enough.

40 ENTRY 40

My writings are from personal experience, which happens to include psychology, philosophy, and many other things, of course. I only truly know what I've experienced, which is so small in the grand scheme of things. Personal examples and thoughts from today. I took a shower, and actually enjoyed it, instead of seeing it as a Herculean task. I played music on my phone, and forgot about life for a few moments. The answers are so simple sometimes. Forgetting about daily life is good in general, but eventually, most people get snapped back to reality, whatever that means. A personal flaw of mine is That I underestimate how intelligent people are. It's not really a conscious thought, it's just that I don't need to explain every little thing to the people in my life. My loved ones are intelligent, considerate, loving, and many great things. I have a desire to be understood I guess, but the people in my life know me better than I know myself sometimes. I don't think my writing is hard to understand in general for people who don't personally know me.

41 ENTRY 41

I THINK I FINALLY FOUND OUT A SIMPLE WAY TO EXPLAIN THINGS. TECHNOLOGY has allowed us to frolic and leap back and forth through time, generations, Etc. #parsimony

42 COMPLETE DIAGNOSIS

Bipolar disorder with psychotic features, OCD, agoraphobia, claustrophobia, panic disorder, PTSD

Sleep disorder called non 24

Neurodiverse brain

#Mentalhealthawareness #brainawarenessweek #sleepdisorders

43 ENTRY 42

My personal friend and USA Today bestselling author Craig A. Price Jr. is reformatting and fine tuning a lot of things about my books and audiobooks, etc. free of charge, simply because he believes in my books and story

#BeRemarkable #GoFlyers #mentalhealthmatters #mentalhealthawareness #authorssupportingauthors

44 ENTRY 43

First, I've had huge, ugly feet my whole life. However, this is a demonstration of how personal hygiene can take a back seat when struggling with mental illness. My feet used to be so full of fluid from being morbidly obese and sedentary that my mom used to cut my toenails, put lotion on my feet, and put socks on for me. As of tonight, I can do it myself. You are not alone. If no one told you today that you matter, I just did. If you feel your mental health failing, please reach out to professional help, the suicide hotline, crisis line, etc. #mentalhealthawareness #suicideprevention #crisisline #18002738255 personal hygiene takes a back seat because mental illness is exhausting in every way, and can often be a full-time job plus all the obligations that come with reality.

ALSO BY JOHN MEDL

Millions Like Me: My Struggle with Mental Illness:
books2read.com/Millions-Like-Me

Poems From a Bipolar Mind: books2read.com/Poems-Bipolar

The Last Day of July: 13 Years of Madness: books2read.com/Last-Day-July

The Entropy of Bipolar Disorder: books2read.com/Entropy-Bipolar

Mental Illness Is An Actual Illness: books2read.com/Mental-Illness-Actual-Illness

Making Bipolar Lemonade: books2read.com/Bipolar-Lemonade

Bipolar Rising : books2read.com/Bipolar-Rising

ABOUT JOHN MEDL

John Medl is an author with over five published books and a mental health advocate from Cincinnati, Ohio. He has suffered from mental illness for more than eleven years. His diagnoses are: bipolar disorder with psychotic features, obsessive-compulsive disorder, Post-Traumatic Stress Disorder, Generalized Anxiety-Panic Disorder, claustrophobia, and agoraphobia.

John has a Bachelor of Arts in Psychology from the University of Dayton, which he finds ironic.

books2read.com/John-Medl

facebook.com/john.medl

twitter.com/johnmedl7

instagram.com/johnmedl7

amazon.com/author/john-medl

www.ingramcontent.com/pod-product-compliance
Lightning Source LLC
LaVergne TN
LVHW052014200926
848481LV00005B/1484